ALASKA

ON-THE-ROAD HISTORIES

ALASKA

Ryan Madden

Interlink Books

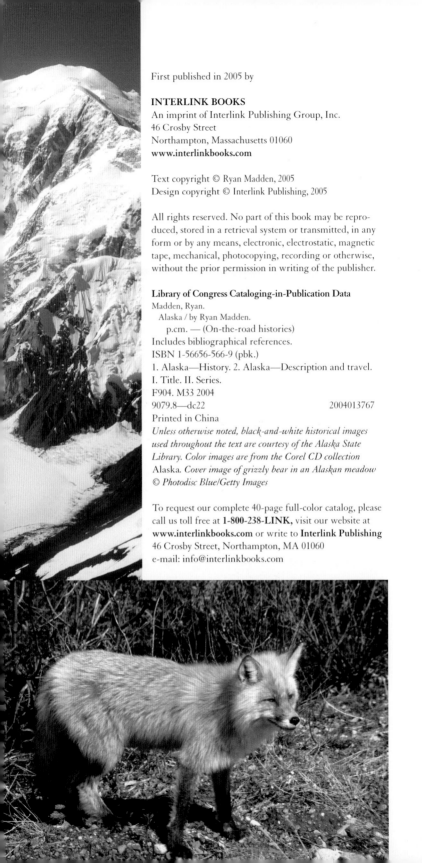

First published in 2005 by

INTERLINK BOOKS
An imprint of Interlink Publishing Group, Inc.
46 Crosby Street
Northampton, Massachusetts 01060
www.interlinkbooks.com

Library of Congress Cataloging-in-Publication Data
Madden, Ryan.
  Alaska / by Ryan Madden.
    p.cm. — (On-the-road histories)
Includes bibliographical references.
ISBN 1-56656-566-9 (pbk.)
1. Alaska—History. 2. Alaska—Description and travel.
I. Title. II. Series.
F904. M33 2004
9079.8—dc22   2004013767
Printed in China
*Unless otherwise noted, black-and-white historical images
used throughout the text are courtesy of the Alaska State
Library. Color images are from the Corel CD collection*
Alaska. *Cover image of grizzly bear in an Alaskan meadow*
© *Photodisc Blue/Getty Images*

To request our complete 40-page full-color catalog, please
call us toll free at **1-800-238-LINK,** visit our website at
www.interlinkbooks.com or write to **Interlink Publishing**
46 Crosby Street, Northampton, MA 01060
e-mail: info@interlinkbooks.com

Contents

Rampart Dam—Iodine 131
Amchitka Island—The Last Great Race

VII. Modern Alaska 241
Oil and Alaska—Toward a Land Claims Settlement
Alaska Native Claims Settlement Act—The Pipeline
ANILCA—Katie John
The Permanent Fund—*Exxon-Valdez* Disaster
The Arctic National Wildlife Refuge—Tourism in Alaska

Map by Skyline Productions

INTRODUCTION

Sunshine streamed through the luminous fringes of the clouds and fell on the green waters of the fiord, the glittering bergs, the crystal bluffs of the vast glacier, the intensely white, far-spreading fields of ice, and the ineffably chaste and spiritual heights of the Fairweather Range, which were now hidden, now partly revealed, the whole making a picture of icy wildness unspeakably pure and sublime.

—*John Muir,* Travels in Alaska, *1914*

During the summer of 1880, famed naturalist John Muir paddled the waters of Glacier Bay in southeastern Alaska in a Tlingit dugout canoe. Muir took copious notes on the natural wonders and fascinating people that he encountered during his journey, writings that were eventually published in his 1914 book *Travels in Alaska*. Through Muir's eyes we see the influence of the lure of gold on individuals as they formed rustic towns in hopes of quick profits. We see majestic glaciers, one of which will come to bear his name. We see a fledgling tourist industry then limited to a wealthy few who could afford an Alaskan cruise. And we see the struggles of Alaska Natives to retain their culture in the face of an onslaught of Americanism. Muir's gospel that wild places can lead to spiritual fulfillment was never more pronounced than in his Alaskan writings. He urged others to go north in a simple phrase: "go, go and see." Over 120 years later, thousands of people from around the world would heed Muir's advice and travel to Alaska to take in its wonders. But along with the spectacular natural beauty goes an interesting and complex human history that is thousands of years old. It is a tale that includes interactions between Alaska Natives, Russians, French, Spanish, English, Americans, Canadians, and Japanese. Alaska is a place where war, poverty, riches, and faith have left an enduring mark on the state's history.

When one mentions Alaska, romantic images of the frozen north abound, from igloos to dog sleds, giant bears to endless tundra. While these images have some factual basis, Alaska is much more. It is a weaving together of cultures and people and their various interactions with the natural world. The surroundings in which these stories have unfolded through the state's history are truly phenomenal. Alaska is a huge landmass with a number of diverse environments. Statistics give some indication: 533,000 square miles, 20 degrees of latitude, three sides surrounded by water, and 33,000 miles of coastline (equal to the rest of the United States). To state it briefly, it is big!

In that vastness there are extremes of climate and terrain. Some areas in southeastern Alaska receive over 200 inches of rain annually. Certain parts of interior Alaska fall to eighty degrees below in the winter and above ninety in the brief summer. In other regions of Alaska, the sun never goes down in the summer and never comes up in the winter. Living has been possible in these extreme conditions due to the abundant natural resources of the sea and land. The indigenous people of Alaska expertly used salmon, moose, deer, caribou, and sea mammals as resources for survival. The image many still have of Alaska as a frozen tundra is contrary to its climatic diversity. There are three major climatic zones in the state. The Japanese current heavily influences the mild and damp rain forests of Southeast Alaska, known as the Inside Passage. Dotted by thousands of islands and home to mountains and glaciers that seem to rise from the sea, this area of Alaska is the most heavily visited part of state. The tundra of western and northern Alaska is actually a relatively dry area with ground-hugging flora and few trees. In contrast, the interior boreal forests of cold winters and short hot summers are filled with spruce, alder, birch, and aspen; the interior is also home to massive rivers and North America's largest mountains.

Ironically, within this large landmass the majority of today's Alaskans live in the urban areas of Anchorage and Fairbanks, surrounded by a vast wilderness. But those large cities are a post-World War II phenomenon. At the time of the U.S. purchase in 1867, Alaska had about 30,000 people, more than 29,000 of them Alaska Natives. Ever since, Alaska has seen a series of boom-and-bust cycles to exploit the land: rushes for fur, gold, copper, salmon, forest products, and oil. In the end some of the people who came stayed, lured by the uniqueness of Alaska. More often, however, those who took the rewards of the natural resources enjoyed them somewhere else. As a result, Alaska's history has not always been cheerful. And for Alaska Native cultures as well as for its animal species, this history has at times been disastrous.

The state's past can be categorized into four major periods: the diversity of Alaska Native history and culture, the influence of the Russians, the early American period and the influence of gold, and Alaska in the twentieth century—how World War II, statehood, and the oil boom impacted the region. The story of Alaska is sometimes tragic, often wonderful, even humorous, but always interesting.

1

ALASKA'S FIRST PEOPLE

THE ORIGINS OF ALASKA'S NATIVE GROUPS

During the most recent Ice Age, immense ice sheets nearly two miles thick covered much of North America. The ice used large amounts of the Earth's water, causing sea levels to fall significantly. As a result, the land masses grew significantly where continental shelves slope gradually, as in the Bering Strait. A sea level drop of approximately 300 feet during the glacial period revealed a relatively flat, low-lying stretch of continental plain linking North America to Asia. The land mass ranged up to 1,000 miles wide and formed a land bridge connecting Asia to North America.

The first entry of humans into the Americas started one of the great migratory events of human history. The descendants of the "First Alaskans" went on to spread across North and South America. As far as Native Americans are concerned, all roads seem to lead back to Alaska. Exactly when people first found the land that would be called Alaska is still an anthropological mystery. Some believe that people migrated from Asia to North America as long as 40,000 years ago. Others argue it was as recent as 15,000 to 10,000 years ago. Whenever it happened, most academics agree that the peopling of the Americas came by way of a northern land bridge that once connected Siberia and Alaska.

The Land Bridge Theory has it that these first migrants were pursuing their subsistence way of life as they followed herds of grazing mammals across the grassy tundra. When the sea level rose and the grassy plain submerged, these new residents moved permanently to what would become Alaska, and then some moved on to other parts of the Americas.

Those who made Alaska their permanent home make up the state's four major Alaska Native groups: Aleuts, Athabascans, Eskimos (Inupiat and Yup'ik), and the natives of the northwest coast. All four groups shared certain basic

similarities in that they all hunted, fished, and gathered food, but they also developed fascinating and distinctive cultures. The image of Alaska as uninhabited wilderness has caused misconceptions about the Alaska Natives' uses of the areas and the types of resources available. People have hunted, fished, trapped, and lived in Alaska for millennia. The notion of wilderness as untouched by human hands is often misleading. Humans have been part of the Alaskan ecosystems for thousands of years.

Anthropologists theorize, based on linguistic, dental, and genetic data, that there were three main waves of immigration across Bering Strait. The first wave passed through Alaska to found the main Amerindian groups of the Americas. The second wave included the Athabascan settlers who occupied the Alaskan interior. The last wave were believed to be the ancestors of the Eskimo/Aleut populations. Some scholars disagree with this theory, since the waves could have been made up of many small groups of people. Because Alaska is so large and diverse geographically and culturally, consensus is difficult.

Denali from Wonder Lake

Today, mainland Alaska is a large projection that sticks out like a thumb from North America toward Siberia. Rivers and mountain chains that lead into the main body of North America bisect the state's interior flatlands, and its rocky southern coast runs into the Pacific Northwest coast of British Columbia. Ten thousand years ago, however, the Alaska mainland was a part of Asia, later severed by the rising seawater that formed the Bering Sea to the south and the Chukchi Sea to the north. The Bering Strait is the connection between the two seas. Alaska's importance to American history is in part the result of its unique geographic position, not just for the early settlement of the continent, but also as the land through which later waves of immigration passed.

Ten thousand years ago northern and central Alaska experienced a lesser amount of glaciations than did much of North America, including the northwest coast. During the height of the last great glaciations, the Alaskan interior formed a relatively ice-free bowl, covered by tundra out of which a narrow, ice-free corridor led eastward and southward into the continental interior.

The geography of Alaska with its mountains and rivers played an important role in settlement. Dominating the north of Alaska is the Brooks Range, which runs east to west into the Yukon Territory. Across the center of Alaska runs the Alaska Range, home to Denali. Southeast Alaska contains the Wrangell Mountains. The Chugach Range runs westward to Prince William Sound and the Kenai Peninsula. In southwest Alaska, the Aleutian Range becomes the backbone of the Alaska Peninsula and continues as the Aleutian Islands, extending about 1,300 miles into the Bering Sea.

The largest river system in Alaska is the Yukon and its tributaries: the Porcupine, the Tanana, and the Koyukon. The Yukon crosses Alaska, emptying into the Bering Sea. Crossing the North Slope is the Colville River, which originates in the Brooks Range and ends in the Arctic Ocean. In northwest Alaska are the Noatak and Kobuk Rivers, with numerous tributaries. The Kuskokwim River, draining the large Kuskokwim Delta, runs south of the Yukon River and also empties into the Bering Sea south of the Yukon and just north of the Alaska Peninsula. The southcentral region is home to the Susitna River, draining into Cook Inlet, and the Copper River, which empties into Prince William Sound. Further south is the Alsek-Tatshenshini system, which drains into the Gulf of Alaska. The landscape is crisscrossed by these mountain ranges and river systems, with which any settlers must learn to cope.

The history of the Alaska Natives is that of a distinct peoples whose cultures formed around their interactions with the land; to study Alaska Native culture is to study the complex way in which humans survive in and relate to their environment. Alaska stretches from the rainy and forested Pacific Northwest to the arid and treeless Arctic coastal plain. The history of Alaska Natives reflects these extremes.

Another source of the complexity of Alaska's history is the interactions that occurred among the various groups. Often people did not stay put, and so there was a constant ebb and flow of cultural groups and traits. For example,

Athabascans apparently expanded out of the interior to dominate a large segment of the southwestern Alaska coast, pushing out Yup'ik Eskimos in the centuries before European contact. Within a few centuries their material culture became difficult to distinguish from that of their neighbors. Trade was also widespread and this promoted new cultural variations. Still another complication, and one not found elsewhere in the Americas, was the continuing contact that existed over the millennia between Alaska Natives and northeast Asia. Ideas, goods, and often people continued to move back and forth across the Bering Strait. Well into the nineteenth century, Siberians were frequent visitors to the shores of Alaska. Within this complex, changing environment, distinct and fascinating native cultures emerged.

Aleuts/Alutiiq

The Aleuts inhabit an island chain strung across 900 miles from the Alaska Peninsula to the island of Attu, 300 miles from Russia's Kamchatka Peninsula. The islands are treeless tundra. The Japanese current's northward-flowing tropical air and frigid, dry air from the Arctic collide there, making the islands foggy and windswept much of the year.

Between ten thousand and forty thousand years ago, the ancestors of Aleuts migrating from Asia to North America settled on these remote islands. Their descendants spoke a language unique to the islands. Most of what we now know about those early Aleuts comes from Russian accounts and from later ethnologists who interpreted those writings.

The indigenous island people lived in underground houses called *barabaras*, some as large as 150 feet long and 25 feet wide with compartments separated by woven grass mats. Each household or barabara had its own male leader. The community measured wealth by the size of one's barabara, the amount and beauty of the clothing, the number of sea mammals one captured, and the number of fish smoked for the winter.

Aleut hearts, minds, and villages focused on the sea. The tidal area along the shore was vital to life. Children, women, and the elderly gathered shellfish, sea urchins, octopi, and seaweed from the tidal waters. Both men and women hunted birds and gathered bird eggs. All the people of a village had a role as food gatherers. They were expert whalers who took advantage of the bi-annual whale migration that passed between the islands during the spring and fall. Using poison-tipped harpoons, they hunted from small boats called *baidarkas*, seeking to drive the poisoned whale up on shore. Whales provided meat, lamp oil, and bones for house supports and tools.

By fully exploiting the marine and few land resources, Aleuts developed a remarkable material culture. The barabaras were close together and blended into the rolling terrain. To warm their dwellings, Aleuts used small grass fires or bowl-shaped lamps burning sea lion or whale blubber. Furnishings included delicately designed sleeping mats, baskets, and cradles that women wove from grass.

Both men and women wore garments reaching to the calf of the leg made of seal or sea otter skins. For protection from moisture they wore hooded waterproof garments made from sea lion intestines, halibut bladder, or the skin of whale tongues. Aleut women sewed clothes with needles of bird bones and thread of fish guts. They embroidered with braided animal hairs, beaks of sea birds, and strips of sea otter fur. They tattooed their faces and hands by pricking them with needles and rubbing black clay into the skin. Through holes pierced in the nose, lower lips, and ears, they wore pieces of tusks, beads, and rings. Necklaces, armlets, and anklets were made from shellfish, walrus ivory, beads, and painted hair.

The resourceful use of materials for boats equaled that for the clothing and ornaments. *Baidars* were large boats that held thirty to forty people for long trips and war parties. Baidarkas, similar to the Eskimo kayak and holding one or two people, were used for hunting and fishing. Aleuts constructed the boats from whale ribs tied together with hoops and covered with sea lion or seal skin. For baidarkas, a skirt of whale gut, drawn around the body of the fisherman, kept out water.

Using darts, spears, and throwing boards, men hunted whales, sea lions, sea otter, seals, and birds; using bone hooks, they fished for halibut, cod, greenlings, sculpins, Atka mackerel, herring, and salmon. Within this marine environment Aleut belief systems, values, and social organization evolved.

In terms of the distribution of products of the hunt, Aleut society was essentially egalitarian, sharing nearly all goods on an equal basis. There were few surpluses; in fact, Aleuts faced periodic food shortages, since their means for storing food were limited. Under these circumstances a hunter had more to gain by sharing his products than by hoarding. Norms that honored generosity and mutual aid while frowning on greed and selfishness reinforced this egalitarian distribution system. The most respected adults were those who shared their last food with guests and who offered possessions to anyone expressing a desire for them.

Ivan Veniaminov, a Russian Orthodox priest who lived in the Aleutians for ten years in the early nineteenth century, kept detailed records of Aleut life and customs. He identified three social classes: the honorables, which included chiefs and their families; the middle class or ordinary Aleuts and liberated slaves; and the lower class or slaves. The honorables were wealthier than the others, in large part because they received a greater share of the bounty of war—rare stones and slaves. Slaves, coming from other islands or other groups from the Alaskan mainland, represented an important source of wealth, since they could be bartered for whatever valuables Aleuts possessed; for example, a pair of slaves was worth a baidarka and a good parka. But perhaps the conclusions of the Russian priest should be taken with some skepticism. His division of Aleut society into classes may say more about Veniaminov's world view than about the Aleuts. Also, by the time Veniamnonv was observing Aleut society, there had already been significant contact with Russians, and the war-like behavior he noticed could have been a result of Russian influence on trade and inter-island relations. Russian domination might have created or exacerbated the conflicts among Aleuts that did exist.

However, Veniaminov did notice that wealth was not the sole criterion of status and prestige. The community respected the wealthy not only for their possessions, but also for personal attributes such as hunting skills and bravery in warfare. A wealthy person who lacked such qualities became the object of mockery. Status depended on demonstrations of the qualities Aleuts valued most highly: generosity, fortitude, patience, industry, self-sufficiency, cooperation, and daring in hunting.

Within the village, Aleuts placed the highest emphasis on cohesion, harmony, cooperation, generosity, and avoidance of conflict. The system of exchange illustrates the emphasis on conflict avoidance. Aleuts conducted trade through a third party, called a *tayanak*, who kept secret the identity of participants precisely to minimize the possibility of hard feelings. To avoid disrupting their community harmony, Aleuts discouraged quarreling, gossip, and theft. When antagonisms did erupt, Aleuts usually managed them by silence or mockery. In fact, physical confrontations were rare, and it was said that Aleuts preferred suicide to receiving a blow. A different set of values governed relationships with outsiders. Displacement of aggression to enemy villages and slaves appears to have been an important means for ensuring an island's cohesion. When attacking another village, Aleuts lauded aggression and brutality as much as cooperation and generosity when within the village. They raided other villages for revenge or to obtain new wives, slaves, and rare stones for charms and weapons. Slave treatment varied. Some became wives or adopted children and were integrated into the community. Others remained in slave status for life.

Aleut religious beliefs before the arrival of Russian Orthodox missionaries were inseparable from their overall philosophy. The supernatural was significant in all important activities. Aleuts believed in a creator and in good and evil spirits. They had sacred and forbidden places. Shamans were endowed with the powers to call on the spirits of their ancestors, foretell the future, and cure the sick.

Aleuts observed numerous rituals to control the unpredictable forces of nature and to protect life. The whale hunter, for example, rubbed human fat or part of a dead human body or menstrual secretion on the tips of spears and darts. After wounding a whale and fastening it with inflated sea lion bladders, the hunter returned to a secluded shelter where he remained three days without food or water, emulating the sighs and groans of a wounded whale in an effort to cause the whale to die and float ashore.

Public celebrations were also an important part of Aleut life in reaction to a special triumph or event, especially when there was a store of food. Lasting for days, celebrations included songs, games, drums, and dancing, along with plays reenacting the cause of celebration.

Sex, marriage, and family relations were flexible. Aleuts did not restrict intercourse for males and females to one marriage partner. There were no marriage or divorce ceremonies. Elders arranged marriages frequently when the intended were young children. While the bridegroom was expected to accept the elders' choice without complaint, the bride's wishes were respected. No couples could marry without the consent of relatives. Once the marriage was approved, the bridegroom gave gifts to his wife's relatives or he provided them with meat for a year or two. To terminate a marriage a man could sell or exchange a wife or simply return her to her relatives.

Both men and women could engage in plural marriage. The majority of Aleuts had one or two partners, although some had as many as six. One wife, the one the husband

Alaska Communities: Unalaska

Unalaska overlooks Iliuliuk Bay and Dutch Harbor on Unalaska Island in the Aleutian Chain. It lies 800 air miles from Anchorage, a two- to three-hour flight, and 1,700 miles northwest of Seattle. The name Dutch Harbor is often applied to the portion of the city on Amaknak Island, which is connected to Unalaska Island by bridge. Dutch Harbor is actually within the boundaries of the city of Unalaska. More than 3,000 Aleuts lived in 24 settlements on Unalaska and Amaknak Islands in 1759. Only nine years later, in 1768, Unalaska became a Russian trading port for the fur seal industry, and in 1787 the Russian American Company enslaved and relocated many hunters and their families from Unalaska to work in the fur seal harvest. The following century saw the construction of the Russian Orthodox Church of the Holy Ascension of Christ in 1825. The founding priest, Ivan Veniaminov, composed the first Aleut writing system with local assistance, and translated scripture into Aleut. Since the Russian Orthodox priests did not force Aleuts to give up their language or culture, the church remained strong in the community. By this time, however, between 1830 and 1840, only 200 to 400 Aleuts lived in Unalaska. In 1880, the Methodist Church opened a school, clinic, and the Jesse Lee Home for orphans, but such efforts to help the natives were undermined when the Japanese attacked Unalalska on June 3, 1942, leading to the U.S. government's decision to intern almost all Aleuts on the island to Southeast Alaska for the duration of World War II. Evacuating U.S. Army troops nearly destroyed the Russian Orthodox Church, the oldest Russian Orthodox cruciform-style church in North America. It is currently undergoing restoration. Unalaska is a rapidly-growing and culturally diverse community, primarily focused on fishing and fish processing activities. Subsistence activities remain important to the Aleut community and many long-term non-native residents as well.

loved best or who produced the most children, was the "first" wife. Family boundaries were loosely defined and did not necessarily coincide with that of the household. In addition to a man, his wife or wives, and his offspring, the household might also include nephews, older married sons and their families, and younger brothers and their families.

The cohesion of traditional Aleut society changed with the Russian conquest of the islands. Of course, their culture prior to the Russian invasion was not static and unchanging, but European contact had dramatic results. In 1725 the Russian government outfitted a scientific expedition commanded by Vitus Bering to seek new trade routes and determine if Asia and America joined. Bering sighted the Aleutians on his second voyage in 1741. At the same time, Russian fur hunters, who had already reached the eastern coast of Siberia, extended their operations eastward to the Aleutians. From Bering's sighting of the Aleutians until the end of the eighteenth century, a continuous stream of Russians invaded and occupied the islands.

ATHABASCANS

> The earth was small at first, and the land gradually increased…A man lived in a village with other men, but no women. Going in his canoe, he heard the noise of talking and laughing, which came from many women. He went up quietly and threw his spear, which passed through the parka of one of them. The rest turned to geese and flew away; but he captured this one and took her home. The other men began to get wives in the same way. They gave their children food and clothes as they grew up, taught them different languages, and sent them away up and down the river, which they peopled.
> —*Ingalik Athabascan origin story, Richard K. Nelson*
> The Athabascans: People of the Boreal Forest

The above legend reveals the crucial role water and animals played in the lives of Athabascans and how those things became part of their story of creation and their spirituality. The Athabascan people lived in the taiga, a land of spruce and birch growth. Their lands were drained by mighty rivers and characterized by climatic extremes ranging from ninety degrees to negative sixty. They were a hunting and gathering people who depended substantially on fish, moose, caribou, and berries. These environmental circumstances forced the Athabascans to live a nomadic lifestyle, moving from place to place as food sources depleted. Summertime would find the Athabascans living near rivers and fish camps, usually in tents. In the winter they tended to live in more permanent dwellings constructed from wood or sod. Athabascans are the people of interior Alaska, an expansive region that begins south of the Brooks Mountain Range and continues down to the Kenai Peninsula. Their language consists of eleven dialects in Alaska, and forms of Athabascan are spoken as far from

Alaska as Arizona. The Athabascans' way of life is tied to
the seasons and to the water. Five major rivers (Yukon,
Tanana, Susitna, Kuskokwim, and Copper Rivers) are
within Athabascan territory. Thus they were highly
nomadic, traveling in small groups to fish, hunt, and trap.

The Athabascan people call themselves *Dena* or "the
people." Groups of 20 to 40 Dena moved systematically
through their resource territories. Annual summer fish camps
for the entire family and winter villages served as base camps.

Tools and technology mirrored the resources of the
regions and the ingenuity of the people. Athabascans used
tools made of stone, antlers, wood, and bone to build
houses, boats, snowshoes, clothing, and cooking utensils.
Birch trees were particularly useful and were the basis of
the famous Athabascan birch bark canoes.

Matrilineal systems in which children belonged to the
mother's clan were the norm for Athabascans, with the
exception of the Holikachuk and the Deg Hit'an. Clan
elders were responsible for decisions concerning marriage,
leadership, and trading customs. Often the core of the
traditional group was a woman, her brother, and their two
families. In such a combination the brother and his sister's
husband often became hunting partners for life. Sometimes
these hunting partnerships started when a couple married.
Athabascan husbands lived with the wife's family during
the first year, when the new husband would work for the
family and go hunting with his brothers-in-law. A central
feature of traditional Athabascan life was a system whereby
the mother's brother takes responsibility for training and
socializing his sister's children so that the children grow up
knowing their clan history and customs.

Clothing also reflected resources. For the most part,
Athabascans made their clothing of caribou and moose
hide, and the resulting moccasins and boots were crucial
parts of one's wardrobe. Both men and women sewed,
though traditionally women did most of the skin sewing.

All Athabascans used sleds (with and without dogs to
pull them), snowshoes, and dogs as pack animals. Trade
was a principal activity of Athabascan men, who formed
trading partnerships with men in other communities and
cultures as part of an intercultural system of diplomacy and
exchange. Traditionally, partners from other tribes were

Multicolored ground cover

also, at times, enemies, and traveling through enemy territory was dangerous.

The Athabascan people lived for thousands of years in relative isolation in the Alaska interior. Except for occasional visits from Eskimos and Tlingits, their homeland was their own. They evolved a way of life well suited to the challenges and resources of their forests, and their subsistence economy met most of their necessities. Athabascans were flexible and adaptive people who incorporated implements, social principles, and ceremonial practices from their non-Athabascan neighbors. Examples include the use of the kayak adopted from neighbors, the use of the community house adopted from Yup'iks, and the use of the large plank dwellings and clan symbols adopted from Tlingits.

Clothing for Athabascans was and still is tailored of tanned caribou or moose hide and decorated with quills, pieces of fur, or trade beads. Their clothes are more than just a covering to protect them from the elements—they are also beautiful works of art. Their richly ornamented garments, as well as their beadwork and embroidery, have gained recognition as being among the finest made anywhere in the world.

Influences from the Western world began filtering into Alaska's interior several hundred years ago. First, metal goods probably came through trade networks with other Alaska Natives, and then in the 1790s, Russian explorers had direct contact with Athabascans in the Cook Inlet and

Alaska Communities: The Athabascan Roots of Nenana and Galena

Nenana is located in interior Alaska, 55 road miles southwest of Fairbanks on the George Parks Highway and 304 road miles northeast of Anchorage. You can also find Nenana at mile 412 of the Alaska Railroad, on the south bank of the Tanana River, just east of the mouth of the Nenana River. Nenana is in the westernmost portion of Tanana Athabascan territory and was first known as Tortella, an interpretation of the native word Toghotthele, which means "mountain that parallels the river." Early explorers such as Allen, Harper, and Bates first entered the Tanana Valley in 1875 and 1885, though by then the Tanana people were accustomed to contact with Europeans due to trading journeys to the village of Tanana, where Russians bartered Western goods for furs. The discovery of gold in Fairbanks in 1902 brought intense activity to the region. In 1903 Jim Duke constructed a trading post/roadhouse to supply river travelers and assist trade with Alaska Natives. St. Mark's Episcopal mission and school was built upriver in 1905. Alaska Native children from other communities, such as Minto, attended school in Nenana. By 1909 there were about 12,000 residents in the Fairbanks area, most drawn by gold mining activities. Then in 1915 construction of the Alaska Railroad doubled Nenana's population. The Nenana Ice Classic—a popular competition to guess the date and time of the Tanana River ice break-up each spring—began in 1917 among surveyors for the Alaska Railroad. The Railroad Depot was completed in 1923, when President Warren Harding drove the golden spike at the north end of the 700-foot steel bridge over the Tanana River. Nenana now had a transportation link to Fairbanks and Seward. According to local records, 5,000 residents lived in Nenana during this time, but an economic slump followed completion of the railroad, and in 1930 officials recorded the population at only 291. In 1961 the government constructed Clear Air Force Station 21 miles southwest, and many civilian contractors commuted from Nenana. Soon a road lay south to Clear, and to the north vehicles were ferried across the Tanana River. In 1967 this same river devastated the community with one of the largest floods ever recorded in the valley. The community gained a $6 million bridge in 1968 across the Tanana River, giving the city a road link to Fairbanks and replacing the river ferry. In 1971 the George Parks Highway provided a shorter, more direct route to Anchorage. The population of Nenana is a diverse mixture of non-natives and Athabascans. The majority of residents participate in subsistence activities, and several Iditarod sled dog race competitors and former champions are residents.

Located on the north bank of the Yukon River, Galena is 45 miles east of Nulato and 270 air miles west of Fairbanks, lying northeast of the Innoko National Wildlife Refuge. The area's Koyukon Athabascans had spring, summer, fall, and winter camps and moved as the wild game migrated. In the summer many families would float on rafts to the Yukon to fish for salmon. On the Yukon, twelve summer fish camps laid stakes between the Koyukuk River and the Nowitna River. Established in 1918 near an old Athabascan fish camp called Henry's Point, Galena became a supply and transshipment point for nearby lead ore mines. In 1920 Athabascans living 14 miles upriver at Louden began moving to Galena to sell wood to steamboats and to work hauling freight for the mines. A school opened in the mid-1920s, and a post office followed in 1932. The U.S. government constructed Galena Air Field during World War II. A few years later, in 1945, the community suffered a major flood. But in the 1950s, military facilities at the Galena and Campion Air Force Stations, airport and road developments, again sparked growth in the community. Another severe flood in 1971 forced the people of Galena to develop a new community site at Alexander Lake, about 1.5 miles east of the original town. Here, at "New Town," they constructed city offices, a health clinic, schools, a store, and more than 150 homes and formed a city government. The military closed the air force station in 1993, but the facilities are still being used by the Galena School District as a boarding school. Many of Galena's residents were originally from Louden or are descendants of Louden, but the population now includes both Athabascans and non-natives. In celebration of its heritage, Galena now holds several traditional festivals, attracting visitors from other river villages.

Lake Iliamna regions. In 1838 they established a trading post among the Koyukon on the Yukon River, and from here they penetrated into the central interior. Meanwhile, other Europeans neared from the east. Men from the Hudson's Bay Company entered the Yukon drainage from Canada and established a post among the Kutchin at Fort Yukon in 1847.

These Europeans were entering Athabascan land in a quest for furs. Initially they came in relatively small numbers and did not take land, offering new goods such as firearms, tea, and tobacco. To obtain these goods on a continual basis, trapping and trading became a way of life throughout interior Alaska. However, as we shall see in the American period, the influence of gold discoveries in Athabascan territory would bring widespread changes.

INUPIAQ

"The Old Woman Who Lives Under the Sea"

Two giants co-existed peacefully alongside the Eskimo. No one knew where they came from or their names. They had a girl child who had an enormous appetite and little concern for what she ate. One night the giants were awaked to the realization that their daughter was chewing on their limbs. Horrified, the giants gathered up the girl and rowed her out to the middle of the sea. There they began to cut off her fingers and toes and throw them into the sea. The fingers and toes turned into whales and seals. On seeing this, the giants threw the entire girl into the sea and paddled furiously for home.

The girl became "Sedna," Mother of the Sea. She controlled all the elements of the sea. She, when angry, could create storms and other bad conditions. She could tell the seals and whales to move away from hunting grounds.

As the above story indicates, the Inupiaq people developed a deep spiritual relationship with the land and sea areas they came to inhabit. Most Americans, unfortunately, still imagine Eskimos as subsisting in a harsh environment, living in igloos made of ice blocks and killing seals to eat them raw. But the reality of the peoples living in a diverse range of environments from interior Alaska to the northern Arctic counters these stereotypes. However, the romanticized view of the Inupiaq continues. In fact, even the error in the translation of the word "Eskimo" has affected our perception of this group of people. Rather than the correct translation of "snowshoe netter," the inaccurate "eaters of raw flesh" remains common.

The Inupiaq are still hunting and gathering in their homelands of north and northwest Alaska. Their lives continue to evolve around whale, walrus, seal, polar bear, caribou, and fish. The north and northwest region of Alaska is vast and extreme in climate. To the people of the north, the extreme climate is not a barrier but a natural provider for a variety of mammals, birds, and fish to be gathered by the people for survival.

The Inupiaq tended to live in small groups of related

families of twenty to two hundred people. Bering Strait, Kotzebue Sound, North Alaska Coast (Tareumiut, people of the sea), and Interior North (Nunamiut, people of the land) were and are the larger main groups of Inupiaq. These people used a variety of technologies, materials, and innovations to survive.

Three key features of Inupiaq life were common. First, they used underground tunnel entrances below the living level to trap cold air. Second, they built semi-subterranean structures that used the ground as insulation. Finally, they used seal oil lamps made from soapstone or pottery, for light, heat, and cooking. Homes were usually made from sod blocks, sometimes laid over driftwood or whalebone and walrus bone frames, and generally dome-shaped. The rectangular houses generally held 8 to 12 people. In the summer many of these houses flooded when the ground thawed, but most people had already moved to their summer camps. Inupiaq settlements used community houses, called qargis or kashims, as work areas.

Traditional subsistence patterns depended upon the location and season of resources, such as whales, marine mammals, fish, caribou, and plants. The Inupiaq hunted whales and sea mammals in the coastal and island villages and caught pink and chum salmon, cod, whitefish, herring, crab, and halibut. Birds and eggs also formed an important part of the diet.

The traditional Inupiaq tool kit had a variety of stone, wood, bone, and ivory tools made for butchering, tanning, carving, drilling, inscribing, sharpening, and flaking. The bow drill was an important tool, used for starting fires and for drilling holes in wood, bone, and ivory. Hunting equipment included a sophisticated package of toggle-headed harpoons, lances, lines, and seal bladder floats used for the bowhead whale hunt. The Inupiaq used seal skin floats for whale hunts as well as water-filled seal bladders, which attracted and led bowhead whales closer to the shore. Other tools included scratching boards for attracting seals to breathing holes, bows, arrows, spears, spear throwers, bolas for taking birds, and snares. Fishing gear included nets, traps made from branches and roots, and hooks.

Inupiaq used a variety of methods of transportation. The *umiaq* was a large open skin boat, fifteen to twenty-five

feet long (although some were nearly fifty feet). It was used for hunting whale and walrus, travel, and bartering. A large umiaq could carry up to 15 people and a ton of cargo. The Inupiaq called the leader or chief of their group the "Umialik." He was a substantial figure who was also the captain of the umiaq and responsible for whale hunts, ceremonies, and trade. The role could be inherited or earned, but those who started with the best whale boats had a clear advantage. The kayak was a closed skin boat typically used by one person. The Inupiaq also used a basket sled for land travel, a flat sled for hauling large skin boats across the ice, and snowshoes in interior regions.

Traditional clothing consisted of outer and inner pullover tops called parkas or kuspuks, outer and inner pants, socks, and boots called *kamiks*. Tops and pants were made of caribou skin, with the fur facing inward on inner garments and outwards on outer garments. The woman's pullover had a larger hood for carrying small children. Various skins provided for gloves, with the fur turned inside and usually connected with a leather strip around the neck. Waterproof outer garments made from sea mammal intestines completed the wardrobe.

Clearly, hunting skill was a premium for Inupiaq, and over time they developed games like the high kick, blanket toss, ear pull, and seal skinning to test strength, stamina, pain thresholds, and agility. Today the Eskimo Olympics still showcases these games. Fairbanks held the first Eskimo Olympics in 1961, drawing contestants and dance teams from Barrow, Unalakleet, Tanana, Fort Yukon, Noorvik, and Nome. The event was a success and has been held annually ever since.

Inupiaq had strong spiritual beliefs in reincarnation and the recycling of spirit forms from one life to the next, both human and animal. Names of those who died recently were given to newborns. Only if animal spirits were released could the animal be regenerated and return for future harvest. This belief explains the elaborate treatment of animals when killed, even today.

Spoken throughout much of northern Alaska, Inupiaq is closely related to the Canadian Inuit dialects and the Greenlandic dialects, which may collectively be called "Inuit" or Eastern Eskimo, as distinct from Yup'ik or Western Eskimo. Alaskan Inupiaq includes two major dialect groups—North Alaskan Inupiaq and Seward Peninsula Inupiaq. North Alaskan Inupiaq comprises the North Slope dialect spoken along the Arctic coast. Seward Peninsula Inupiaq was found principally in Teller and in the southern Seward Peninsula and Norton Sound areas.

Alaska Communities: The Inupiaq of Kotzebue, Point Hope, and Wainwright

Kotzebue is on the Baldwin Peninsula in Kotzebue Sound, on a 3-mile-long spit, which ranges in width from 1,100 to 3,600 feet. It is located near the discharges of the Kobuk, Noatak, and Ssezawick Rivers, 549 air miles northwest of Anchorage and 26 miles above the Arctic Circle. The Inupiaq occupied this site because of its coastal location near a number of rivers. The German Lt. Otto Von Kotzebue sailed into Kotzebue Sound in 1818 for Russia, and the community was named after the sound in 1899 with the establishment of its first post office. Decades later, an air force base and White Alice Communications System followed. The residents of Kotzebue are primarily Inupiaq, with subsistence activities being an integral part of their lifestyle. Each summer, the North Tent City fish camp is set up to dry and smoke the season's catch.

Point Hope is located near the tip of Point Hope peninsula, a large gravel spit that forms the westernmost extension of the northwest Alaska coast, 330 miles southwest of Barrow. Point Hope peninsula is one of the oldest continuously occupied Inupiaq areas in Alaska. The peninsula offers easy access to marine mammals, and ice conditions allow boat launchings into open leads early in the spring whaling season. By 1848 commercial whaling activities brought an influx of westerners, many of whom employed Point Hope villagers. By the late 1880s the whalers established shore-based whaling stations, such as Jabbertown, though these disappeared with the demise of whaling in the early 1900s. Due to erosion and periodic storm-surge flooding, the village moved to a new site just east of the old village in the early 1970s, transporting most of the houses on runners and building others. Point Hope residents are dependent upon marine subsistence, and they retain strong cultural traditions after more than a century of outside influence.

Wainwright is located on the Chukchi Sea coast. In 1826 Capt. F.W. Beechey named the Wainwright Lagoon for his officer, Lt. John Wainwright, but a map of 1853 indicates the original name of the village itself as Olrona. Its Inupiaq name was *Olgoonik*. Traditionally, the region around Wainwright was well-populated, though the present village was not established until 1904, when the Alaska Native Service built a school here and instituted medical and other services. When delivering school construction materials, the captain of the ship reportedly chose the site because sea ice conditions were favorable for landing. Wainwright established its first post office in 1916, though officially the city didn't form until 1962. Coal from several nearby mines served the village, the closest about seven miles away. Today, though, fuel oil heats most houses. A U.S. Air Force Distance Early Warning (DEW) Station also stands near the city now, but such advances have not broken the traditions of the majority Inupiaq population there who continue to practice a subsistence lifestyle.

The name "Inupiaq," meaning "real or genuine person" (inuk "person" plus -piaq "real"), is often spelled "Iñupiaq," particularly in the northern dialects. It can refer to a person of this group ("He is an Inupiaq") and can also be used as an adjective ("She is an Inupiaq woman"). Alaska is home to about 13,500 Inupiaq, of whom about 3,000, mostly over age 40, speak the language. The Canadian Inuit population of 31,000 includes about 24,000 speakers. In Greenland, a population of 46,400 includes 46,000 speakers.

The Inupiaq's philosophy of life was that each generation learned their mores by observing the way their parents lived. The elders of the community were the teachers. If there were problems to discuss, the elders got together, discussed it, and came to a consensus. Sometimes it was a man who headed the group and sometimes it was a woman. In these group discussions, anyone who expressed their wisdom and common sense always impressed, and the elders included that person in any decision-making thereafter.

Traditionally, parents communicated with their children through their language, facial and body expressions, and tone of voice. Children began learning the Inupiaq language at a very young age, and the Inupiaq preferred quiet or unspoken forms of correction, considering loud, verbal disciplining inappropriate and disrespectful. Yelling at a child too much would make the child "deaf" to talk or reasoning as time went on. It was also disrespectful to the name and being of the child, whereas a spanking when necessary was more favorable. A spanking hurt the skin, but constant yelling hurt the spirit.

Parents who admired particular persons would in turn take the name of that person and give it to their child, often consulting grandparents who knew their forebears for additional names. In other instances a couple would give the child a name of a recently deceased person or a name common within the family. Boys had a community house where the elders taught them the skills for hunting and how to make implements. An adolescent boy's teacher permitted him to follow the hunters in any season. Adolescent girls learned from women the skills of sewing, childcare, cooking, and household management. The girls

Famous Alaskans: Howard Rock

Howard Rock was born in Point Hope where he learned the subsistence lifestyle of his ancestors and became an activist for his people. He served in Europe during World War II, and when he returned started a career as an artist. Later, he helped prevent the Atomic Energy Commission from performing above-ground nuclear tests in a harbor near his village, edited *The Tundra Times*, and helped lead the Alaska Native land claims struggle which led to the Alaska Native Claims Settlement Act.

also brought food to the boys at the community house during the appropriate times.

The Inupiaq could solve conflicts among individuals in an interesting way, often holding a "song duel." In this event a man who felt wronged by another could challenge him to an exchange of belittling songs. The group would witness the song display. The men would take turns singing songs which through wit and derision would show the wrongdoing of the other. The audience responded with laughter until one withdrew in shame. The matter was thus settled.

In some instances a village might perform ceremonies throughout the year, but for individuals life was a continuous flow built upon levels of responsibility. Customs might vary between villages, but the increasing expectation of responsibility continued until death. At puberty a youth might be sent to an elder for a year of training. Elders sat in designated areas up front during a community activity with a public path behind them. The people so respected their elders that no one walked in front of them.

The Inupiaq held whale ceremonies prior to a hunt which revealed their philosophy of renewal. They ate all the meat from the previous year to show the whale that it was needed to sustain the village. They also displayed new clothes and equipment made during the winter before beginning the hunt. Animal spirits were thus crucial, for only if they were released could the spirit be regenerated so as to return for future use. Therefore, many ceremonies centered on these animals, such as the cutting of throats and breaking open of skulls to release spirits, taking care to thank the animal, and making maximum use of it.

Today food is still shared by all Inupiaq. When a whale is killed in Barrow, the hunters will send some of the meat and blubber to relatives, whether they live in Anchorage or Seattle, keeping alive kinship and cultural connections.

YUP'IK

The people of the two St. Lawrence Island villages of Gambell and Savoonga still speak Siberian Yup'ik, a language nearly identical to that spoken across the Bering Strait on the tip of the Siberian Chukchi Peninsula. The total Siberian Yup'ik population in Alaska is about 1,100, and of that number about 1,050 speak the language. Children in both Gambell and Savoonga still learn Siberian Yup'ik as their first language at home. Of a population of about 900 Siberian Yup'ik people in Siberia, there are about 300 speakers.

The southwest Alaska Natives are named after the two main dialects of the Yup'ik language, known as Yup'ik and Cup'ik. The Yup'ik and Cup'ik still depend upon subsistence fishing, hunting, and gathering for food. Elders tell stories of traditional ways of life as a way to teach the younger generation survival skills and their heritage.

Historically the Yup'ik people were very mobile, traveling with the migration of game and fish and planting seasons. The ancient settlements and seasonal camps contained small populations, with numerous settlements throughout the region consisting of extended families or small groups of families.

All males in the Yup'ik community lived in a *qasgiq*, or men's house. Boys old enough to leave their mothers joined male relatives in the qasgiq, where they lived, worked, ate, bathed, slept, and learned how to be men. Women prepared and brought food there, and ceremonies, singing, dancing, and events usually occurred in the qasgiq, making it a community center.

Women and girls lived in an *ena*, which had architectural features similar to the qasgiq, although the qasgiq was twice as large. Bearded seal or walrus intestine provided a removable "skylight" window. Like most other winter dwellings, the qasgiq and the ena shared the distinctive, semi-subterranean winter entrance passageway—which in the ena also provided space for cooking.

The Yup'ik adapted technology to survive in the sub-arctic environment, fine-tuning it through the centuries by trial and error and gearing it toward the marine

environment along the coast and the river habitats in the
delta regions. Women's important household items
included the versatile, fan-shaped slate knife called an
uluaq, the stone seal oil lamp, and implements for sewing
skins made from stone, bone, and walrus ivory. Men had
tools associated primarily with hunting, and these they
elaborately decorated with appropriate spiritual symbols to
aid in hunting success. These items included a variety of
spears, harpoons, snow goggles, ice canes, and bows and
arrows for hunting and warfare.

The Yup'ik geared all social norms and behavior
toward survival and compatibility among family-village
groups, determining roles and social rank largely by gender
and individual skills. Successful hunters, or *nukalpiit*,
usually became group leaders. Women's roles included
child rearing, food preparation, and sewing. The Yup'ik
used birds, fish, and marine and land animals to make
clothing and designed hunting clothes to be insulated and
waterproof, using fish skin and marine mammal intestines
for waterproof shells and boots, and grass to make insulated
socks and as a waterproof thread.

Coastal villages traded with the inland villages for
items not locally available. Inland villagers highly desired
seal oil, usually bartering moose and caribou meat, and furs
such as mink, marten, beaver, and muskrat for seal oil and
other coastal delicacies, such as herring and herring eggs.

Yup'ik is the largest of the state's native languages, both
in the size of its population and the number of speakers. Of a
total population of about 21,000 people, about 10,000 are
speakers of the language. Children still grow up speaking
Yup'ik as their first language in 17 of 68 Yup'ik villages, those
mainly located on the lower Kuskokwim River, on Nelson
Island, and along the coast between the Kuskokwim River
and Nelson Island. The main dialect is General Central
Yup'ik, and the other four dialects are Norton Sound,
Hooper Bay-Chevak, Nunivak, and Egegik.

The Yup'ik Eskimos of the Yukon-Kuskokwim Delta
area in western Alaska lived in an environment that was
very different from our stereotyped images of a place
barren, icy, and harsh. They lived on a mostly flat, marshy
plain crisscrossed by many waterways, which the Yup'ik
used in place of roads. Because this region is below the

Alaska Communities: Gambel and Savoonga

The village of Gambell is located on the northwest cape of St. Lawrence Island in the Bering Sea, 200 miles southwest of Nome and 36 miles from the Chukotsk Peninsula, Siberia. Sivuqaq is the Yup'ik name for the village and for the island. The city was renamed for Mr. and Mrs. Vene C. Gambell. During the 1930s, some residents moved to Savoonga, 39 miles southeast of Gambell, to establish a permanent settlement there, and the city was incorporated in 1963.

St. Lawrence Island has been inhabited by Yup'iks for thousands of years. The island had 35 villages with a total population of around 4,000 by the 19th century, but a tragic famine between 1878 and 1880 decimated the population. In 1900 a government plan moved a herd of reindeer to the island and by 1917, the herd had grown to over 10,000 animals. President Roosevelt established a reindeer camp in 1916 at the present site of the Savoonga village, where grazing lands were better and the herd tended to remain. Good hunting and trapping attracted more residents, and the area earned its first post office in 1934.

When the Alaska Native Claims Settlement Act passed in 1971, Gambell and Savoonga decided not to participate and instead opted for title to the 1.136 million acres of land in the former St. Lawrence Island Reserve. The island is now jointly owned by both. Gambell is a traditional Siberian Yup'ik village with a subsistence lifestyle focusing on walrus and whale hunting, while Savoonga is hailed as the "Walrus Capital of the World." Whale, seal, walrus, and reindeer comprise 80% of the islander's diets. The isolation of both villages has helped to maintain their culture and language. Residents are almost completely bilingual and still use walrus-hide boats to hunt.

Arctic Circle, temperatures are more moderate and hunting and fishing continued most of the year. During the summer, edible greens and berries grow prodigiously, and spruce and birch trees are common along streams. The Yup'ik used these trees and driftwood to build partially subterranean, permanent winter homes. In the spring and summer, groups of families moved to sealing and fishing camps but returned to the permanent camps for the winter. These permanent communities comprised large groups of up to 300 persons.

Due to the relatively moderate climate, a wide variety of vegetation grows in the area, supporting a rich population of birds and mammals, and larger game animals including bear, moose, and caribou live inland. The sea and various waterways provide whales, seal, walrus, and many varieties of fish. The abundance of food enabled the Yup'ik in the region to form a more settled lifestyle with larger groups of people, although yearly fluctuations in food availability and weather conditions necessitated some degree of mobility. Village groups, tied together by blood and marriage, varied in size from 50 to 250 persons. Marriages also occurred beyond the village, but remained within the bounds of the larger regional group. Prior to the arrival of Russian explorers and missionaries in the 1800s, bow and arrow warfare between regional groups was a regular part of Yup'ik life.

The Yup'ik traditionally believed that no one ever truly died, but that the soul was part of a cycle in which it was reborn in another generation. This cycle of life extended to animals in the traditional belief that the souls of seals killed by hunters must be properly cared for so that they, too, could be reborn. They believed that a seal recognized the merits of a hunter and allowed itself to be killed; when this happened, the seal's soul retracted to its bladder. Although its body died and provided food for the hunter, its soul would stay alive in the bladder until it was returned to the sea.

The Bladder Festival celebrated the Yup'ik belief in the cycle of life and their relationship with their environment. The Yup'ik hunter collected the bladders from seals killed during the season. When the Bladder Festival was held in the winter, all of the bladders caught by hunters were inflated and hung together in the qasgiq, where they were celebrated for five days. On the fifth day, each family took the bladders of the seals they had killed to the sea and pushed them through a hole in the ice, allowing the souls of the seals to be reborn.

The Yup'ik Eskimos had contact with outsiders much later than their northern Arctic counterparts. It was not until the 1800s that Russian explorers encountered them.

Alaskan birch trees

Famous Alaskans: Molly Hootch & Anna Tibeluk

Prior to 1976, many rural native villages in Alaska lacked educational facilities beyond the 8th grade. Students who wished to attend high school were forced to fly long distances and live nine months of the year away from their homes. In 1972 a number of native students joined together in a suit against the state of Alaska to provide high schools in over 100 native villages. While the case's official name is Tibeluk v. Lind for the Eskimo girl who joined the list of plaintiffs in 1975, most refer to it as the Molly Hootch case for the student who headed the original list of plaintiffs. In 1976, the court ruled in the plaintiffs' favor, granting high schools to 126 villages and revolutionizing education in Native Alaskan villages.

This late contact is largely the result of the lack of resources deemed commercially valuable by outsiders. Consequently, change inherent to outside contact did not happen until the late 1800s. Unlike earlier explorers of the seventeenth century who characterized the northern Arctic Eskimos as savages, the Russians described the Yup'ik in more favorable, but romanticized, terms. Russian Orthodox missionaries came to live among the Yup'ik in the late 1800s, introducing Christianity to the Yup'ik. The Yup'ik were selective as to the elements of Christianity they accepted, depending on whether or not the elements were compatible with their traditional beliefs.

Because contact with the outside world was relatively recent, the Yup'ik were able to retain many of their original ways of living. Many still speak the traditional Yup'ik language, and the focus on the extended family as the center of social life remains. They still locate their communities along water, and much of their subsistence comes from traditional harvesting of these resources. Recent interest in documenting and maintaining cultural traditions has led to a focus on the Yup'ik way of life, resulting in support of scholarly study and performances and demonstrations intended to explore, record, and share their culture.

Southeast Alaska Natives: Tlingit, Eyak, Haida, and Tsimshian

Raven thought over all kinds of plans for getting this light into the world and finally he hit on a good one. The rich man living there had a daughter and he thought, "I will make myself very small and drop into the water in the form of a small piece of dirt." The girl swallowed this dirt and became pregnant. When her time was completed, they made a hole for her, as was customary, in which she was to bring forth, and lined it with rich furs of all sorts. But the child did not wish to be born on those fine things. Then its grandfather felt sad and said, "What do you think it would be best to put into that hole? Shall we put in moss?" So they put moss inside and the baby was born on it. Its eyes were very bright and moved around rapidly. Round bundles of varying shapes and sizes hung about on the walls of the house. When the child became a little larger it crawled around back of the people weeping continually, and as it cried it pointed to the bundles. This lasted many days. Then its grandfather said, "Give my grandchild what he is crying for. Give him that one hanging on the end. That is the bag of stars." So the child played with this, rolling it about on the floor back of the people, until suddenly he let it go up through the smoke hole. It went straight up into the sky and the stars scattered out of it, arranging them as you now see them. That was what he went there for. Some time after this he began crying again, and he cried so much that it was thought he would die. Then his grandfather said, "Untie the next one and give it to him." He played and played with it around behind his mother. After a while he let that go up through the smoke hole also, and there was the big moon. Now just one thing more remained, the box that held the daylight, and he cried for that. His eyes turned around and showed different colors, and the people began thinking that he must be something other than an ordinary baby. But it always happens that a grandfather loves his grandchild just as he does his own daughter, so the grandfather said, "Untie the last thing and give it to him." His grandfather felt very sad when he gave this to him. When the child had this in his hands, he uttered the raven cry, "Ga," and flew out with it through the smokehole.

He made all the different races, as the Haida and
the Tsimshian. They are human beings like the Tlingit,
but he made their languages different.

He also made the dog. It was at first a human being
and did every thing Raven wanted done, but he was too
quick with everything, so Raven took him by the neck
and pushed him down, saying, "You are nothing but a
dog. You shall have four legs."

—*John R. Swanton,* Tlingit Myths

To the Tlingit, the power of the Raven was such that he
created the people and the environment in which natives of
the Alaskan Panhandle inhabited. He was a creature to be
respected. Southeast Alaska Natives share a similar
Northwest Coast Culture with important differences in
language and clan systems. Anthropologists use the term
"Northwest Coast Culture" to connect these Alaska
Natives with other peoples indigenous to the Pacific
Northwest coast, extending as far as northern Oregon. The
Southeast Alaska Natives have a complex social system
consisting of moieties, phratries, and clans. Eyak, Tlingit,
and Haida divide themselves into moieties, while the
Tsimshian divide into phratries. All subdivide these
moieties and phratries into clans.

The region from the Copper River Delta to the
southeast Panhandle is a temperate rainforest with
precipitation ranging from eight inches per year to almost
two hundred inches per year. Here the peoples depended
upon the ocean and rivers for their food and travel.
Although these four groups were neighbors, their spoken
languages were not mutually intelligible.

The Tlingit language has four main dialects: Northern,
Southern, Inland, and Gulf Coast, with variations in accent
from each village. The Haida people speak an unrelated
language, Haida, with three dialects: Skidegate and Masset
in British Columbia, Canada, and the Kaigani in Alaska.
The Tsimshian people speak another isolated language,
Sm'algyax, which has four main dialects: Coast Tsimshian,
Southern Tsimshian, Nisga'a, and Gitksan. Eyak is a
language with no living speaker.

The Eyak occupied the lands in the southeastern
corner of southcentral Alaska. Their territory ran along the
Gulf of Alaska from the Copper River Delta to Icy Bay.

Alaska Communities: The Native Villages of Kake, Metlakatla, & Angoon

Kake is located on the northwest coast of Kupreanof Island along Keku Strait, 38 air miles northwest of Petersburg and 95 air miles southwest of Juneau. Historically, the Kake tribe of the Tlingits controlled the trade routes around Kuiu and Kupreonof islands, defending their territory against other tribal groups in the region. Ventures into the region by early European explorers and traders resulted in occasional skirmishes between Tlingits and the foreigners. Tensions between locals and outsiders had been escalating when, in 1869, a non-native sentry at the settlement in Sitka shot and killed a Kake native. In accordance with their traditional custom, the Kakes then killed two prospectors in retribution. In turn, the U.S. Navy sent the *USS Saginaw* to punish the Kakes by shelling their villages and destroying their homes, boats, and stored foods. The Kake people survived this onslaught, but were forced to disperse and live with other tribes to continue. Over the following 20 years, the Kakes regrouped at the current village site. In 1891 a government school and store took root there, as did a Society of Friends mission. In the early part of this century, Kake became the first Alaska Native village to organize under federal law, resulting in U.S. citizenship for community residents. In 1912 Alaska built its first cannery near Kake, and after the second World War, timber harvesting and processing became a major local industry. Kake is a Tlingit village with a fishing, logging, and subsistence lifestyle. The world's largest totem pole was commissioned by Kake and carved by Chilkats in 1967 for Alaska's centennial celebration. The 132-foot totem pole now stands on a bluff overlooking town.

Metlakatla, meaning "saltwater channel passage," is located at Port Chester on the west coast of Annette Island, 15 miles south of Ketchikan. A group of Canadian Tsimshians who migrated from Prince Rupert, British Columbia in 1887 seeking religious freedom founded the village. They were led by a Scottish lay priest in the Anglican Church (Church of England), Reverend William Duncan, who had begun his missionary work with the Tsimshians at Fort Simpson, B.C., in 1857 and continued to inspire and lead his followers until his death in 1918. Rev. Duncan traveled to Washington, D.C. around 1886 to personally request land from President Grover Cleveland for the Tsimshians. A local search committee selected the island, and by 1890 there were 823 residents. Congress declared Annette Island a federal Indian reservation in 1891. Residents soon built a church, school, sawmill and cannery, and constructed homes in an orderly grid pattern. A hydroelectric plant followed in 1927. During World War II, the U.S. Army constructed a large air base a few miles from town, which was later used for commercial amphibian flights to Ketchikan. The U.S. Coast Guard also maintained a base on the island until 1976. The Annette Island Reserve remains the only federal reservation for indigenous peoples in Alaska. Metlakatla is a traditional Tsimshian community with an active economy and subsistence lifestyle, relying on salmon, halibut, cod, seaweed, clams, and waterfowl. The 86,000 acre Island reservation and surrounding 3,000 feet of coastal waters are locally controlled and not subject to state jurisdiction. The community regulates commercial fishing in these waters and also operates its own tribal court system, including a tribal juvenile court and tribal appellate court.

The Tlingit community of Angoon is the only permanent settlement on Admiralty Island, located on the southwest coast at Kootznahoo Inlet, 55 miles southwest of Juneau and 41 miles northeast of Sitka. Admiralty Island has long been the home of the Kootznoowoo Tlingit tribe (*kootznoowoo* meaning "fortress of bears"). From the 1700s to the mid-1800s, fur trading was the major money-making activity in the area. In 1878 the Northwest Trading Company established a trading post and whaling station on nearby Killisnoo Island and employed villagers to hunt whales. Whaling, a Bureau of Indian Affairs (BIA) school, and a Russian Orthodox Church attracted many Tlingits to Killisnoo. In 1882 a whaling vessel's harpoon charge accidentally misfired and exploded, killing a native crewmember—a Tlingit shaman, or medicine man. Villagers demanded payment of 200 blankets to the man's family, as was customary. The Northwest Trading Company felt threatened and sought assistance from the U.S. Navy at Sitka, and the village and a summer camp were subsequently shelled and destroyed by the Navy Cutter *U.S.S. Corwin*. Native accounts of the attack claim six children died of smoke inhalation. In 1973 the federal government granted a $90,000 out-of-court settlement for the 1882 bombardment. Whaling did not last long, and the company switched to herring processing. During this time, many Tlingits moved to Killisnoo for employment at the plant. In 1928, fire destroyed Killisnoo, and many Tlingits returned to Angoon, forming a city in 1963.

Oral tradition tells us that the Eyak moved down from the interior of Alaska via the Copper River or over the Bering Glacier. Until the eighteenth century, the Eyak were more closely associated with their Athabascan neighbors to the north than with the North Coast Cultures.

Traditional Tlingit territory in Alaska includes the southeast panhandle between Icy Bay in the north and the Dixon Entrance in the south. Tlingit people have also occupied the area to the east inside the Canadian border. This group is known as the "Inland Tlingit." The Tlingits have occupied this territory for a very long time, for 10,000 years according to western scientists, though the natives themselves say it has been since time immemorial.

The original homeland of the Haida people is the Queen Charlotte Islands in British Columbia, Canada. Prior to contact with Europeans, a group migrated north to the Prince of Wales Island area within Alaska. This group is known as the "Kaigani" or Alaska Haidas. Today, the Kaigani Haida live mainly in two villages, Kasaan and the consolidated village of Hydaburg.

The original homeland of the Tsimshian is between the Nass and Skeena Rivers in British Columbia, Canada, though at contact in Southeast Alaska's Portland Canal area, there were villages at Hyder and Halibut Bay. Presently in Alaska, the Tsimshian live mainly on Annette Island, in Metlakatla, Alaska, in addition to settlements in Canada.

Housing styles in Southeast Alaska reflected the forest resources of the area. The people built their homes from red cedar, spruce, and hemlock timber and planks. Roofed with heavy cedar bark or spruce shingles, the rectangular houses ranged in size from forty by sixty feet, with some Haida houses being seventy by one hundred feet. All houses had a central fire pit with a centrally located smoke hole. A plank shield framed the smoke hole in the roof.

The people had winter villages along the banks of streams or along saltwater beaches for easy access to fish-producing streams. The location of winter villages gave protection from storms and enemies and provided drinking water and a place to land canoes. Houses always faced the water, with their backs to the mountains or muskeg/swamps. Most villages had a single row of houses, but some had two or more rows, one behind the other.

Each local group of Eyak, Tlingit, Haida, and Tsimshian had at least one permanent winter village, with various seasonal camps close to food resources. The houses held twenty to fifty people, usually of one main clan. In each Eyak village, there were two potlatch houses, outside each one of which was a post topped with an Eagle or a Raven. The dwelling houses were unmarked. The southern Tlingit had tall totem poles in front of their houses. The northern Tlingit houses had fewer and shorter frontal totem poles.

Southeast Alaska's environment is a temperate rainforest, producing many tall and massive trees. Wood was the most important commodity for the people, from which they made houses, totem poles, daily utensils, storage and cooking boxes, transportation, ceremonial objects, labrets (worn by high status women), and clothing. Tools such as adzes, mauls, wedges, digging sticks, and, after contact, iron made the wood into usable items. To cut the wood the people used chipped rocks, bones, beaver teeth, and shells. For light, the Eyak set out a clamshell with seal oil or pitch and a lump of fat for a wick in the sleeping room. They also used dried ooligan (a type of smelt) as candles or hollowed sandstone with cotton grass fashioned into wicks.

Southeast Alaska Natives created various ways by which to harvest the seasonal salmon runs. They placed fish weirs and traps in streams, built holding ponds in the inter-tidal region, and used dip nets, hooks, harpoons, and spears. A specialized hook, shaped in a "V" or "U" form, allowed the people to catch specific-sized halibut.

These communities also made various baskets for cooking and storage and for holding clams, berries, seaweed, and water. The Tsimshian used baskets in the process of making ooligan oil, and they incorporated basket weaving techniques for mats, aprons, and hats. Mats woven of cedar bark were used as room dividers and floor mats, as well as to wrap the dead prior to burial or cremation. They pounded the inner cedar bark to make baby cradle padding, as well as clothing such as capes, skirts, shorts, and blankets. Historians credit the Nass River Tsimshian with originating the Chilkat weaving technique, which spread throughout the region.

Alaskan Dall sheep

No central government existed. Each village and each clan house resolved its differences through traditional customs and practices. Decisions were made at the clan, village or house level and affected clan members of an individual village or house. The people had a highly stratified society consisting of high-ranking individuals/families, commoners, and slaves. Unlike present day marriages, family members arranged all unions. Slaves were usually captives from war raids on other villages.

All four groups had an exogamous (meaning they married outside of their own group), matrilineal clan system, so that the children traced their lineage and names from their mother (not their father, as in the European system). Thus the children inherited all rights through the mother, including the use of the clan fishing, hunting, and gathering land, and the right to use specific clan crests as designs on totem poles, houses, clothing, and ceremonial regalia.

The Eyak were organized into two moieties, dividing their clan system into two reciprocating halves or "one of two equal parts." Their moieties, Raven and Eagle, equated with the Tlingit Raven and Eagle/Wolf and with the Ahtna Crow and Sea Gull moieties. The names and stories of the clans in Eyak moieties show relationships with the Tlingit and Ahtna.

In the Tlingit clan system, one moiety was known as Raven or Crow, the other as Eagle or Wolf, depending upon the time period. Each moiety contained many clans. The Haida have two moieties, Eagle and Raven, and also have many clans under each moiety. The clans that fall under the Haida Eagle would fall under the Tlingit Raven, for example: Tlingit Raven/Frog; Haida Eagle/Frog. The Tsimshian had phratries (four groups, instead of the two groups in moieties). There were four crests: Killerwhale (Blackfish), Wolf, Raven, and Eagle. However, Fireweed, Wolf, Raven, and Eagle were the Gitksan's phratry names. The Tsimshian Killerwhale and Wolf constituted one side and their opposite side comprised of the Eagle and Raven. The Gitksan, however, had Fireweed and Wolf as their opposites to Eagle and Raven.

All four groups used animal fur, mountain goat wool, tanned skins, and cedar bark for clothing. Hats made of spruce roots and cedar bark kept the rain off the head. After western trading, wool and cotton materials were common.

The main means of travel was canoes. The people traveled regularly for seasonal activities such as subsistence and trading. The Haida canoes, made from a single cedar log of up to sixty feet in length, were the most highly prized commodity.

Contemporary subsistence activities and traditional ceremonies are still essential to the cultural identity of Alaska Natives of the Southeast. The ocean supplied their main food which was salmon. There are five species: King (chinook), silver (coho), red (sockeye), chum (dog salmon), and pink (humpback or humpy). Southeast natives also caught and ate steelhead, herring, herring eggs, and ooligans. Southeast waters produce an abundance of food, including a variety of sea mammals, deepwater fish, and sea

Famous Alaskans: Elizabeth Peratrovich Peratovich

Elizabeth Wanamaker Peratrovich was born July 4, 1911, in Petersburg. Her Tlingit name was Kaaxgal.aat. As Grand Camp President of the Alaska Native Sisterhood, Elizabeth provided the crucial testimony that cultivated passage of the Anti-Discrimination Bill. The Senate passed the bill, which mandated equal treatment for all citizens in public accommodations, 11 to 5. A new era in Alaska's racial relations had begun. Elizabeth Peratrovich died on December 1, 1958, after a lengthy battle with cancer. She is buried in Evergreen Cemetery in Juneau.

plants such as seaweed (black, red), beach asparagus, and goose tongue. Land resources for food included plants (berries and shoots) and land mammals (moose, mountain goat, and deer).

Salmon were part of ceremonial life in Southeast Alaska, and the natives commonly believed that salmon were a race of people that would come up from the sea to sacrifice themselves so that the people on the land could live. Salmon ceremonies, therefore, respected and acknowledged that sacrifice and returned unused salmon parts to the stream. This act also aided the salmon, as the nutrient-poor streams of Southeast Alaska needed the salmon carcasses to produce nutrients for the next generation.

Traditionally, clans owned the salmon streams, halibut banks, berry patches, land for hunting, intertidal regions, and egg harvesting areas. As long as the clan used the area, they owned it. The food was seasonal and therefore had to be preserved for the winter months and early spring by smoking it in smokehouses or drying it, either by wind or sun. These subsistence patterns are still a crucial part of Southeast Alaska Native people's cultural identity.

Southeast Alaska Natives are known for a formal ceremony called the potlatch, and tribe members expected high-ranking clans and/or individuals to give them. However, a commoner could also give a potlatch and raise his position by doing so. Except in the Haida tradition, the host would not raise his personal status, but rather the status of his children. Natives held potlatches for the following occasions: a funeral or memorial honoring the dead; the witness and validation of the payment of a debt, or the naming of an individual; the completion of a new house; the completion and naming of clan regalia; a wedding; the naming of a child; the erection of a totem pole; or as an attempt to rid the host of a shame. Potlatches might last days and would include feasting, speeches, singing, and dancing. Guests witnessed and validated the events and the host paid them with gifts during the ceremony. A nineteenth century observation by a Russian named Sutkoff of a Tlingit potlatch provides some insight into the magnitude and ethics of the ceremony:

> When the chief is dressed, he comes to the door and addresses the guests. "You all know that my uncle was a great hunter, also my ancestors were great hunters, they killed a great many wild animals and wounded a great many. The latter have gone back to the woods and are alive at the present time." After he has finished speaking he calls the slave that dressed him and gives him the end of a stick and he tells him he can go free, and so he frees all who dressed himself and his children. After this they have a dance. They start in to dress the guests by giving them pieces of blankets, and call each one's name as they make the gift. They don't eat this day, but eat the next day; hair seal, berries preserved in eulachon grease, dried fish, and with feasting the festival ends. Often the guests eat so much that they vomit, for the host tries his hospitality by making his guests sick, and then it is to his honor afterwards that they got sick. And if no one should get sick, it would speak badly for the food. And those who vomit and get sick are made extra presents of blankets. All guests bring with them spoons, and dishes, and they carry away all the food their dishes hold.

The potlatch had an important function in the class-based systems of Alaska Natives in the Southeast. The ceremony promoted social cohesion, gave a creative outlet for dancing and theater, and distributed surplus wealth among all the classes. By holding a potlatch and giving away much more than people needed, upper-class Tlingits raised their status in their community.

Alaska Native Traditions and Today's Alaska

Richard Nelson, author of *The Island Within*, writes here about the relevance of Tlingit beliefs in the modern world:

In Alaska today, it may be true that what we take from the land and waters is less important than what we leave here to grow and thrive. Trees, bears, salmon, and deer might also have a kind of spiritual value—not just for Sitkans but for everyone who comes to experience them. For many thousands of years, the Tlingit Indians and other Native people in Alaska treated everything in the natural world as a community of beings possessed of spiritual power. These traditions also teach that all of nature must be treated with humility, respect, and restraint, acknowledging that plants and animals are the source of human life.

—*Richard Nelson*
Lecture During the Recreation of the Harriman Expedition, 2001

Regalia worn at potlatches were the Chilkat and Raven's Tail woven robes, painted tanned leather clothing, tunics, leggings, moccasins, ground squirrel robes, red cedar ropes, masks, rattles, and frontlets. Other items used at potlatches included drums, rattles, whistles, paddles, and staffs. Only clan regalia named and validated at a potlatch could be used for formal gatherings.

The Southeast Alaska Natives made Chilkat robes of mountain goat wool and cedar warps. The Chilkat weaving style is the only weaving that can create perfect circles. The Raven's Tail robe they made of mountain goat wool. Some of the headpieces had frontlets that would also have sea lion whiskers and ermine. After contact, the natives made robes of blankets obtained by trade and adorned with glass beads and mother-of-pearl and abalone shells.

Totem poles are strongly associated with Alaska Natives, but only those of Southeast Alaska carve them. Originally an important part of the potlatch ceremony, totem poles were once carved and raised to represent a family-clan's kinship system, dignity, accomplishments, prestige, adventures, and rights and prerogatives. A totem pole served, in essence, as the emblem of a family or clan and often as a reminder of its ancestry.

Clans raised totems for several reasons: in honor of a deceased elder who meant a great deal to the band; to show the number of names and rights a person acquired over their lifetime; to record an encounter with a supernatural being; or to symbolize the generosity of a person who sponsored a potlatch ceremony. Today, totem poles have come to represent the tradition and pride of Northwest Pacific Coast Natives.

Clans identified very strongly with the crests and figures carved on their totem pole. Some poles embodied one-of-a-kind stories or unusual symbols. Only a pole's owner and the carver of the totem pole knew these stories or symbols in their entirety, and only if they gave an account to a relative, granted interviews to academics, or left a written record would these unique messages be known.

Alaska Native history did not end with Euro-American contact. Their story continues to the present day, and they are still an important and vital part of present-day Alaska. As the following chapters reveal, Alaska Natives came to face difficult obstacles after Euro-American contact, but they endured.

2

Russians Come to Alaska

Russian interest in Alaska did not occur in a vacuum. To provide some historical context we need to go back several centuries before 1741. Russia's move east can be traced to 1480, when Moscow gained liberation from the Golden Horde of Mongols who invaded Russia and set up the princes of Moscow as their tax collectors. By 1480 those princes had gained enough power to force out the invaders. But the experience of invasion left a deep scar upon the Russians' psyche. An almost xenophobic tendency to protect their eastern borders pushed Russians further east to shore up defenses and avoid yet another Mongol attack.

In 1552 Ivan the Terrible conquered Kazan and ended the Mongol threat, thus removing a major roadblock to Siberia. The Stroganov family then established a private colony east of the Ural Mountains. This move showed the Russian government that Siberia was not only accessible and vulnerable but that riches could be had through the exploitation of furs.

From the late 1550s to the early 1700s, a combination of government forces and frontier traders moved into Siberia all the way to the Kamchatka Peninsula. Fur traders, perhaps equivalent to American cowboys in myth and legend, became a type of frontier hero archetype. These *promyshlennik* were sometimes tough, sometimes nasty, folks who were out to make a quick profit and have an adventure.

Russia's expansion brought power and territory and satisfied a longing for defense. The advance set the stage for Russians to go as far east as they could until they came to the sea, and then they wondered what lay beyond.

But the indigenous people of Siberia paid the cost of Russian expansion. The Russians killed or bought out their leaders, wrecked their subsistence economies, introduced disease and alcohol, and plundered furs by over-hunting, setting a pattern that would be repeated in parts of Alaska for years to come.

Vitus Bering

In 1724 Peter the Great decreed that Siberia and neighboring regions must be explored. At the time, Russians did not even know whether Asia and North America were separated. The Danish seafarer Vitus Bering (1681–1741) had joined the Russian service in 1704 and became a second lieutenant in the newly formed Russian navy, where he distinguished himself during the Great Nordic War and was promoted to commander. Peter the Great hired Bering in 1725 to explore Kamchatka and beyond at a time when it was an epic adventure just to reach Kamchatka. Russia brought the peninsula under control only in 1697, and the area was still largely a wilderness. Bering and his men traveled five thousand miles from St. Petersburg to Kamchatka using sleds with dog teams and building makeshift boats along the way. His team divided into threes, and, amazingly, all three teams arrived in Kamchatka a little over a year after their departure. Once they arrived, having been unable to bring an ocean-going vessel with them, they built a boat to explore what was to them the largely unknown northern Pacific. The *Gabriel* was launched in July of 1728, three years after Peter's decree. Despite the long preparation, the voyage was short, from July to August. Bering ordered the ship back for fear of becoming ice-bound. But he did come away from the voyage convinced that Asia and America were separated by the water that would eventually be named the Bering Strait.

In 1730 Bering returned to St. Petersburg, where there had been chaos after Peter the Great's death. Russia was under its third ruler in five years, the Empress Anna. From 1730 to 1733, Bering lobbied for further exploration, and in 1733 Russia appointed him leader of a great expedition to coordinate the work of scientists, explorers, scholars, and government officials. The expedition had multiple tasks: to explore and map the Arctic coast, to study the plant and animal life of Siberia, to study the customs, folklore, and language of Siberia's indigenous people, to sail to Japan and open relations, and finally to explore North America. The latter would be Bering's expedition.

Many problems arose with coordination and money issues, so Bering did not leave for Siberia until 1737. His expedition arrived at Kamchatka in 1740 and built two ships. On June 4, 1741, the ships set sail to America. Vitus Bering commanded the *St. Peter* with 75 men, and Aleksay Chirikov commanded the *St. Paul* with 76 men.

Unfortunately by June 20, the two ships had lost sight of each other—a precursor to some very difficult times ahead.

Chirikov's *St. Paul* is believed to have sighted Alaska on July 15, perhaps near Prince of Wales Island. Scurvy struck his crew, and when he neared land he sent a boat ashore to find fresh water

\.Н. ЧИРИКОВ
Alaska State Library PCA 20-241

in hopes of helping the sick sailors. The boat did not return so Chirikov sent out another boat, which also did not return. The men's fate was unknown. Chirikov spent several days trying to find them but failed. Eventually the *St. Paul* headed back to Kamchatka. Several of the crew died from scurvy on the way and Chirikov died of tuberculosis shortly after his return.

The voyage of the *St. Peter* fared little better. Georg Steller was a German scientist who persuaded Bering to allow him to go on the expedition. Bering permitted him to go ashore for only brief periods to look for cures for scurvy among local plants and to observe wildlife. A bird and a marine mammal, Steller's jay and Steller's sea lion, carry his name, but Steller grew increasingly frustrated with the expedition and with Bering. He recorded in his journal that he had done "ten years of preparation for ten hours of exploration."

Storms hounded the *St. Peter* and wrecked the ship on what is now Bering Island. Forced to winter over until 1742, many of the crew died, including Bering. Steller and

the others lived by eating seals and fish. Somehow they recrafted a crude ship and navigated it back to Kamchatka. Bering's grave on the island was later discovered in 1991 by Danish archeologists taking part in a Russian expedition.

From 1740 to 1784 there was little formal interest by Russian government officals in Alaska, but Bering's voyage had established in their minds a claim on the land. For the most part, private individuals looking for profit ventured to Alaska in search of fur riches. Some of the survivors of Bering's voyage had brought back sea otter pelts. The luxurious fur was a favorite of the Chinese nobility, who would pay handsomely for it, and it could be traded through Mongolia. The *promyshlennik*, in search of sea otters, conquered and exploited the Aleut. This was a very difficult period in Aleut history. From Bering's sighting of the Aleutians until the end of the eighteenth century, a continuous stream of Russians invaded and occupied the islands.

Aleuts resisted invasion. On Iliaka Island, for example, they fought for decades, employing surprise attacks, until the Russians, in a series of brutal retaliations, finally

Alaska Communities: Diomede

Located on the west coast of Little Diomede Island in the Bering Straits, Diomede is 1,135 miles northwest of Nome and only 2.5 miles from Big Diomede Island, Russia. The international boundary lies between the two islands. Vitus Bering named both in 1728 in honor of Saint Diomede. When the Iron Curtain closed, Big Diomede became a Soviet military base and Russia moved all native residents to the mainland. During World War II, Little Diomede residents who strayed into Soviet waters were often taken captive. Diomede incorporated in 1970, though today some residents are interested in relocating the village due to the rocky slopes and harsh storms, lack of useable land for housing construction, and the obstacles to building a water/sewer system, landfill, or airport. Over 90 percent of the population is Alaska Native or part native. Diomede is a traditional village with a subsistence lifestyle, relying primarily on seal, polar bear, blue crab, and whale meat. Mainland Alaska Natives come to Diomede to hunt polar bears. Residents use seal and walrus hides to make individual clothing items, parkas, hats, mukluks, and furs and skins for trade.

Interior Alaska near Denali National Park
Photo from the personal collection of the author

Famous Alaskans: Captain James Cook

The navigator Captain James Cook was born in Marton, North Yorkshire, England, in 1728. He spent several years as a seaman in North Sea vessels, then joined the navy in 1755, becoming master in 1759. He surveyed the area around the St. Lawrence River, Quebec, and then carried the Royal Society expedition in the *Endeavor* to Tahiti to observe the transit of Venus across the sun (1768–71). He also circum-navigated New Zealand and charted parts of Australia. In his second voyage (1772–75), he sailed around Antarc-tica and discovered several Pacific island groups. Thanks to his dietary precautions, there was only one death among the crew. His third voyage (1776–79) aimed to find a passage around the north coast of America from the Pacific, but he was forced to turn back, and on his return voyage was killed by natives on Hawaii.

subdued them. Russian crews, consisting primarily of runaway peasants, ex-convicts, debtors, and drunkards shanghaied by ships' captains treated the Aleuts ruthlessly, taking hostages, murdering and kidnapping women, robbing possessions, demanding tribute, forcing Aleuts to work for them, and sending them on voyages from which most never returned. As with other Native American populations throughout North America after the invasion period, massacres and epidemics decimated the Aleut population, which fell, according to Russian estimates, from 12,000 at the time of Russian contact to 1,500 by 1825.

Soft Gold

With many individuals searching for wealth in the Russian Far East and Alaska, Grigori Shelekhov became the man to try to control the sea otter trade. Shelekhov established the first permanent Russian settlement in North America on Kodiak Island in 1784, which was also the first European settlement in the North Pacific. The first group consisted of Shelekhov, his wife, and 192 men and was essentially a private company with a charter from the tsar. Shelekhov's settlement was important to the Russians in the context of global nationalism and their fear of other European powers laying claim to Alaska—a fear that was not without some merit.

By 1774 Juan Perez of Spain had sailed north to the

Queen Charlotte Islands, just north of Vancouver Island, but scurvy forced him to turn around. Later, in 1778, James Cook, sailing for England, ventured north to 70 degrees in the Arctic Ocean until ice forced him back. An ill-fated trip to Hawaii was next for Cook. Altercations there between Cook's expedition and Hawaiians left many dead on both sides, including Cook. Survivors on the British vessels sailed north again but found no passage. They returned along the China coast and found that trade in sea otter pelts, relatively worn ones by this time, brought huge financial returns. There was almost a mutiny when the profits became evident to the crew and they wanted to go back to Alaska. Officers eventually regained control of their men and returned to England. Publication of the exploration in 1784 placed the Pacific Northwest in the commercial sights of England for the first time, making for competing European claims to Alaska.

Conflicting imperial claims in 1789 led to the Nootka Sound controversy. In the 1780s Nootka, on the west coast of Vancouver Island, was a busy place with European and even American ships making port and trading iron, muskets, skins, and the like. Russia had already established itself in the north, but Spain claimed Nootka and the entire west coast of North America. England used Cook's voyage as their claim, and the United States was also interested.

In 1789 the Spanish erected a post to claim formal possession of Nootka. Soon a British ship arrived under Captain Colnett and started to erect a trading post. The Spanish seized the British vessel and arrested Colnett and the crew who were then sent to Mexico as prisoners. England and Spain were yet again on the verge of warfare. How would possession of Nootka be determined? Of course the Nootkans were not consulted. Spain's claim lay in a planted cross and bottle buried with writing. England's lay in the written record of Cook's third voyage.

In 1790 the countries averted war. Spain agreed to limit its domain and compensate England for damages but would continue to trade in Nootka Sound. The downfall of the Spanish Empire was evident in the agreement and would be accelerated over the next few decades. England, Russia, and the United States would have to figure out their boundaries with respect to Alaskan issues in the coming years. The result for Shelekhov and his fur company was that they could expand their domain in Alaska without fear of Spanish interference.

THE BARANOV ERA

Aleksandr Baranov

Aleksandr Baranov was the leading personality in Russian American history. He was first and foremost a businessman whose main objective was to make a profit for his employer. Baranov was born in 1747 in Kargopol, Russia, near the Finnish border, and lived until 1819. He was a successful merchant in Irkutsk, Siberia, but Alaska's rapidly expanding fur trading industry lured him to the area. In 1799 he became chief manager for the profitable and influential Russian American Company and oversaw the fur trade for all of Alaska, including the Aleutian and Kurile Islands. Activity in the region flourished as trading in sea otters and seals boomed. In addition to establishing trading centers and presiding over vast expanses of territory, Baranov organized the company to expand its range to include the coast of California. At the age of 33 Baranov left behind his wife and daughter to try his luck in Siberia with furs, and from 1786 to 1790 he made his way across Russia and Siberia to Kamchatka. By the time Grigori Shelekhov met him there, Baranov had failed to make his fortune and was broke. But Shelekhov offered him employment working in and managing his fur company.

Baranov agreed to a five-year stint in 1791. The difficulty of his journey to Alaska would foreshadow the problems he would need to overcome in his new job. He became ill, and then his vessel shipwrecked on Unalaska and he took his first *baidarka* ride to get to Kodiak. When Baranov arrived he confronted a laundry list of problems that would require inventive solutions.

The company feared foreign competition for the sea otter riches, seeing the Americans and British as the most pressing threats. Shelekhov also feared competition from rival Russian fur traders. Food and supplies were a constant worry, and their arrival was inconsistent at best. Relations with Alaska Natives were not very good, though the reasons for this were not difficult to ascertain: Shelekhov had fired a cannon ball at Alaska Natives on Kodiak, and Aleuts were suffering from years of abuse

Grigori Shelekhov

by Russian fur traders. Among the Russians, worker morale was low. Some of the men were convicts or had been shanghaied into service. The role of the Russian Orthodox Church at this time was almost non-existent.

Baranov's solutions to these problems revealed his knack for the practical. Trade was forbidden with foreigners, but the British and Americans could provide valuable goods and food, so Baranov decided to bend the rules and trade for necessities. The Kodiak settlement built a ship, the *Phoenix*, so they could travel to areas where trade could be readily accomplished. The ship was also symbolic of what the settlement could achieve.

Worker morale would need a quick fix if the infant company were to succeed. Workers usually signed on for seven-year stints and received stocks and profits upon their return after their cost of living was taken out. However, some spent more than they earned and were forced to sign up for another seven-year cycle. This situation hardly made for happy employment.

To use modern vernacular, the solution was to "party." The workers consumed Kvass, a homemade concoction of whatever would ferment, and Baranov took charge of brewing and dispensing it. The men could drink as much as they wanted for free as long as they did not consume during working hours. Nonetheless, saints days, birthdays, and ship arrivals were all occasions for a party of singing, dancing, drinking, and sometimes fisticuffs. Baranov himself participated in all these activities to boost company morale.

Relations with Alaska Natives needed to be addressed as well. Baranov invited Alaska Natives to the parties and encouraged relations between Alaska Native women and his men, even taking the daughter of a Kenai chief for his own mistress. He did not allow prostitution, and the obligation to provide for any children from these unions lay on the Russian men while the children themselves belonged to the mother. Baranov also took a paternalistic attitude toward Aleuts and promised them better treatment from his company than they had received from previous Russian traders.

Rival Russian companies also presented Baranov with problems. In 1794 employees of the Lebeder-Lastockhin Company were causing turmoil in the Cook Inlet region by attacking villages, stealing furs, and burning homes. Baranov had no real authority to act against a rival company, but after an appeal by Alaska Natives, he felt his reputation was on the line. He took a party of men to Cook Inlet and arrested seven of the Lebeder-Lastockhin employees, shipping them off to Siberia. All were eventually acquitted. But their company folded and Baranov escaped sanctions for overstepping his authority.

To solve religious issues, Baranov requested that missionaries from the Russian Orthodox Church be assigned to Kodiak, and in 1794 eight monks arrived. Unfortunately, this move was not as successful as Baranov's others. The monks refused to take part in the colony's work and accused Baranov of exploiting both Alaska Natives and his employees. The monks also condemned him as a drunkard and a sinner for living with an Alaska Native woman while already married.

Baranov decided to expand in 1796 to Southeast Alaska, as the fur resources around the Aleutians and Kodiak were already diminishing. The settlement at Yakutat was an effort to bring permanent settlement to Southeast Alaska and to supply both furs and food for the company. The Yakutat Tlingit chief gave permission to use the area. Shelekhov secured thirty serf families and ten convicts for the Yakutat colony.

In 1796, when the ship made its way into Prince William Sound and the serfs saw what they were in for—the terror of the mountains, forests, and the Tlingits—they mutinied. The attempt, however, was unsuccessful, and Baranov ordered lashings for many. Such a start did not bode well for the fledgling colony's future.

The Yakutat settlement lasted from 1796 to 1805 and was a failure. The land was not very productive for farming and relations with the Tlingit were poor. Eventually the Tlingit destroyed the settlement in 1805. Much more important to the history of Russian America was the founding of New Archangel.

Baranov was impressed with the location of what would become the settlement of Sitka, deeming it a good ice-free port that held promising trade possibilities. He paid the Sitka Tlingit tribe a sum of money to build a small fort six miles north of the hill overlooking present-day Sitka, which would later become Castle Hill. (The Sitka Tlingit were certainly not willing to give up the prime overlook location to the visiting Russians.)

In 1799 Baranov returned to the island that would eventually bear his name to build the fort for which he had bargained. Five hundred Aleuts and about 100 Russians arrived with him to build and then man the post, which he named St. Mikhail. Afterwards, in 1800, Baranov returned to Kodiak.

In Baranov's absence from 1800 to 1802, relations between the local Tlingit and the Russians of St. Mikhail Post deteriorated. Some historians speculate that the Americans or British caused many of the problems by spreading rumors that the Russians were planning to take over all of the Tlingit territory.

On a June day in 1802 the Sitka Tlingit, led by Chief Katlian, attacked St. Mikhail Post and inflicted heavy damage, killing 130 Aleuts and 20 Russians and destroying the post. An English trading vessel conveniently arrived to rescue survivors. Captain Henry Barber took them back to Kodiak and demanded a ransom of 50,000 rubles for saving them. Baranov haggled and eventually paid 10,000 rubles for their return.

Baranov refused to accept the defeat at St. Mikhail and in 1804 returned to the site with more Aleuts, more Russians, and a Russian warship, the *Neva*. Baranov and his crew landed near Castle Hill and took possession of it. He met with Tlingit leaders and demanded permanent possession of the hill in exchange for St. Mikhail's destruction. Tlingit leaders did not consent and prepared for an attack.

Sitka in 1905

The Tlingit, under Chief Katlian, built a fort about a mile away (now a national park) where they hoped shallow waters would make the fort safer from cannon fire from ships. On October 1st the Russians attacked, and after several days of fighting, they destroyed the Tlingit fort. The surviving Tlingit decided upon a strategic retreat over steep mountains to set up a settlement on the other side of the island.

Baranov had the upper hand, but in reality he was able to control only a small part of the island, and the existence of New Archangel, named in honor of the destroyed St. Mikhail fort, always depended on the Tlingit. In 1805 he signed a treaty with the Tlingit, and by 1808 New Archangel was the largest town in Russian America. In 1818 it became Russian America's capital.

REZANOV AND THE RUSSIAN AMERICAN COMPANY

In 1795 Shelekhov died and in 1797 Nikolai Petrovich Rezanov, his son-in-law, took over the company. He was a member of the nobility and had connections to the tsar, and thus in 1799 Rezanov obtained a charter granting a monopoly on the fur trade in Alaska to the newly named Russian American Company. His model was the British

Alaska Communities: Seward and Kodiak

Seward is situated on Resurrection Bay on the east coast of the Kenai Peninsula, 125 highway miles south of Anchorage. It lies at the foot of Mount Marathon and is the gateway to the Kenai Fjords National Park. Baranov named Resurrection Bay in 1792. While sailing from Kodiak to Yakutat, he found unexpected shelter in this bay from a storm and named the bay Resurrection because it was the Russian Sunday of the Resurrection. Seward was named for U.S. Secretary of State William Seward. In the 1890s, Capt. Frank Lowell arrived with his family. About a decade later, in 1903, John and Frank Ballaine and a group of settlers arrived to build a railroad, which they constructed between 1915 and 1923. By 1960 Seward was the largest community on the peninsula, though tsunamis generated after the 1964 earthquake destroyed the railroad terminal and killed several residents. As an ice-free harbor, Seward has become an important supply center for interior Alaska. It is primarily a non-native community, although the Mount Marathon natives are very active. Seward's annual Fourth of July celebration and its grueling Mount Marathon race attract participants and visitors from southcentral Alaska and beyond.

Kodiak is located near the eastern tip of Kodiak Island in the Gulf of Alaska, 252 air miles south of Anchorage, a 45-minute flight, and a four-hour flight from Seattle. The island itself, inhabited for at least 8,000 years and otherwise known as "the emerald isle," is the largest in Alaska. Kodiak National Wildlife Refuge encompasses nearly 1.9 million acres on Kodiak and Afognak Islands. The first non-Alaska Native contacts were in 1763 by the Russian Stephen Gloto, and in 1792 by Alexander Baranov. Sea otter pelts were the primary incentive for exploration, and Russia established a settlement at Chiniak Bay, the site of present-day Kodiak, which later became the first capital of Russian Alaska. Sea otter fur harvesting, once a major commercial enterprise, eventually led to the near extinction of the species. However, in 1882 a fish cannery opened at the Karluk spit. This sparked the development of commercial fishing in the area. During the Aleutian Campaign of World War II, the Navy and the Army built bases on the island, constructing Fort Abercrombie in 1939, which later became the first secret radar installation in Alaska. Development continued, and the 1960s brought growth in commercial fisheries and fish processing, but the 1964 earthquake and subsequent tidal wave virtually leveled downtown Kodiak, destroying the fishing fleet, processing plant, canneries, and 158 homes—$30 million in damage. The infrastructure was rebuilt, and by 1968, Kodiak had become the largest fishing port in the U.S. in terms of dollar value. The Magnusson Act in 1976 extended the U.S. jurisdiction of marine resources to 200 miles offshore, which reduced competition from the foreign fleet, and over time allowed Kodiak to develop a groundfish processing industry. The local culture surrounds commercial and subsistence fishing activities. The Coast Guard comprises a significant portion of the community, and there is a large seasonal population. Kodiak is primarily non-Alaska Native, and the majority of the Alaska Native population are Alutiiq. Filipinos are a large subculture in Kodiak due to their work in the canneries. A Russian Orthodox Church seminary is based in Kodiak, one of two existing seminaries in the U.S.

Nikolai Petrovich Rezanov

East India Company, which was also a private business with the powers of a government in the areas it controlled.

The new company's authority gave it sanction to buy arms at cost, make Alaska Natives loyal subjects of the tsar, and act as the arm of the Russian government from the Aleutians to Northern California.

Rezanov had grand plans for the colony, and in 1805 he visited New Archangel, meaning to implement his vision. He wanted to build the population and recruit more workers by making jobs there more attractive and to use ideas from the Enlightenment to reform the company. He sought to improve working and living conditions, bring in a wage system of payment, add bonuses, build homes for the aged, schools for children, and a people's court for minor offenses, and stop excessive drinking. He also reprimanded the clergy for interfering with Baranov and for their lack of missionary zeal and their feeble efforts to learn the local languages. Rezanov wanted long-term stability for the colony and warned against over-hunting sea otters and destroying the company's profit base. He also realized that Baranov had done an admirable job under the circumstances, and he reaffirmed him as the man for the job of governor of Russian Alaska.

However, New Archangel was suffering hard times when Rezanov arrived in 1805, and his reforms would have to be put on hold while the problems of survival were addressed. The settlement was near famine, with no supply ships arriving, and most feared foraging outside the fort because of the Tlingit presence. Rezanov decided to go to San Francisco to resupply the settlement. This proved to be a very interesting voyage, for despite language barriers and contrasting cultural backgrounds, the Russian explorer and a young Spanish girl would fall in love and would spawn a legend that lives on today.

Born February 19, 1791, on the Presidio of San Francisco, Maria de la Concepcion Marcela Arguello (often simply referred to as Concepcion) was the daughter of Presidio

Comandante Don Jose Dario Arguello. On April 8, 1806, Nikolai Petrovich Rezanov sailed into the Bay of San Francisco aboard the *Juno*, a vessel sent from the struggling fur-trading Russian settlement at New Archangel, Alaska. The Russians were in desperate need of supplies and provisions for their starving settlement. Comandante Arguello was visiting Monterey, and his son, Don Luis, was in temporary command. He gladly welcomed the Russian soldiers to the Presidio. The language barrier complicated matters, but the German doctor on board the ship, Georg Heinrich von Langsdorff, and the Presidio's priest, Franciscan Father Uria, were able to converse in Latin.

Rezanov's main mission was to establish a barter system for grain and provisions for Sitka. He was not very successful, as the comandante and governor would not allow trade. Rezanov did manage, however, to catch the eye of fifteen-year-old Concepcion. Von Langsdorff wrote of Concepcion's attractiveness in his journal:

> She was distinguished for her vivacity and cheerfulness, her love-inspiring and brilliant eyes and exceedingly beautiful teeth, her expressive and pleasing features, shapeliness of figure, and for a thousand other charms besides an artless natural demeanor.

Von Langsdorff went on to detail Rezanov's interest in Concepcion: "The bright sparkling eyes of Dona Concepcion had made upon him a deep impression, and pierced his inmost soul." Concepcion quickly grew enamored of Rezanov as well. A later pupil of Concepcion recalled, "How she loved him and how they planned for a life of love and happiness in far-off Russia." The two spent the weeks they had together exploring the Presidio and Bay Area, in addition to planning their future lives in Russia.

Rezanov proposed to Concepcion and noted the response: "My proposal shocked her parents, raised in fanaticism—the difference in religion and the future separation from their daughter were like a thunder clap to them." The Arguellos later warmed to the idea, but the religious differences still worried them. It was agreed that Rezanov would head back to St. Petersburg in order to gain consent from the Russian emperor and the Pope for the mixed Russian Orthodox and Roman Catholic wedding.

Von Langsdorff did note in his journal further incentive for the union:

> A close bond would be formed for future business intercourse between the Russian American Company and the provincia of Nueva California. He [Rezanov] therefore decided to sacrifice himself, by wedding Dona Concepcion, to the welfare of his country and to bind in friendly alliance Spain and Russia.

During this period, Russia and Spain were vying for control of the Northern Pacific Coast. Rezanov felt that a marriage to the Spanish comandante's daughter could prove politically beneficial as a link between Russia and Spain. On May 21, the *Juno* sailed out of the San Francisco Bay toward Alaska as the Arguello family and new friends bid Rezanov and the other soldiers farewell from the shore. This would be the last time Concepcion would ever see her beloved Rezanov.

During his overland attempt to reach St. Petersburg, Rezanov caught pneumonia three times. Each time he failed to allow himself to heal completely before beginning his journey again. While ill with fever during his third relapse on March 1, 1807, in Krasnoyarsk, he fell from his horse and died. Concepcion waited patiently for her true love to return and was left struggling with doubt—ridden with thoughts of tragedy or disloyal love. It was not until five years later that Concepcion learned from an officer that Rezanov was dead. This young officer returned the locket that Concepcion had given to Rezanov prior to his trip. With this, Concepcion turned to caring for others for consolation. She looked after her parents and became involved in charity work throughout California and even in Guadalajara, Mexico. Her family encouraged her to get married, and it was rumored that she had many suitors. Instead she dedicated herself to religion, joining the Dominican sisterhood in Benicia until her death in 1857.

Supplies continued to be a major problem. Baranov became harsher in trying to control his men and included whipping and exile to small isolated islands as punishments. In 1809 nine men tried to take power and assassinate Baranov. The plot was uncovered and the men arrested and sent to Siberia. The company kept news of these problems secret from its shareholders as profits continued.

In 1818 Baranov finally retired from the Russian American Company and left Alaska. His journey home took him around the Cape of Good Hope where he took ill, and in 1819 he died at sea along the coast of Java. More than any other person, he ensured the survival of the Russian American Company and the small Russian colony in Alaska.

The Aleuts and the Russians

The first charter granted to the Russian American Company in 1799 included no guidelines concerning the treatment of Aleuts. Because the company's survival depended on Aleut skill in hunting sea otters, it was crucial to keep the indigenous people under control. Thus, a second Russian American Company charter in 1821 included a section called "Concerning the Islanders" requiring the Aleuts to labor for the company. It also stipulated that the company could commandeer no more than half the males in a village between the ages of eighteen and fifty. In addition, the second charter established a joint system of administration by the chief of the Aleuts and a company superintendent.

P. A. Tikhmenev, a Russian historian who was a member of the Russian American Company's board of directors, and Father Ivan Veniaminov, considered to have been in the indirect employ of the company that supported his missions, reported amicable relations between the company and the villagers. But S.B. Okun, a contemporary Russian historian, claimed that company brutality and exploitation of Aleuts was unceasing. No government officials were stationed in the colony, and according to Okun the company simply ignored government stipulations regarding the treatment of Aleuts. Okun also wrote that Aleut leaders lacked independence, merely performing policing actions for the company. It does seem likely, however, that Aleuts had some bargaining power with the company, stemming from their monopoly on sea otter hunting skill. Russian workers never succeeded in learning to pilot baidarkas to hunt otter or to process the furs without damage.

The company desperately needed skilled workers, such as joiners, coopers, blacksmiths, carpenters, bricklayers, bookkeepers, navigators, and physicians. It was unable to rely completely on a Russian labor force, primarily because serfdom in the mother country tied peasants to the land. In addition, the government limited the timespan of Russian residence in the American settlement to seven years to protect the interests of the nobility, who feared that lifting restrictions might lure serfs to the new colony.

Then the Russian Orthodox church stepped in. Mission schools not only taught the Russian language and converted the Aleuts, but also taught skills needed by the company. In 1825 Father Veniaminov founded the first Russian Orthodox church-school in the Aleutians at Iliaka, and with the help of converted Aleuts like Ivan Pan'kov, the new religion spread across the 1,500-mile chain of islands. Several factors attracted the Aleuts to the Russian church. First, church membership exempted them from paying tribute for three years. Second, Russian church ceremonies substituted for aboriginal ones, which Russian missionaries suppressed. And finally, the church adapted certain procedures to Aleut customs and conducted services in both Russian and Aleut. Veniaminov also encouraged traditional Aleut interests in art, music, and basketry. The efforts of Russian missionaries to convert Aleuts were probably further aided by the declining power of the shamans. Russian-introduced diseases proved beyond the shamans' curing abilities, and their spiritual power diminished.

In addition to altering the Aleuts' religion, education, and ceremonial life, Russian missionaries had a profound impact on their family organization. Appalled by the Aleuts' sexual "promiscuity," polygamy, and the practice of sharing wives with guests, missionaries subjected Aleuts to constant pressures to become monogamous and to abstain from sex outside marriage. In the 1830s Veniaminov wrote that "after the acceptance to Christianity by the Aleut, polygamy and the custom of regaling guests has been stopped," although he noted that the impulse to engage in these acts remained strong.

Pressures to alter family organization also came from other sources. Rezanov, the chief shareholder in the Russian American Company, considered the large multifamily units to be unhealthy and ordered Aleuts to build smaller single-family dwellings. Although the nuclear family had been a recognized entity in Aleut culture, it had not been separated by residence. The pressures exerted by missionaries and other Russians led to the Aleut's widespread adoption of monogamy and the nuclear family residence, although the pressures appear to have had less influence on Aleuts' casual and open attitudes toward sex.

Along with the other changes, the Aleuts were introduced to *kvass*. Alcohol was unknown in the Aleutians before Russian contact. Anthropologists theorize that its quick adoption by Aleuts may have been due to the suppression of Aleut ceremonies during this period. Aleut drinking assumed forms that resembled ancestral behavior before ceremonies. Drinking was social rather than solitary, occurring periodically, and involving group celebrations. The parties lasted until all the liquor was consumed. Much like their their ceremonial behavior, Aleuts who drank indulged impulses and abandoned restraints, but violence was still rare.

The Russians also disturbed the ancient relationship among Aleuts between production and consumption by introducing the barter system of exchange. Instead of using all products for personal consumption, Aleuts were now required to exchange furs for money and then purchase merchandise from the company store (at prices set by the company).

Despite these widespread changes during the Russian administration, many aspects of the old culture survived. At the time of the United States's purchase of Alaska, most Aleuts still lived in barabaras, hunted and fished in baidarkas, and relied on their ancient technology. The sea remained the primary source for food, shelter, boats, and equipment. However, Russia's own interest in her American colony was waning as the sea otter population was diminishing.

RUSSIAN NAVAL PERIOD, 1821–1867

Baranov's retirement in 1818 ushered in a new period for Russian America. When the charter was renewed in 1821, it included a provision that required all the company's chief managers/governors to be Russian naval officers. The Russian Navy had campaigned for the provision, alleging abuses in Alaska and a failure to protect Russian interests in the Pacific.

The officers would spend five-year terms in Alaska. They were not necessarily businessmen, but they brought more control to the area. One Russian historian summed up this period as "more order, less pelts." Tsar Alexander agreed to the naval provision because he was disturbed by reports that during Baranov's tenure foreigners were making inroads into Alaska. Trade with these groups took profits from the company. Thus the new policies of 1821 reflected a hard line.

Trade with non-Russians in the territory was again forbidden. No furs could be sold to the Americans or the British. Only Russian ships were to supply the colony, and no foreign vessel could come within 100 miles of Russian-claimed territory. Bluntly, these policies failed. Furs that otherwise could have been sold rotted on the docks. Russian goods cost more and took more profits, leaving colonists underfed.

In 1825 the Russians entered into a new agreement that included trade with the Americans and British and eventually made a pact with the Hudson's Bay Company in 1839. Farms of the Puget Sound Agricultural Company and the Willamette Valley sprang up, in part, to supply the Russians. The compromise worked well and the food and supplies were more consistent and cheaper.

Most of the naval men were from the aristocracy and thus stayed apart from the workers and Alaska Natives.

Baranov's Castle, circa 1890

Gone were the days of Baranov drinking with his workers. The officers dealt with the natives more formally, using rank and file discipline and allowing bureaucrats and administrators to run the business of the company. Naval officers were most interested in exploration, mapping Alaska, and making scientific observations. Despite lower profits, there was a building boom of a sort in New Archangel that consisted of officers' homes, a new home for the Russian Orthodox bishop, some new workers' homes, and a two-story fortress, known as Baranov's Castle.

During this period, the Russians did establish labor reforms and in 1835 made colonial citizens of the workers who had been with the company for twenty years. Russian guaranteed pensions for these new citizens as well as a small piece of land in Alaska, with hunting and fishing rights. In spite of these policies, however, the Russian population never grew past 700. By 1860 the Creole population was three times that of the Russians. Education was possible to obtain, but not without service to the company.

Social changes could be seen in New Archangel as well. If it ever was the "Paris of the Pacific," it was during this period. Baroness Wrangell and her followers gave elaborate balls and parties. The community gained a school for navigation as well as a finishing school for girls. But there was a great disparity between the wealthy and the rest of the people, and visitors who looked beyond the fancy entertainment were generally not impressed. Sir George Simpson called it the "most miserable place I have ever visited" and noted "the odor and lack of sanitation." All the while the fur trade was on the decline as over-hunting continued and the market in China suffered.

In an attempt to diversify and continue profits during the era, the company put new ideas into play. In the 1840s it dug coal and shipped it to the south. But labor and transport costs made the endeavor unprofitable. Ice, on the other hand, was a profitable commodity, and the company shipped 3,000 tons per year to America.

RUSSIAN ORTHODOXY IN ALASKA

After the establishment in 1784 of the first Russian settlement on Kodiak Island, Grigori Shelekhov petitioned Catherine II and the Russian Orthodox Church to send missionaries to care for the spiritual needs of the Russian settlers as well as those Alaska Natives who had been baptized by the *promyshlenniki* (Russian for "hunters"). Their mission was also to spread Russian Orthodox Christianity to other Alaska Natives. The Church responded by assembling a missionary team of four priests, two deacons, and two monks from the Valaam Monastery north of St. Petersburg. The Church charged Joseph Bolotov with the supervision of the mission, and after a perilous journey of 293 days across European Russia and Siberia, the team reached Kodiak Island on September 24, 1794.

In 1794 the Three Saints Church was founded in Old Harbor, the first Russian Orthodox church on the North American continent. Church records reveal that the monk Macarius settled on Unalaska (the largest island in the Aleutian chain) but soon extended his work to twenty-four more islands. Macarius baptized some 2,500 Alaska Natives and blessed more than 536 marriages. Another monk, Juvenaly, penetrated to the inner regions of Alaska and converted some 5,000 people to the Russian Orthodox faith until he was killed in 1796 near Lake Iliamna, thus becoming the first martyr for Russian Orthodoxy in the New World. By 1796, the missionaries had baptized a total of 12,000 Alaska Natives. The success of the initial mission prompted the Holy Synod to set up an auxiliary bishopric for Alaska (attached to the see of Irkutsk, the main see for all of Eastern Siberia). Archimandrite Joseph was elected as the first Russian Orthodox bishop of America. On the return trip to Alaska, however, the *Phoenix*, the ship on which Bishop Joseph was traveling, shipwrecked off the coast of Unalaska with no survivors. The work of the mission continued, and in Kodiak the Church established a school for both Russian and Alaska Native children. However, when two more monks were called to Irkutsk, the only member of the original team who remained in America was Father Herman. Father Herman founded a hermitage on Spruce Island near Kodiak. He retired from active missionary work, but his exemplary life and acts of charity spread his fame throughout Alaska. Father Herman was not afraid to stand up to colonial authorities to defend the rights of the Alaska Natives, and when disease or famine struck the Aleuts, he whole-heartedly cared for the

Russian steeple and cross

people. During his lifetime and after his death in 1837, miracles were attributed to him, and in 1970 Father Herman was canonized by the Russian Orthodox Church in recognition of his saintly life and work in North America.

Russian Orthodoxy continued to grow and gain roots in Alaska Native communities. Proof of this gain came when the Spanish authorities in Northern California captured a party of Russian Orthodox Aleuts on a hunting expedition. The Spanish pressured the Aleuts to convert to Catholicism, but the Aleuts refused, citing their previous conversion to Russian Orthodoxy. One of the Aleuts, Peter, was tortured to death because of his refusal to renounce the Russian Orthodox faith. An order by the Spanish governor later released the other Aleuts unharmed. Peter therefore became the second Russian Orthodox martyr in the New

Father Ioann Veniaminov

World, and the first Native American to be canonized by the Russian Orthodox Church.

The Russian Orthodox mission received new life with the arrival of Father Ioann Veniaminov in 1824. Father Ioann and his family settled in Unalaska, where he continued Macarius' work; he devised an alphabet for the Aleuts and then proceeded to translate the Scriptures into Aleutian. He also composed a catechism in Aleutian entitled, "A guide to the Kingdom of Heaven."

In 1834 Father Ioann moved to Novoarkhangelsk (New Archangel, now Sitka) to work among the Tlingit natives. After the death of his wife, the church consecrated him as bishop of Alaska in November 1840. Following Russian Orthodox custom, he had first been tonsured as a monk and assumed the name of Innocent. Upon his return to Alaska, Bishop Innocent founded a seminary (1841) in New Archangel, which included coursework in Latin, trigonometry, navigation, medicine, and six years of native languages. He also continued to open more orphanages and schools for the children of the region, the later of which offered reading, writing, and arithmetic, biblical history, penmanship, music, and, at times, as many as four languages simultaneously: Russian, Old Church Slavonic, English, and an Alaska Native language. He allowed any Alaskan resident, regardless of ethnic background, to enroll in these schools and receive an education and saw to it that instruction came in both Russian and local languages. Certainly, the stories of the many remarkable graduates of the church system, mostly Creoles like the priest Iakov Netsvetov, who helped to preserve the culture of languages of Alaskan Natives, and the explorer-soldier Alexander Kashevarov, who mapped America's northern coast up to Point Barrow in 1838, are among the most intriguing in the history of Russian America.

Bishop Innocent also expanded the territory covered by the Alaskan diocese, setting up new mission centers deep in the Alaskan interior at Nusagag on the Kuskokwim River (1842) and Kenai on the Yukon (1845). By 1850 the Alaskan diocese consisted of 36 parishes with 12,000 communicants. Father Elias Tiskov and Father Nadejdin helped to expand the work of translating the Scriptures, the service books, and the catechism into Tlingit, Aleutian, and other local languages.

The church gave Bishop Innocent responsibility for the Kamchatka Peninsula and the Far Eastern Siberian territories, and in order to better serve the entire region, he moved his see to Yakutsk in the winter of 1851–1852. He thereupon consecrated Father Peter, the rector of the seminary in New Archangel, to be the auxiliary bishop for Alaska. In 1868 Bishop Innocent was elected to be Metropolitan of Moscow, becoming the highest-ranking clergyman within the Russian Orthodox Church. After his election, Innocent continued to support the missionary activities of the Russian Church in Asia and America and established the Siberian Missionary Committee to oversee mission staffing. In order to ensure a supply of high-caliber clergy for the missions, this committee asked for clerical volunteers to serve ten years in the mission field. In return, the committee paid generous salaries and guaranteed a full pension on retirement. As a result, the missions of the Russian Church received a steady stream of well-educated and motivated priests who were able to leave Russia and their homes because the committee gave them the financial independence necessary for them to concentrate on mission work. Metropolitan Innocent died in 1879 and was canonized in 1977 as the "Apostle to America" because of his mission and labors.

The primary goal of the Alaska mission had been to convert the Alaska Native population to Orthodox Christianity. Education and pacification of Alaska Natives, despite their importance to the Russian American Company, were adjuncts to this goal. Both the Tsar, as head of the Church, and the Church hierarchy encouraged conversion. Unlike some other missionaries in North America, the rules of Russian Orthodoxy for converting Alaska Natives strictly forbade using coercion. The emphasis was on voluntary acceptance and participation in church life—often difficult, since many Alaska Natives continued to subsist on hunting and fishing.

Russian Orthodox missionaries were generally successful in their conversions, though more so among the Aleuts and Eskimos than among the Tlingits. But with the purchase of Alaska by the United States in 1867 and the coming of Catholic and Protestant missionaries, competition for converts became keen. Of course, Alaska Natives who had been converted to Orthodoxy often tried other denominations—at times to avoid Russian Orthodox formalities—and then returned. Equally often, they returned to their own traditions.

One of the most pervasive challenges faced by Orthodox missionaries, in addition to the elements, insufficient resources, and language and cultural barriers, was that of the traditional Alaska Native practice of shamanism. The shaman, a term which originated in Siberia and means "he who knows," possessed quasi-magical powers and could protect his followers from the powerful, often destructive forces believed to permeate the universe. Often serving as chief, priest, physician, and judge, the shaman was perhaps the most influential of tribal members. As the priests noted time and again in their journals, Alaska Natives often returned to their traditional beliefs in shamans or synchronized Russian Orthodoxy with pre-existing beliefs. Distinctive Alaska Native beliefs in totems in Southeast Alaska and mummification, among the Aleuts, were discouraged by Orthodox missionaries. Whole villages sometimes renounced Christianity and returned to shamanism—a phenomenon abetted by the increasing competition among various Christian sects that occurred after the sale of Alaska to the United States in 1867.

In the course of exercising their charge to evanglize Alaska Natives, Russian priests became intimately involved with natives' lives. In addition to attending baptisms, births, deaths, and marriages and teaching children in the church schools, clergymen would, with parental permission, often "adopt" Alaska Native and creole children, usually with the idea of training them for the priesthood or as translators. In fact, a significant number of Creoles and Alaska Natives became priests, deacons, officials in the Russian American Company, as high-ranking military officers. They also contributed financially and decorated churches with the carvings and icons they produced.

Still, the bulk of the Alaska Natives who converted were influenced by shamans seeking to return them to traditional ways. The infrequent visits of parish priests, whose districts often spanned hundreds of miles, and the need to hunt and fish for survival inevitably weakened commitment to the Church. Nonetheless, the Russian priests' success is witnessed by the deeply-rooted presence today of Russian Orthodoxy in the state.

Second in importance to the conversion of Alaska Natives was their education. On the founding of the first Russian colony on Kodiak Island in 1784, the colony immediately established a school as well as a church. Significantly, the school, supported by the Russian American Company, was bilingual, and Bishop Innocent's work in the next century only sustained and expanded these methods. But the Russian American tradition of bilingualism contrasted sharply with the American system, dominated by the Presbyterian minister Sheldon Jackson. Appointed the first federal superintendent for public instruction in 1885, Jackson decreed that only English could be taught at schools. His antagonism toward the Russian Orthodox Church prevented his recognizing the unusual success of the bilingual Russian program, whose effects are still evident today.

Among the most enduring legacies of Russian America are the works written and published in Alaska Native

Alaska Communities: Russian Orthodoxy in Kenai and Eklutna

Kenai is located on the western coast of the Kenai Peninsula, fronting Cook Inlet. It lies on the western boundary of the Kenai National Wildlife Refuge, on the Kenai Spur Highway, approximately 65 air miles and 155 highway miles southwest of Anchorage. Prior to Russian settlement, Kenai was a Dena'ina Athabascan village. Russian fur traders first arrived in 1741. At that time, about 1,000 Dena'ina lived in the village of Shk'ituk't, near the river. The traders called the people "Kenaitze," or "Kenai people." In 1791 Russia constructed a fortified trading post, Fort St. Nicholas, for fur and fish trading—the second permanent Russian settlement in Alaska. In 1849 the Holy Assumption Russian Orthodox Church was established. Through the 1920s, commercial fishing was the primary activity, and in 1940, homesteading enabled the area to develop, providing the first dirt road from Anchorage in 1951. In 1957 prospectors discovered oil at Swanson River, 20 miles northeast of Kenai—the first major Alaska oil strike. In 1965 offshore oil discoveries in Cook Inlet fueled a period of rapid growth, and Kenai has been a growing center for oil exploration, production, and services ever since. The Kenai River is a major sport fishing location for Anchorage residents and tourists and is world renowned for trophy king and silver salmon.

Eklutna is located at the head of the Knik Arm of Cook Inlet, at the mouth of the Eklutna River, 25 miles northeast of Anchorage and within the boundaries of the Anchorage Municipality. The area was the site of many Athabascan villages as long as 800 years ago. Today's residents are descendants of the Danaina tribe. Russian Orthodox missionaries arrived in the 1840s, and a railroad station was built in 1918. The Eklutna Power House supplies hydroelectric power to Anchorage. The Russian Orthodox religion is prevalent and can still be seen in the village's ornate gravesites.

languages: translations of Christian texts, dictionaries of Alaska Native words, grammars, primers, and prayer books. The tradition among Russians of giving literary form to spoken languages dates back to the fourteenth century, when St. Stephen of Perm created an alphabet for tribes in northeastern Russia. The tradition was not universally applied, as political factors sometimes required the suppression of native tongues.

Soon after the founding of Russian America, many attempts were made to learn native languages. As early as 1805, Nikolai Rezanov of the Russian American Company compiled a dictionary of some 1200 words in six Alaska Native languages. The greatest proponent of multilingualism was, of course, Father Veniaminov. Besides his alphabet for the Aleut language, his 1834 Aleut catechism, which he wrote and published with the help of the Aleut Chief Ivan Pan'kov, was the first book published in an Alaska Native language.

The Sale of Alaska

By the early nineteenth century, America was becoming a commercial force in the Pacific. Merchant ships sailed the northwest coast of the continent in search of furs, and the North Pacific became a region of interest to businessmen, explorers, and statesmen alike. In 1864 Western Union was developing a plan to run a cable from California through British Columbia to Alaska and then across the Bering Strait to Russia, then India, and finally to Europe. Unfortunately for Western Union, another cable company ran a cable under the Atlantic in 1866, thus ending Western Union's hopes. But the plan had stimulated America's curiousity about Alaska. A Smithsonian expedition had already gone to Alaska, and Harry Bannister testified before Congress concerning Alaska's potential mineral resources and the profits still to be had in the Pribilof seal industry.

American political leaders had expressed interest in acquiring Alaska as early as the 1840s, during the height of the nation's fascination with its "Manifest Destiny" to expand its control across the continent. American traders and whalers were frequent visitors to Alaska's shores, and many spoke highly of its resources.

The U.S. took exploratory steps in 1860 to determine whether Russia would sell Alaska, but the question had to await the conclusion of the Civil War. In 1866, a year after the war's end, the Tsar's advisors indicated that the Russian American Company would need direct government aid to survive. The Russian treasury could not afford to either rescue the company or go to war with the United States or Britain over a colony on another continent. In early 1867 Russia's minister to the United States, Edward de Stoeckl, opened negotiations for the sale.

On March 29, 1867, Stoeckl informed Secretary of State William Henry Seward that the Tsar had agreed to sell Russian interests in Alaska to the United States. The Russian minister and Seward drafted a treaty that same night. On June 20 President Andrew Johnson signed the treaty and sent it to the United States Senate for confirmation.

The treaty provided for a purchase price of $7.2 million in gold. All private property was to be retained by its owners—there wasn't much—and Russian Orthodox Church members were to assume title to churches built in Alaska by the Russian government or the Russian American Company.

At that time, in 1867, Russian leaders were convinced they had gotten the better of the deal, while many Americans suspected that their government had foolishly bought worthless property. Within Congress there was considerable opposition to the Alaska purchase, and proponents feared that either the Senate would fail to ratify the Alaska treaty or the House would not appropriate the money needed to buy this vast northern territory.

The chief architect of the Alaska purchase was Secretary of State William H. Seward, who was 66 years old in 1867. During his long political career he had served as New York governor and senator and had become a founding member of the new Republican Party. In 1860 he narrowly lost the Republican nomination for president to Abraham Lincoln. Seward then became Lincoln's secretary of state, and he continued in that role after Andrew Johnson became President in 1865.

Always an avid expansionist, Secretary Seward had been unable to pursue his goals until after the Civil War had ended. Shortly after the war, he said in one speech that if he had thirty to fifty more years of life, he would work to give the United States "possession of the American continent and the control of the world." Seward's expansion aimed south into the Caribbean, where he negotiated to buy the Virgin Islands, and considered building naval bases on Santo Domingo, Haiti, Cuba, and Puerto Rico. Congress, however, rejected the Virgin Island treaty, and nothing came of his plans for naval bases. Seward also looked

Secretary of State
William H. Seward

west to the Pacific. In 1867 the United States took over the uninhabited Midway Island and negotiated a reciprocal trade treaty with Hawaii, which Seward hoped would serve as a step toward annexation. The Senate failed to ratify the treaty and for the most part, Seward's expansionist policies were rebuffed by a Congress and a public weary from war and already possessing vast territories in the American West.

Why did Russia want to sell its holdings in Alaska? In 1861 the Russian American Company was near bankruptcy. Its stock had dropped sharply in value. Its fur trading had declined and was actually losing money. Coal mining, lumbering, and ice operations had failed. The Russians also suffered from competition with the British Hudson's Bay Company, based in Canada, and feared that Britain might try to seize control of Alaska. Alaska was too far away for Russia to defend successfully. One way or another, Russia seemed destined to lose Alaska. Selling the territory to the United States, therefore, offered several positive solutions to Russian problems. It would raise revenue that Russia badly needed, stop British expansion into the North Pacific, and maintain Russia's good relations with the United States.

To William Seward, the possibility of purchasing Alaska was tremendously exciting. He firmly believed that the United States would someday spread over all of North America, including Alaska and Canada, but wanted such expansion to come peacefully rather than through warfare.

He saw commercial value in the territory and its future fishing, fur, and mining operations. Some supporters of the purchase saw it in terms of beating back the competition of the British Hudson's Bay Company in Canada, but Seward's vision was more expansive. He believed Alaska could be a important naval base on the path to Asia. And like the Russians, he knew the purchase would help strengthen relations between the two countries.

Against these positive factors, Seward had to weigh the negatives. Not only were the press and public cool to the idea, but many were overtly hostile to spending seven million dollars to purchase a frozen territory they knew almost nothing about during post-Civil War Reconstruction. Previously, Congress had rejected Seward's other expansionist treaties, and Seward had many opponents in his own party. Radical Republicans, who were moving to impeach President Andrew Johnson because of his Reconstruction policies, also disliked Seward as one of the President's allies. As a result, they were suspicious of anything he proposed. Newspaper headlines were already calling the idea "Seward's Folly" and "Seward's Icebox" and dismissing Alaska as a barren, worthless land of "short rations and long twilight."

Seward was so adamant about purchasing Alaska that he started negotiating with the Russian minister, de Stoeckl, before President Johnson authorized him to do so. His original offer was for five million. While the Russian minister was taking the offer to the Tsar, Seward asked the Cabinet for authority to offer seven million. By March 23, both parties had reached an agreement on the main points of the purchase. Stoeckl cabled St. Petersburg about the seven million figure and asked for authority to sign the treaty. On March 29, Stoeckl received approval from Tsar Alexander with minor revisions.

Seward wanted so much for the treaty to be signed that he opened the State Department that evening after hours and made the Russian delegation welcome. Stoeckl asked to improve some of the smaller points, but Seward refused to consider them, offering in turn another $200,000 to the purchase price. This translated into approximately 2.5 cents per acre for 586,400 square miles of territory, a land area twice the size of Texas.

Secretary Seward refused to lose this opportunity. He launched a campaign in both the press and the Congress to help win passage of the treaty. Seward's case was greatly strengthened when he won the support of Senator Charles Sumner, chairman of the Senate Foreign Relations Committee. Because of Sumner's efforts, the Senate quickly passed the Alaska treaty by a vote of 37 to 2. The House of Representatives was more suspicious and waited over a year before voting 113 to 43 in favor of appropriating the necessary money. Afterwards, rumors spread through Washington that the Russian ambassador had bribed key members of the House to win the appropriation. The press made much of this scandal, but a congressional investigation failed to discover any evidence proving the charges true. Nevertheless, because the Alaska purchase was so controversial from start to finish, no expansionist proposal succeeded in the United States for the next thirty years.

Seward prevailed in completing the purchase, but he became the butt of popular jokes. When asked what was the most significant act of his career he declared, "The purchase of Alaska! But it will take a generation to find that out." In America, the purchase of Alaska elicited a range of reactions from praise to ridicule. The *New York Tribune* coined the term "Walrussia" for what was presented as a worthless, frozen territory. But other newspapers, east and west, praised the acquisition for the commercial and strategic benefits it would bring.

Without a major economic lure the Americanization of Alaska proceeded slowly. Although Alaska was brimming with wildlife, the fur trade had long been in decline. The North Pacific had rich seal fisheries, but international compe-tition threatened to destroy the harvests.

On the misty after-noon of October 18, 1867, at the city of Sitka on the desolate Alaska coast and amongst the commemorative firing of Russian and Amer-ican cannon, the Imperial Russian flag came down over Russian America. The Stars and Stripes was raised up the 90 foot flag pole, and "Seward's Icebox" became a territory of the United States.

The United States did not roll out the red carpet for remaining Russians, ordering many out of their homes and even assaul-ting some. Consequently, most went back to Russia, California, or other parts of the northwest. The U.S.

Alaska Communities: Fort Yukon

Fort Yukon is located at the confluence of the Yukon and Porcupine rivers, about 145 air miles northeast of Fairbanks. Alexander Murray founded Fort Yukon in 1847 as a Canadian outpost in Russian Territory, and it became an important trade center for the Gwich'in Indians who inhabited the vast lowlands of the Yukon Flats and River valleys. The Hudson Bay Company, a British trading company, operated at Fort Yukon from 1846 until 1869, and the outpost gained a mission school in 1862. The U.S. purchased Alaska in 1867, and two years later determined that Fort Yukon was on American soil. Moses Mercier, a trader with the Alaska Commercial Company, took over operation of the Fort Yukon Trading Post, and a post office was established in 1898. The fur trade of the 1800s, the whaling boom on the Arctic coast (1889–1904), and the Klondike gold rush spurred economic activity and provided some economic opportunities for the Alaska Natives. However, major epidemics of introduced diseases struck the Fort Yukon population from the 1860s until the 1920s, and in 1949 a flood damaged or destroyed many of their homes. During the 1950s, the U.S. established a radar site and Air Force station. At the end of the decade, in 1959, Fort Yukon incorporated as a city. Most residents are descendants of Gwich'in Athabascan tribes, in which subsistence is an important component of the local culture.

government named General Jeff Davis (not to be confused with the President of the Confederacy) commander of the military in Alaska, making it a district of the United States under military rule. Thus, General Davis became the virtual ruler of Alaska. Interestingly, in Sitka there is an intersection labeled Jeff Davis and Lincoln, which may be the only intersection so marked in the country; it must give pause to some tourists.

With no civil government, Alaska remained under military rule until 1884. Meanwhile, Congress spent little time on Alaska. Some historians refer to this period as the era of federal neglect. A San Francisco company named the Alaska Commercial Company purchased the buildings, ships, and equipment of its Russian predecessor. Their main focus would become the Pribilof Seal industry, as the sea otters were nearly wiped out. Some proposals for the Alaskan District were to make it a county of Washington Territory or a penal colony similar to Australia. Sitka (a form of "Shee Atika," the name of the Tlingit tribe of the area) became the military headquarters. Promoters and boosters tried to sell land in the area to other Americans. Many squatted in the vicinity of Sitka, and one individual even recorded a claim for the Russian Orthodox Church and for the Church lands.

Sitka elected a town council and mayor and started a newspaper called the *Sitka Times*, but by 1873 the brief boom was ending. People started moving out, many blaming the government for their exit. They did not like military rule and complained of unruly soldiers. There was also no federal help with mail or transport and land titles were not being issued.

The real power of the district lay with the Alaska Commercial Company. By 1870 the company had acquired a twenty-year lease to catch seals on their breeding grounds on the Pribilof Islands. On the Pribilofs the Alaska Commercial Company ran a company town and controlled the Aleuts already living there. The Company generally opposed development in Alaska to preserve their fur trade. By 1880 the Company was making good profits on the seals and on the sale of ice. But soon other forces from America would have important impacts on the new territory.

3

SEWARD'S "FOLLY" — THE EARLY AMERICAN PERIOD

The first three or four decades of American ownership of Alaska are widely defined as a period of neglect, if not blatant abuse, of the new district. Virtually from the day of the transfer of Alaska from Russian to American hands, the residents were petitioning Congress for some form of civil government.

Washington, however, saw no reason to spend any money in a district where the population in 1867 comprised of about 31,000 Alaska Natives and 900 whites, with virtually all of the whites at Sitka. The situation had changed little by 1880, when the U.S. hired Ivan Petroff to conduct the first census. Although he could not have covered much of Alaska, he reported finding 33,426 people, with only 430 whites (excluding military personnel). Negative descriptions of the residents by visiting government agents only compounded the problem of small population. For example, William Morris of the Treasury Department reported in 1881 that "there are in this country as God-abandoned, God-forsaken, desperate, and rascally a set of wretches as can be found on earth. Their whole life is made up of fraud, deceit, lying, and thieving, and selling liquor to the Indians which they manufacture themselves."

Since the arrival of the Russians, the Tlingit natives had generally maintained an uneasy truce with the white invaders. In 1879, however, following the closure of the Army fort at Sitka, the situation there worsened to the point where the whites appealed to the British Royal Navy at Victoria for help. Captain Holmes A'Court immediately took the man-o'-war *Osprey* to Sitka and stood guard over the settlement until a humiliated U.S. Navy sent the *Alaska* up, seven weeks later. The American Revenue Cutter Service had dispatched the *Oliver Wolcott*, but this had neither the armaments nor the manpower to provide sufficient protection, so the *Osprey* remained.

Two years later, the residents of Juneau went so far as to elect a representative and send him to Washington. Although he was not recognized, the move helped to show Alaska's resolve that Washington must either take responsibility or legally pass responsibility over to the territory to manage its own affairs.

Finally, in 1884, the residents of Alaska were successful in convincing legislators in Washington that some form of local government was necessary for development of the country's extensive resources. The First Organic Act created the District of Alaska and allowed for the appointment of a skeleton bureaucracy. Although the act allowed for a school system, district and circuit courts, and the enforcement of mining laws, it had a lengthy list of shortcomings. The president appointed all officials, the act did not allow for an Alaskan representative in Washington, the handful of officials appointed could not hope to govern a territory the size of Alaska, and no provision was made for either a system of land laws or for the collection of taxes.

The Organic Act was remarkable in its simplicity, but the biggest problem arose not from that simplicity but from the men who were appointed as officials under the act. Never before had so interesting a group tried to govern a state or territory; alcoholism, fraud, and just plain incompetence were widespread among the members of the new government. Less than a year after they had received their appointments, President Grover Cleveland fired Governor John Kinkead, Judge Ward McAllister Jr., U.S. Attorney Edward W. Haskett, and U.S. Marshal Munson C. Hillyer for a wide range of mistakes they had made, with the final mistake being the arrest of the Presbyterian minister, Sheldon Jackson, who had been presidentially appointed as Alaska's first general agent of education in 1885.

SHELDON JACKSON

In 1877, a soldier stationed at Wrangell wrote to General Oliver Howard pleading for a Christian mission in Alaska. General Howard forwarded the letter to his friend, the Reverend Al Lindsey, a Presbyterian minister in Portland, Oregon. At the General Assembly of the Presbyterian Church in Chicago, Sheldon Jackson received the letter and had it published in the *Chicago Tribune*, as well as in a number of church publications. Jackson pushed the Mission Board to do something about the need for missionaries in Alaska. He clearly wanted to go there and tackle the new job himself. The Home Mission Secretary Henry Kendal, however, told Jackson that he should finish his work in Montana, Idaho, and Washington first. The enthusiastic Jackson, however, went to Portland, Oregon, where he met with Mrs. Amanda McFarland, whom he had known when her late husband had worked in the American southwest. McFarland was planning to go to Alaska to establish a school in Wrangell, and Jackson decided that he would accompany her.

Wrangell offered few amenities for a traveler from the lower states, but Jackson found land available for McFarland to set up a school. After seeing to it that McFarland was safely ensconced, Jackson set off in a canoe with several local Alaska Natives to explore Southeast Alaska. After what he found to be an informative and exciting trip around the region, he returned to Wrangell and then went home with a plan to raise money for the school. Soon after his return, Jackson raised $12,000 in support of McFarland's work.

In 1881 the Jackson family moved their residence to New York City. He also made another trip to Alaska in 1881 and established several mission stations in the Southeastern part of the district. He named one of these Haines, after Francis Haines, an old friend and Secretary of the Woman's Executive Committee of Home Missions. In 1882 Jackson raised and delivered $5,000 to John Brady at Sitka for a school building project. Brady sponsored an industrial school for Alaska Native boys at Sitka. As a result of the combined efforts of Brady and Jackson, a school building was completed in 1882.

In 1883 the Jackson family moved to Washington, D.C. It was likely that Jackson, who could not stand the idea of a sedentary office job, made this move to avoid working in the Home Mission Board Office. Moreover, his new interests in Alaska required lobbying efforts with the federal government. That same year Senator Benjamin Harrison, a friend of Jackson's and a fellow Presbyterian, introduced a bill to Congress to provide funding for the

Alaska Communities: Sitka

Sitka is located on the west coast of Baranof Island fronting the Pacific Ocean, on Sitka Sound, 95 air miles southwest of Juneau, 185 miles northwest of Ketchikan, and 862 air miles north of Seattle. An extinct volcano, Mount Edgecumbe, rises 3,200 feet above the community. A major tribe of Tlingits originally inhabited Sitka, calling the village "Shee Atika." In 1799 a site seven miles from present day Sitka became "New Archangel." Baranov, the manager of the Russian-American Company, built St. Michael's Redoubt Trading Post and fort there, but Tlingits burned down the fort and looted the warehouse in 1802. In the Battle of Sitka in 1804, the Russians retaliated by destroying the Tlingit Fort in present day Totem Park. This was the last major stand by the Tlingits against the Russians, and the tribe evacuated the area until about 1822. By 1808, Sitka was the capital of Russian Alaska, and during the mid-1800s, Sitka was the major port on the north Pacific coast, with ships calling from many nations. Furs destined for European and Asian markets were the main export, but salmon, lumber, and ice were also exported to Hawaii, Mexico, and California. After the purchase of Alaska by the U.S. in 1867, Sitka remained the capital of the territory until 1906, when the seat of government moved to Juneau. A Presbyterian missionary, Sheldon Jackson, started a school, and in 1878 the area earned one of the first canneries in Alaska. In the early 1900s, gold mines contributed to its growth, and the city was incorporated in 1913. During World War II, the U.S. fortified the area and built an air base on Japonski Island across the harbor, with 30,000 military personnel and over 7,000 civilians. After the war, the BIA converted some of the buildings for a boarding school for Alaska Natives, Mt. Edgecumbe High School. The U.S. Coast Guard now maintains the air station and other facilities on the island. A large pulp mill began operations at Silver Bay in 1960 but is now closed. Sitka offers abundant resources and a diverse economy, and Tlingit culture, Russian influences, arts and artifacts remain a part of the local color. Sitka has year-round access to outdoor recreation in the Gulf of Alaska and Tongass National Forest.

education of Alaskan children. Jackson was keen on this legislation and lobbied hard for its passage.

In July of 1884, Jackson led a tour of 150 delegates from the National Education Board to southeastern Alaska. The Board of Home Missions had also designated him as a missionary to the congregation in Sitka. After the National Education tourists returned home, Jackson stayed in Sitka and organized the First Presbyterian church of Sitka and the Presbytery of Alaska.

Jackson's lobbying and tour leading proved successful, and later in 1884 Congress appropriated the funds for the education of children in Alaska. At the same time, fellow Presbyterian and friend, Commissioner of Education John Eaton, appointed Jackson as General Agent of Education for Alaska. The annual salary was twelve hundred dollars.

Jackson had an ambitious plan not only to start schools but also to work for "good government" in the district. His political efforts to ensure the latter made Jackson controversial in Alaska. In fact, in May of 1885, Jackson was arrested in Sitka for obstructing a public road in an expansion effort for the Sitka Industrial School. Eventually he was cleared of the charges, but the incident made it clear that Jackson's power did not please everyone in the territory.

During a trip to Point Barrow in 1890, Jackson grew convinced that the Inupiat were in danger of becoming extinct. He believed that the traditional food source of Siberian Natives, reindeer, must be introduced to northern Alaska. To this end, he raised over two thousand dollars and set out for Siberia in 1891 to procure reindeer. While in Siberia he purchased sixteen animals which he placed with Eskimo people on an island near the Alaska mainland. In 1891, aboard the U.S. Revenue Cutter *Bear*, Jackson purchased one hundred seventy-five more reindeer, which he brought to Alaska. In 1893, given this success, Jackson got money to bring even more reindeer to Alaska.

To many, Jackson was making good progress, but others thought he was far exceeding his authority. In 1898 Congress appropriated two hundred thousand dollars for the purchase of reindeer in order to relieve miners who were in danger of starvation in the Yukon Valley. Jackson this time went to Lapland to purchase the reindeer, and bring them across the United States to Alaska. By the time

Jackson got back with the reindeer the miners were out of trouble. The reindeer were moved to Alaska anyhow, and Jackson was considered to be in charge. When the reindeer finally arrived in Alaska only 141 of the original 538 remained alive, and the blame for the fiasco fell on Jackson.

Jackson came in for more criticism when his old friend John Brady became the governor of Alaska in 1897. Some people worried about the creation of a Presbyterian dynasty. The rumors finally influenced President Theodore Roosevelt, and in 1905 he appointed an investigator to look into the state of things in Alaska. The investigator, Frank Churchill, published his report in 1906. Churchill criticized Jackson for favoring church schools (particularly Presbyterian schools) and blamed Jackson for the reindeer debacle. He also saw it as inappropriate for Jackson to receive a salary from the Board of Home Missions while at the same time holding a government position. Still, he found no reason to question Jackson's honesty. Churchill concluded by noting that Sheldon Jackson was not in good health and that, as a result, his judgment may have been questionable.

Sheldon Jackson was a man of his times, and in spite of his vigorous religious bent, he was as ambitious and powerful as many of the nation's most influential politicians and leaders of industry. There is no doubt that he was a man of almost unlimited energy and tenacity who seemed willing to endure almost any hardship in his quest to win the West for Christ. Many saw Jackson as a hero and a brave man who sacrificed much for his fellow man. Many of his activities are recorded in numerous governmental and religious reports as well as in his book *Difficulties at Sitka in 1885* (1886).

But in order to fully appreciate his contributions and accomplishments, it is necessary to examine Jackson's life in the context of nineteenth century frontier America. He, like most of his contemporaries, held views about segregation and religion that we now would consider intolerant. Despite his many accomplishments, he was, at best, condescending toward Alaska Native values and beliefs, and he always believed his own culture, faith, and point of view to be superior. It is easy to admire the single-mindedness of his life-long mission, but his insistence on the forced assimilation of Native American children created a legacy of ambivalence and even anger and resentment that continues to plague relationships even a century later. Interestingly, his legacy lives on at Sheldon Jackson College in Sitka, which is still associated with the Presbyterian Church but contains a strong Alaska Native Studies program headed at this writing by an Alaska Native leader who attended Sheldon Jackson College when it was a high school. Also, many of the leaders of the Alaska Native Brotherhood were Sheldon Jackson High students who went on to fight for Alaska Native rights.

JAMES WICKERSHAM

James Wickersham was another remarkable figure in the early American period of Alaskan history. Born on August 24, 1857, in Illinois, he moved in 1883 with his wife Deborah to Tacoma, Washington Territory. There he served as county probate judge and Tacoma city attorney and, in 1898, was elected to the Washington Territorial House of Representatives.

The 65th Congress passed the Civil Code of Alaska in 1900, creating the second and third judicial districts for the northern portion of Alaska. President McKinley appointed James Wickersham district judge for the Third Judicial District, headquartered at Eagle City. In June of 1900, Wickersham was sworn in, becoming the first judge to sit in the Interior of Alaska.

The new district covered some 300,000 square miles; it had no roads, no public buildings, and almost no U.S.

Famous Alaskans: Amanda McFarland

McFarland was the first woman missionary to Alaska. Her first calling to be a missionary was at her home church in Portland Oregon, when a missionary came to the church to speak. He pleaded with the congregation to go to Alaska. At the time, the hardships she heard of about Alaska missionary work kept her home. Instead she married Reverend McFarland, and she and her husband became missionaries in Illinois. But when her husband died, she at last decided to go to Alaska as a missionary. In 1877 McFarland went to Alaska with Dr. Sheldon Jackson. She started a home and school for girls in Fort Wrangell. After the school burned, all the girls joined a boys' industrial school in Sitka.

James Wickersham

currency. The district court and its officials were the only civilian government, besides town functionaries, in the whole of the Interior. In addition to traveling his circuit, the district judge was expected to procure land and materials to construct his own courthouse and jails. It was fortunate that his duties also included the collection of mercantile and saloon license fees, for Congress had provided no other funds for the construction and operation of the court.

Wickersham covered his circuit by boat in summer and by dogsled in winter. When claim-jumping disputes at Rampart required the attention of the court in 1901, Wickersham traveled from Eagle City to preside, a round-trip journey of over 1,000 miles of dog mushing made in 45 days, including six days of court. The following summer he traveled to Unalaska in the Aleutians to try a murder case. In the spring of 1903, following a gold strike in the Tanana Valley and the ensuing stampede, Judge Wickersham loaded the court records into a dogsled and moved his headquarters to the new population center, Fairbanks, a collection of tents and a few log cabins.

Wickersham greatly appreciated the beauty and resources of the Tanana Valley, frequently citing its agricultural potential. He found time to enjoy hunting and hiking, stopping at Alaska Native encampments to hear their history and learn about their culture. In the summer of 1903 he led the first attempt to climb Denali, taking directions from Olyman Cheah of the Tena band of Athabascans.

Wickersham resigned as district judge in 1908 and became Alaska's delegate to Congress. He served until 1920 and was re-elected in 1930. Wickersham was crucial in securing the passage of the Organic Act of 1912 that granted Alaska territorial status. Also, he introduced the Alaska Railroad Bill, the legislation to establish McKinley Park, and was responsible for the creation of the Alaska Agricultural College and School of Mines, which later became the University of Alaska. Finally, in 1916 he introduced the first Alaska Statehood Bill.

Frequently at the center of controversy, Wickersham perhaps exerted a greater influence on events during the formative years of the Alaskan Territory than any other individual. He was the author of many articles about Alaska, on subjects ranging from the salmon industry to Alaska's need for self government. He compiled the first edition of the Alaska Reports, a record of all decisions of the Alaska courts, and, after retiring from Congress at age 76, he assembled the first index of all material published about Alaska, *The Wickersham Bibliography*.

Wickersham died in Juneau on October 23, 1939. In 1949, the Alaska Territorial Legislature paid tribute to his memory by designating his birthday, August 24, Wickersham Day. James Wickersham was a statesman, author, historian, and scholar. One historian said of Wickersham: "No other man has made as deep and varied imprints on Alaska's heritage, whether it is in politics, government, commerce, literature, history or philosophy. A federal judge, member of Congress, attorney and explorer, present-day Alaska is deeply in debt to him."

Harriman Expedition

It has been almost 100 years since Edward Henry Harriman assembled an elite crew of scientists and artists and took them on a two-month survey of the Alaskan coast. The 1899 expedition was the largest and most famous of its day. Enthusiastic crowds cheered their departure, and newspapers all over the world featured the story on their front pages.

The voyage produced a few new scientific discoveries, for example, a previously unknown fiord and glacier, but its value as an assessment and survey of an Alaskan environment in flux is unparalleled. The scientists produced thirteen volumes of data that took twelve years to compile.

The expedition arrived when Alaska's coastal beauty was beginning to tarnish from heavy use of its natural resources. The Gold Rush was in full swing, salmon canneries were working round the clock, and fur seal rookeries exported thousands of skins every year. The Alaska Native populations in some areas had already been reduced dramatically; in other places, the natives competed with Chinese laborers for low-wage jobs in fish factories.

In many instances, the expeditioners observed and catalogued the flora and fauna of a pristine, idealized wonderland. Yet the signs of so-called progress were difficult to ignore. The Harriman Expedition chronicled an Alaska on the brink of alterations devastating to the environment.

The passengers on the expedition ship were some of the most famous and influential people in America at the time. Edward Harriman was one of the nation's most powerful railroad magnates, and C. Hart Merriam was one of its most prominent scientists. John Burroughs was the best selling nature writer of the day, and John Muir was the much-admired father of the American conservation movement. With these men traveled an eminent assembly of nature artists, geologists, botanists, foresters and zoologists. One can only imagine what the dinner-time conversation must have been like in such an assemblage.

The boat left Seattle on May 31, 1899. For the next two months, the *Elder* steamed almost 9,000 miles along the coasts of British Columbia and Alaska. They made some fifty stops, sometimes brief visits that lasted an afternoon, sometimes longer excursions. At several places, several of the travelers went ashore with camping equipment and stayed overnight, so they could collect more specimens or hike into a forest or across a glacier. The *Elder* would steam off to some other spot and then return and pick the campers up at an agreed upon time.

Perhaps a precursor to today's luxury ship cruises, life on the boat was lavish by any standard. The cabins and salons were newly remodeled and a chef prepared gourmet meals. Harriman even provided space for work on specimen preservation and simple laboratory spaces for research. There was a library with over 500 books about Alaska, and on many days, one or another of the scientists would lecture about his area of expertise.

This extravagance was certainly a contrast to life in Alaska in 1899. The population numbered 63,000 and included many Alaska Natives struggling to maintain their traditional cultures in the face of Russian and then

Alaskan forest

American occupation. Neither the Russians nor the Americans had been particularly wise in their dealings with the Alaska Natives, and in some cases, they had been ruthless. Life was also difficult for the hundreds of prospectors who had come to Alaska during the Gold Rush. For every man who made a fortune there were many hundreds more who left penniless.

The Harriman Expedition differed from other surveys and expeditions to Alaska in that the scientists and artists on board did not stay very long at any one spot, and there was little chance for in-depth scientific exploration. Yet they were careful observers and eager specimen gatherers. Their records and collections gave us a way to assess one-hundred years of change along the Alaskan coast. The fact that there were so many scientists of the first rank on board the *Elder* makes their observations all the more valuable.

Another difference stood out: this was one individual's project. Edward H. Harriman conceived, planned, and paid for the trip himself. Newspapers of the time praised him highly for this, and several editorial writers called for other American millionaires to sponsor such trips. And Harriman certainly put his own mark on the voyage. It was he who insisted the boat sail through the narrow, shallow inlet in Prince William Sound that opened up into a previously undiscovered fiord. It was he who chose to include stops at Kodiak and Siberia, and, when the trip was over, it was he who paid for the publication of the participants' scientific writing.

It took 50 specialists the better part of a decade to study, catalogue, edit and publish the thirteen volumes that cover the scientific observations and findings from the trip. Some of the volumes are simply listings of field notes and specimens collected. Other volumes, particularly the glacier study, were judged to be important reports that broke new ground in scientific study. All told, these volumes, along with diaries, letters, newspaper accounts, and scientific reviews, form a monumental record of this two month trip to Alaska.

Of equal interest is the vast collection of animal and plant specimens from the trip. There were 8,000 insects, 344 of which had been previously unknown to scientists. The collections included thousands of shellfish, birds, small mammals, and even a small number of large mammal specimens. This natural history treasure trove, much of it now at the Smithsonian Institution, retains great research value. Even today these specimens give us information about Alaska's ecosystems of a century ago.

One interesting aspect of these collections is the way in which our ideas about this kind of collecting have changed. Consider the case of large mammals. It would be unthinkable nowadays that the leader of a scientific expedition would shoot a female grizzly and cub out of season on Kodiak Island, but that is what happened in early July on the Harriman expedition. Another kind of collecting, taking Alaska Native artifacts from the uninhabited village at Cape Fox, violates the standards we would find acceptable today. Native American artifacts are now protected by law, and, in fact, some items taken in the late nineteenth and early twentieth centuries were returned to the tribes that once owned and produced these objects. Other ships that cruised to Alaska during this time period were not interested in scientific discoveries or scenery; instead they went north in search of profits.

WHALING IN ALASKA

Whaling has a long, significant, and colorful history in Alaska. From both subsistence and commercial perspectives in the western Arctic, the bowhead and to a lesser degree the belugas were the primary focus of attention. Baleen whales are generally larger and slower than toothed whales, making them easier prey for traditional hunters, while European and American society placed a high value on both the oil and baleen obtained from these whales.

Alaska Natives of the Bering Sea are known to have hunted the bowhead for at least the past 2,500 years. Hunters went to sea in walrus-hide umiaks or the smaller kayaks, with toggle-head harpoons and seal-bladder floats as tools. The float served to both slow and tire the whale after it had been harpooned, and to mark the kill; a wounded whale could sometimes run for days, and it was a true test of endurance for the umiak crew to keep up. When the hunt was successful, these men achieved enormous stature in their communities.

Writings from the Harriman Expedition

The voluminous collection of scientific and natural writings that the expedition spawned is simply titled *Alaska: The Harriman Expedition, 1899*. Below is an excerpt from the book's preface, written by Edward H. Harriman himself:

> Our Comfort and safety required a large vessel and crew, and preparations for the voyage were consequently on a scale disproportionate to the size of the party. We decided, therefore to include some guests who, while adding to the interest and pleasure of the expedition, would gather useful information and distribute it for the benefit of others.

Among the "guests" that Harriman spoke of was nature writer Iohn Burroughs. Toward the end of his journey through the inside passage, he visited the brand new Yukon Gold Rush town of Skagway, and traveled to the border between the US and Canada at White Pass on the still-incomplete White Pass and Yukon Railroad. Excerpts of his account of his visit are as accurate today as they were 101 years ago:

> In the afternoon we steamed up Lynn Canal over broad, placid waters, shut in by dark smooth-based mountains that end in bare serrated peaks. Glaciers became more and more numerous; one on our right hung high on the brink of a sheer, naked precipice, as if drawing back from the fearful plunge. But plunge it did not and probably never will.
>
> We were soon in sight of a much larger glacier, the Davidson, on our left. It flows out of a deep gorge and almost reaches the inlet. Seen from afar it suggest the side view of a huge white foot with its toe pressing a dark line of forest into the sea.
>
> Before sunset we reached Skagway and landed at the long, high pier (the tides here are sixteen or eighteen feet). The pier was swarming with people. Such a gathering and such curiosity and alertness we had not before seen. Hotel runners flourished their cards and called out the names of their various hostelries before we had touched the dock. Boys greeted us with shouts and comments; women and girls, some of them in bicycles suits, pushed to the front and gazed intently at the strangers. All seemed to be expecting something, friends or news, or some sensational occurrence. No sooner had we touched than the boys swarmed upon us like ants and began to explore the ship, and were as

promptly swept ashore again. Skagway is barely two years old. Born of the gold fever, it is still feverish and excitable. It is on a broad delta of land made by the Skagway river between the mountains, and, it seems to me, is likely at any time by great flood in the river to be swept into the sea. It began at the stump and is probably still the stumpiest town in the country. Many of the houses stand upon stumps; there are stumps in nearly every dooryard, but the people already speak of the "early times" three years ago.

The next day the officials of the Yukon and White Pass Railroad took our party on an excursion to the top of the famous White Pass, twenty-one miles distant. The grade up the mountain is in places over two hundred feet to the mile, and in making the ascent the train climbs about twenty-nine hundred feet. After the road leaves Skagway River its course is along the face of precipitous granite peaks and domes, with long loops around the heads of gorges and chasms; occasionally on trestles over yawning gulfs, but for the most part on a shelf of rock blasted out of the side of the mountain. The train stopped from time to time and allowed us to walk ahead and come face to face with the scene. The terrible and the sublime were on every hand. It was as appalling to look up as to look down; chaos and death below us, impeding avalanches of hanging rocks above us. How elemental and cataclysmal it all looked! I felt as if I were seeing for the first time the real granite ribs of the earth; they had been cut into and slivered, and there was no mistake about them. All I had seen before were but scales and warts on the surface by comparison; here were the primal rocks that held the planet together, sweeping up into the clouds and plunging down into the abyss. Over against us on the other side of the chasm we caught glimpses here and there of the "Dead Horse Trail." Among the spruces and along the rocky terraces are said to have perished several thousand horses on this terrible trail. The poor beasts became so weak from lack of food that they slipped on the steep places and plunged over the precipices in sheer desperation, and thus ended their misery.

On the summit we found typical March weather: snow, ice, water, mud, fog, and chill…. Even in this bleak spot we found birds nesting or preparing to nest: the pipit, the golden-crowned sparrow, and the rosy finch. The vegetation was mostly moss and lichens and low stunted spruce, the latter so stunted by snow that one could walk over them.

The first half of the nineteenth century was the so called Golden Age of whaling, with about 740 Atlantic whaling ships operating from East Coast American ports alone. During this period, the sperm whale was the most sought-after, because of the quantity of oil it contained and because it floated when killed, whereas most other species sank to the bottom. The first whalers entered the Pacific Ocean in 1788 in their quest for new territory, but not until trans-continental railways allowed quicker access to the large markets of Europe and the eastern U.S. did whaling expand into the Northwest coast.

The arrival of Russians in Alaska in pursuit of sea otters and fur seals forced many Alaska Natives into market hunting, often in conditions that they knew were too dangerous. In 1800, 64 men in 2-man baidarkas were lost in one storm while whale-hunting for the Russians.

In 1848 the first American whale ship, the *Superior*, entered the Bering Sea, and the huge population of bowhead and other whales astounded its crew. A maritime gold rush ensued; the following year, 154 ships joined the chase, and in 1850, 200 ships took 1,719 whales with another 348 killed but not recovered. The year 1852 was the peak season, with 2,682 bowheads killed. Catches after that were extremely erratic, with none caught in 1855 or 1856; never again did the catch reach 600 animals in a season.

In one of the more bizarre events in Alaska's whaling history, a Confederate Navy raider, the *Shenandoah*, extended the Civil War to the Arctic for seven days, from June 22–28, 1865, when she captured 24 American whale ships that were registered in New England states and burning 20 of them, taking the crews prisoner and sending them to San Francisco.

While whaling could be extremely profitable, it was also very dangerous; in September 1871, early ice trapped 32 of the 41 ships whaling in the Bering Sea, forcing 1,200 people, including some women and children, to flee in small boats across up to 60 miles of ice-choked seas to reach safety. All but one of the ships, the *Minerva*, were crushed by the ice and lost the following spring. Salvage crews were, however, able to save 1,300 barrels of oil and $10,000 worth of baleen from the wrecks; the local Alaska Natives also salvaged a great deal of the material, but some of them died after drinking from bottles they found in the ships' medicine chests. Five years later, another twelve whale ships were lost near Point Barrow; this time, 50 men died trying to escape.

The efficiency of commercial whaling increased dramatically in 1880 with the arrival of the *Mary and Helen*, the first whaler equipped with both sails and a steam engine to operate off the Alaskan coast. Not reliant on the wind, this type of ship could follow the whales more closely and stay on the hunting grounds longer.

Most whalers considered venturing east of Point Barrow particularly hazardous as the short ice-free season would force the ship to winter over in the ice. By 1888, however, whale populations had dropped to the point where new hunting grounds were needed. That summer, the Pacific Steam Whaling Company sent the first whalers into Canadian waters. They returned the following summer to report that bowhead whales were "thick as bees" near what would soon become the primary whaling base of the Beaufort Sea, Herschel Island.

In 1890 the company's ships docked at San Francisco with a cargo of whale oil and baleen valued at $400,000; it remains the most valuable U.S. whaling cargo ever.

The socioeconomic structure aboard a whale ship was a study in contrasts and resulted in frequent serious conflicts. Ships recruited many of their seamen from among the waterfront drifters in ports around the Pacific, including many from Hawaii, and the violent lifestyle that many of them were used to continued to some degree on board. The officers, though, were often well educated and cultured; despite the brutal weather conditions, many of the captains brought along their wives, and sometimes their children, on these multi-year voyages. In some instances they were able to develop a rather close approximation to life at home, with amateur variety shows and theatre productions and well-equipped game rooms and lounges, either on board the ships or on shore.

Soon after the turn of the century, the signs became clear that the boom years of whaling were gone forever. By 1907 the price of baleen had dropped from a high of $7 per pound to 50 cents; two years later, the market had virtually disappeared as spring steel and other metals replaced baleen. At the same time, improved petroleum distillation techniques were rapidly lowering demand for whale oil. Some recovery in the market for whale products gained only by using various parts of the whale for dog food and grinding up the rest for fertilizer.

Whaling vessel, circa 1910

Although the Bering and Beaufort Seas were two of the prime whaling grounds in the world, virtually the entire handful of remaining whale men gave up in 1912 due to the dwindling market and increasing costs of doing business in the Arctic. Operating costs, however, were much lower in Southeast Alaska, and dozens of whaling stations operated there well into the 1930s.

Greatly improved equipment in the 1920s and 1930s, including the use of huge factory ships which could process the whales at sea, increased the slaughter to such a degree that world-wide attention began to focus on the possibility of hunting several species of whales to extinction. In 1937 several nations, including the United States, signed the first International Whaling Agreement. The International Whaling Commission however, allows Alaskan Eskimos to kill 50 bowhead whales each year.

Along the southeast coast of Alaska, sightings of humpbacks, gray whales, and orcas are now a common occurrence, and dozens of companies offer close-up encounters.

Captain Healy and the Revenue Cutter Service

On April 23, 1790, Treasury Secretary Alexander Hamilton asked Congress to provide ten boats for "securing the collection of the revenue." On August 4th that year, Congress authorized the construction of the boats, and the Revenue Cutter Service formed. Thus began the service which reorganized as the Coast Guard in 1915. The early cruises of Revenue Service cutters in Alaskan waters are legendary for the extent of the voyages, the conditions they operated under, and the courage of the crews. The conditions often demanded that the men push themselves to their limits, and the captains of the cutters enforced those demands.

The most famous of Alaska's Revenue Cutter Service captains was Michael Healy. Healy was an African-American born in 1839 with pale skin that allowed him to "pass" as white when he left the South. He was the fifth of ten children born to a Georgia plantation owner, and his wife Mary Eliza was a former domestic slave. Mr. Healy had purchased her in 1829 and took her as his common-law wife, despite the fact that such a marriage was illegal in Georgia and that their children would be legally classified as slaves. Unable to send their children to school in the South, they instead sent the three oldest boys to a Quaker school in Flushing, New York, and later to Holy Cross in Massachusetts, where Michael joined them in 1850, following the death of both of his parents within a few months of each other. Most of the Healy children had fairly light skin coloring, and their black heritage seems not to have been widely known. All of the Healys identified themselves as white.

In 1854 Michael was sent to school in France, but he soon ran away to sea, sailing for Calcutta on a British ship in July 1855. On the oceans he found a career that suited his temperament, and he rose quickly through the ranks. In September 1863, he joined the Revenue Cutter Service, and with a great deal of help from lobbying efforts by family contacts, he was commissioned as third lieutenant in January 1865.

Healy was initially posted to the East Coast, but by the mid-1870s he had arrived in California to work on the Arctic patrols. Based in San Francisco Bay, the cutters would go north each spring and patrol the Alaskan coast and Bering Sea from a base at Unalaska. Their main duties in the early years were protecting seals from poachers who were decimating the herds and offering assistance to the fleet. In 1881, as second-in-command of the *Thomas Corwin* under Captain Hooper, Healy visited the Siberian coast during a search for the lost exploration ship *Jeanette*. During that visit, they noticed that the Chukchi people were able to sustain themselves by raising reindeer, and a few years later, Healy used that knowledge to work with Sheldon Jackson to import reindeer to Alaska.

In March 1883, Healy was promoted to captain and in 1886 was given command of the largest cutter in Arctic service, the *Bear*. The *Bear* was the most important ship to operate in Northern waters, and Healy and the *Bear* became the prime symbol of American sovereignty in Alaska. It is an interesting irony that a person of African-American decent, "passing" as white, came to symbolize America to so many Alaska Natives. The *New York Sun* noted that the powers given to Captain Healy for these patrols made him "a good deal more distinguished person in the waters of the far Northwest than any President of the United States, or any potentate of Europe."

Long voyages under brutal conditions, however, often caused tempers to flare on board the ships. Successful captains could not tolerate any breach of discipline when such slips could mean the loss of the ship with all hands. Harsh punishment controlled such situations, and while Captain Healy earned praise in some quarters, he was denounced for his brutality in others. One of his punishments was to order men "triced up," tied up with their hands behind them and their toes barely touching the deck. The punishment lasted fifteen minutes and the pain was excruciating. They were then tied with their backs to posts with their arms around them for forty-two hours. Sometimes he ordered men ashore for two days to shift for themselves. Meanwhile, some seamen accused Captain Healy himself of drunkenness and gross incapacity.

Captain Healy was court-martialed twice for his treatment of crew members, in 1890 and in 1895–1896. Tricing, as described above, was still technically legal in the Revenue Cutter Service, but more damning were the charges that he had been drunk on several occasions. Captain Healy had acquired the nickname "Hell Roaring Mike" as a result of adventures in the saloons of San Francisco, and his superiors acknowledged the problem by allowing him to take his wife along on his voyages.

U.S.R.C. Bear, surrounded by ice

Although he was acquitted in the 1890 trial, 25 officers of the Revenue Cutter Service proffered charges against him in 1895 and proved that Healy did indeed have a drinking problem, a decision that removed him from command of the *Bear* and dropped his name to the bottom of the captain's list. In 1900, he was restored to service and given command of the *McCulloch* for her Alaskan patrols. In July, however, he snapped and was confined to a hospital for a time. Although he returned to the sea, he seems never to have fully recovered, and a few months after his retirement in 1903 he died.

The controversy surrounding Michael Healy's actions during his Alaskan service were eventually laid to rest with the naming of the Coast Guard's newest Polar-Class icebreaker in his honor. The 420-foot, 16,300-ton *Healy* joins three other icebreakers in the Coast Guard fleet and is mainly used as a research ship

THE CREATION OF GOLD FEVER

Gold!

I wanted the gold, and I sought it,
I scrabbled and mucked like a slave.
Was it famine or scurvy—I fought it;
I hurled my youth into a grave.
I wanted the gold, and I got it—
Came out with a fortune last fall,

Yet somehow life's not what I thought it,
And somehow the gold isn't all.

No! There's the land. (Have you seen it?)
It's the cussedest land that I know,
From the big, dizzy mountains that screen it
To the deep, deathlike valleys below.
Some say God was tired when He made it;
Some say it's a fine land to shun;
Maybe; but there's some as would trade it
For no land on earth—and I'm one.

—*Robert W. Service*
The Spell of the Yukon and other Verses

The gritty poetry of Robert Service, the poet laureate of the Klondike Gold rush, revealed the adventure and hardships of many would-be miners who risked all to find their fortune in the North Country. Some, like Service, developed a romantic relationship with the environment, while others succumbed to "gold fever" and chased an elusive fortune across northern Canada through interior Alaska all the way to Nome, over one thousand miles from Dawson City. The migration of these miners dramatically impacted the Alaskan District's population, its relationship to the federal government, and the extent of white incursions into Alaska Native territory.

In 1897 a newspaper in Ottawa, Canada, published an editorial for "fortune hunters" headed to Alaska and then to the Yukon. The editorial asked the reader to take an eleven-question self-examination before proceeding on their journey:

Have I a capital of at least $500 dollars?
Am I subject to any chronic disease or organism, especially rheumatism?
Am I physically sound in every way and able to walk thirty miles a day with a fifty pound pack on my back?
Am I willing to put up with rough fare, sleep anywhere and anyhow, do my own cooking and washing, and mend my own clothes?
Can I leave home perfectly free, leaving no one dependent on me in any manner for support?
Can I do entirely without spirituous liquors?
Can I work like a galley slave for months, if need be, on

poor fare and sometimes not enough of that, and still
keep up a cheerful and brave spirit?
Am I pretty handy with tools and not subject to lazy fits?
Can I swim and handle boats?
Can I put up with extremes of heat and cold?
Can I bear incessant tortures from countless swarms of
mosquitoes, gnats and sand flies?

One cannot help but wonder how many of the over two
hundred thousand souls who set out for the Yukon could
answer yes to all of these questions. Perhaps it was precious
few. Nevertheless, set out they did, and of that original
number, thirty-four thousand eventually arrived in the
Klondike. Why would so many otherwise sane individuals
risk all and head north, convinced that their fortune
awaited them? Historical context perhaps provides some of
the answer. Gold was very much on the minds of
Americans in the late nineteenth century. The 1897-98
Gold Rush was the culmination of a fifty-year search for the
yellow metal in the west that had progressed steadily
northward. The search had gone from California in 1849,
to Fraser River, British Columbia in 1859, to Juneau in
1880, and then the Yukon in 1897. Previous success by a few
convinced many others that it just might be possible for
them to hit the jackpot. This became an infectious disease
of the mind called "gold fever."

The west coast press did much to encourage the spread
of that fever. When the S.S. *Portland* arrived in Seattle in 1897
with Klondike gold, the newspapers did not waste time.
Soon headlines spread across the country announcing the
Yukon discovery. In the depressed economy of 1897, the
temptation must have been great for many to see if they could
be the next ones to make headlines.

An immediate competition arose between west coast
cities to prosper from those who followed the lure. San
Francisco, Seattle, Tacoma, Portland, and Victoria, British
Columbia, all vied for their share of benefits as the miners
headed north. A good example of this competition could be
found in a San Francisco merchant's window in 1897. A
huge poster display showed two gold stampeders on their
way to the Klondike riches. In one frame the miner was
tired, dirty, and beaten down, unable to continue, and
collapsed in a heap at the foot of Chilkoot Pass. The caption

below his picture read, "I outfitted in Seattle." In the other frame the prospector was happy, fresh, and clean at the top of Chilkoot Pass. His caption of course read, "I bought my goods in San Francisco."

Despite that advertisement, in the end it was Seattle that put out the most advertising and lured the most folks to its city and then to Alaska. In many ways the Klondike Gold Rush is just as much a Seattle story as an Alaskan one. The money brought in by the stampeders is credited with building the foundations of what became the metropolis of Puget Sound. The Rush also cemented a relationship between Seattle and Alaska that lasts to the present day.

One week after the arrival of the *S.S. Portland* in Seattle, the chamber of commerce put together an advertising committee to sell the Gold Rush and Seattle as the place to outfit before the journey. The head of this committee was Erastus Brainerd who, according to noted gold rush historian Pierre Berton, was the driving force behind Seattle's success in attracting stampeders. Brainerd was a Harvard graduate and a former art curator before becoming what we would call in modern parlance a "PR" man.

Brainerd employed a variety of schemes that successfully sold the Gold Rush. He had advertisements inserted into small-town papers to reach rural America. He also had the *Seattle Post Intelligencer* edition announcing the riches in the Klondike sent to post offices, libraries, mayors offices, and railroads. In an ethically dubious move he persuaded Seattleites to send letters to friends and relatives about the Gold Rush. His team wrote the letters and left blanks for the names and signatures. They also supplied postage and took the letters to the post office. Brainerd even internationalized his plan by sending "Klondike Christmas Cards" to European leaders. Interestingly, the German Kaiser refused to open his due to a fear of letter bombs.

Brainerd's advertisements portrayed the Klondike trip as a casual stroll, the Whitehorse rapids as akin to wading, and transportation to Alaska and goods in Seattle as fair and cheap. In other words one would take a cruise, a leisurely walk, and a nice raft trip, pick up some gold, and head home rich. "Let the buyer beware" were never truer watchwords.

Independence Mine

Alaska Communities: The Cities of Juneau, Fairbanks, and Nome

Located on the mainland of Southeast Alaska, opposite Douglas Island, Juneau began to flourish at the heart of the Inside Passage along the Gastineau Channel and lies 900 air miles northwest of Seattle and 577 air miles southeast of Anchorage. The area was a fish camp for the indigenous Tlingit people. In 1880, nearly 20 years before the gold rushes to the Klondike and Nome, Chief Kowee of the Auk Tribe led Joe Juneau and Richard Harris to Gold Creek. There they found mother lode deposits upstream, staked their mining claims, and developed a 160 acre incorporated city they called Harrisburg, which brought many prospectors to the area. The city of Juneau formed in 1900, and the state transferred its capital from Sitka to Juneau in 1906 while Alaska was a U.S. Territory. The Treadwell and Ready Bullion mines across the channel on Douglas Island became world-scale mines, operating from 1882 to 1917, and in 1916 the Alaska-Juneau gold mine was built on the mainland, becoming the largest operation of its kind in the world. In 1917 a cave-in and flood closed the Treadwell mine on Douglas, though it had produced $66 million in gold in its 35 years of operation. Fishing, canneries, transportation and trading services, and a sawmill contributed to Juneau's growth through the early 1900s. The A-J Mine closed in 1944 after producing over $80 million in gold. In 1970 Juneau and Douglas were unified into the city and borough of Juneau, making the third largest community in Alaska. As the state capital, Juneau is supported largely by State and federal employment and by tourists cruising the Inside Passage. About one-third of residents live downtown or on Douglas Island; the remaining two-thirds live elsewhere along the roaded area. Juneau has a Tlingit history with a strong historical influence from the early prospectors and boom town that grew around full-scale gold mining operations.

Fairbanks is located in the heart of Alaska's interior, on the banks of the Chena River in the Tanana Valley. Three hundred and fifty-eight road miles north of Anchorage, by air the city is only a 45 minute trip and 3 hours from Seattle. Koyukon Athabascans have lived in this area for thousands of years. In 1901 Capt. E.T. Barnette established a trading post on the Chena River. A year later, gold was discovered 16 miles north of the post. The town grew as the Chena steamboat landing brought many prospectors during the Pedro Dome gold rush. Fairbanks got its name from Indiana Senator Charles Fairbanks, who later became vice-president. In 1903 Judge Wikersham moved the seat of the Third Judicial District from Eagle to Fairbanks, and the population continued to increase with the addition of the court, government offices, a jail, a post office, and the Northern Commercial Company. Fairbanks elected Barnette as its first mayor in 1903, and he helped to establish telephone service, fire protection, sanitation ordinances, electric lights, and steam heat. He also opened and became President of the Washington-Alaska Bank. By 1910 the official population had grown to 3,541, although more than 6,000 miners lived and worked their claims on creeks north of town. The U.S. military built Ladd Field (now Fort Wainwright) in 1938. Construction of the Alcan Highway in the 1940s and the Trans-Alaska oil pipeline in the 1970s fueled growth and development. The Fairbanks area continues to be the second-largest population settlement in Alaska. Residents are primarily non-Alaska Native, though diverse.

Nome was built along the Bering Sea on the south coast of the Seward Peninsula, facing Norton Sound. It lies 539 air miles northwest of Anchorage, a 75-minute flight, 102 miles south of the Arctic Circle, and 161 miles east of Russia. Western Union surveyors seeking a route across Alaska and the Bering Sea reported gold discoveries in the Nome area as far back as 1865. But it was a $1,500-to-the-pan gold strike on tiny Anvil Creek in 1898 by three Scandinavians—Jafet Lindeberg, Erik Lindblom, and John Brynteson—that brought thousands of miners to the "Eldorado." Almost overnight an isolated stretch of tundra fronting the beach transformed into a tent-and-log cabin city of 20,000 prospectors, gamblers, claim jumpers, saloon keepers, and prostitutes. The gold-bearing creeks had been almost completely staked when some entrepreneur discovered the "golden sands of Nome." With nothing more than shovels, buckets, rockers, and wheel barrows, thousands of miners descended upon the beaches. Two months later the golden sands had yielded one million dollars in gold (at $16 an ounce). The area gained a narrow-gauge railroad and telephone line from Nome to Anvil Creek in 1900. By 1902 prospectors had exhausted the more easily reached claims, and large mining companies with better equipment took over operations. Since the first strike on tiny Anvil Creek, Nome's gold fields have yielded $136 million. The gradual depletion of gold, a major influenza epidemic in 1918, the depression, and finally World War II, each influenced Nome's population, and a disastrous fire in 1934 destroyed most of the city. The population of Nome is a mixture of Inupiaq and non-Alaska Natives, with the former villagers from King Island also living in the area. Although many employment opportunities are available, subsistence activities remain prevalent in the community. The city is also famous for being the finish line for the 1,100-mile Iditarod Sled Dog Race from Anchorage, held each March.

The campaign certainly worked. In 1898 Seattle had twenty-five million dollars worth of Klondike-related trade. All the other west coast ports combined for just five million in Klondike trade that same year. Seattle's bounty compares rather favorably to the mere ten million dollars worth of gold that came out of the Klondike in 1898. Brainerd himself became a victim of his own propaganda and in 1898 headed for the Klondike to make his fortune.

Another way that gold fever spread throughout the United States was through the development of "syndicates" which sent individuals to the gold fields representing many investors. In 1898 alone, eighty-five syndicates were in operation from twenty-two different cities. These groups invested over one hundred sixty five million dollars and sent thousands of young men to the north, but only a few had success that paid off for their investors.

Along with the advertising and syndicates came new devices and schemes designed to make getting to the gold and getting it out a breeze. In reality their main design was to separate stampeders from their money. A few examples will suffice. The automatic gold pan, which looked like a phonograph with a gold pan strapped to it, would supposedly speed up one's panning rate to beat the competition. The "Klondike bike" could help one bike through mountain passes, and the rider could attach floats to drift down rivers. X-ray machines would help one see the gold underground that others would miss. Even trained gophers were sold to dig tunnels to the gold for the prospectors. Needless to say, many of these "inventions" were left strewn along the trail to the Klondike.

A bicycling feat of note did come out of this gold rush era. Ed Jesson left Dawson on a Klondike bike someone had abandoned for Nome on February 29, 1900. He had not found riches in the Klondike, and despite having learned to ride a bike only the week before, he believed he could ride the bike down the frozen Yukon River to Nome, the site of the next gold rush. One month later, on March 29, 1900, he arrived in Nome, over a thousand miles from his starting point. He had ridden the bike the entire distance down the frozen Yukon and was quoted as saying, "I didn't even puncture a tire the whole trip and it didn't require dog food."

What were the effects on Alaska of these thousands of gold seekers passing through the area? By 1896 Alaska had been in American hands for almost thirty years, most of that time under military rule. Recent gold finds in Juneau had increased the population to approximately thirty thousand.

The search for gold expanded beyond the Klondike after 1898. Nome in 1899 and Fairbanks in 1902 experienced smaller versions of the Klondike rush, and people spread into areas beyond Southeast Alaska. Many thousands who did not make it in the Klondike crossed the border into Alaska. Towns like Iditarod, McGrath, Bethel, and Flat were developed as smaller offshoots of larger gold rushes occurred. Other towns, like Eagle and Valdez, did not grow up as mining towns but felt mining's impact. Eagle was on the Yukon River only a few miles from the Canadian border and came to serve as a port of entry for those coming from the Yukon. It became a trading center for a large area and a communications point. Valdez developed as an ice-free port that even had a telegraph to Eagle for communications.

The Gold Rush focused attention on Alaska as nothing else could. Alaska was front-page news, but not all of it was positive. Rumors and reports said people were starving along the trails. This was when Sheldon Jackson made his doomed journey, receiving two hundred thousand dollars from Congress to bring reindeer to Alaska to transport supplies to the miners. The reindeer themselves traveled from Norway to New York City, then overland by railroad to San Francisco, then by boat to Skagway. The last leg included a stop in Seattle where they munched on park grass. That debacle of the reindeer that did make it to Alaska, too few and too late, did not stop the federal government from continuing an interest in Alaska.

The United States Army built new posts at Eagle, Nome, and Haines, and the government extended the Homestead Act to Alaska, appointing judges as the population grew. The U.S. also allowed for some self-government on the town level, with a council and mayor, installed taxes on liquor as prohibition was repealed, and developed plans for an Alaska Railroad. In essence the Gold Rush brought Alaska to the attention of the federal government as perhaps a useful area.

Gold-seekers crossing the Chillcoot Pass, 1897

The Gold Rush greatly impacted Alaska Natives. Skookum Jim, who was half Tlingit, helped discover the Klondike gold. But prospectors spread disease and illness throughout Alaska, trespassed upon forests, and took fish

Famous Alaskans: Characters of the Gold Rush

"Soapy" C. Smith, perhaps the best-known person connected with the gold rush, controlled a well-organized underworld of thieves, thugs, and con-men during gold's heyday. Born in Georgia in 1860, Smith came from a prosperous family fallen on hard times. As a young man he drifted west and became an expert at manipulating three walnut shells and a pea. For the next 20 years he perfected the con-man's trade in various Colorado towns. Upon hearing news of the Klondike rush, he joined the northbound migration and eventually settled in Skagway, a thousand miles from law and order. By late January, 1898, he was the uncrowned king of the Skagway underworld. Six months later surveyor Frank Reid gunned him down on the Juneau Company Wharf in Skagway harbor. Smith's operations extended from the ships plying the Inside Passage to the summits of the White Pass and Chilkoot. His cohorts posed as helpful fellow travelers. Gang members quickly located those with the fattest wallets and steered them into Smith's bogus business operations. Along the Chilkoot Trail, the gang set up warm fires and tents to lure stampeders into shell-game tables and phony poker games.

Skookum Jim Mason, as he was known to white men, was another famous gold rush character. "Skookum" means "strong" in the west coast trading language called Chinook, and "Mason" was added by a Mr. Mason who was trading at the village of Tagish, Yukon, where Jim spent much time. He appears to have been at ease in both the traditional world of the Tagish people and that of the white man, and was successfully able to combine the best of both worlds to help his family and ultimately his people. He thoroughly enjoyed watching the white man's greed for gold and would throw nuggets out of the window of his hotel room when he was in Seattle just to watch the near-riot that would erupt on the street below. When he died on July 11, 1916, he left a trust fund to be used for the benefit of Yukon natives. That money was finally used in the 1970s to build the Skookum Jim Friendship Centre in Whitehorse.

After the infamous shootout in Tombstone, Arizona, Wyatt Earp would live almost another 50 years. He was never able to settle down and was mining almost to his death at age 80 in 1929. He spent several years in Nome during the gold rush of the late 1890s. Earp built the Dexter Saloon in Nome and did well with his businesses in Alaska, leaving in 1901 with $80,000—a massive fortune in those days. While in Nome, he was arrested for interfering with an officer while off duty. Wyatt's story is that he was attempting to assist the deputy marshal and his actions were misconstrued. He was released without charges. Later the *New York Tribune* falsely reported that Earp was killed with the headlines "Wyatt Earp Shot at Nome; The Arizona 'Bad Man' Not Quick Enough With His Gun." The story went on to tell what a terror Wyatt was to the good citizens of Nome.

and game without regard to aboriginal rights. New communities created by the Rush, along with an increased white population, brought a form of Jim Crow to Alaska. Prejudice and racism forced many Alaska Natives into second-class status in their own land. Some, however, found entrepreneurial opportunity. Chilkoot natives worked as packers for the stampeders and charged from five to fifteen dollars per one hundred pounds carried. The Chilkoot also charged a one dollar per head fee for every person passing through their territory.

While the gold rush did draw people to Alaska, most remained only a few years, but enough stayed to double the previous population from thirty thousand to sixty thousand, where it remained until World War II. The Gold Rush did kindle interest and create optimism concerning the area as the twentieth century began.

KENNICOTT

The towns of Kennicott and McCarthy played significant roles in the early American period of Alaskan history. In 1900, two prospectors spotted a large green patch on the steep hillside above present-day Kennicott. What was thought to be a grassy hillside ended up being one of the richest copper deposits ever found.

The Kennicott Mine Company formed in 1906 and later became the Kennicott Copper Corporation. To move the copper ore from Kennicott to Cordova, the Copper River Northwestern Railway began construction in the spring of 1906 in Cordova, and the line eventually stretched 196 miles to Kennicott. Before the mine closed in 1938, the railroad had transported an amazing 220 million dollars' worth of copper ore.

During the peak of operations, Kennicott was home to more than 600 miners and mill workers. McCarthy was founded five miles down the hill. During the copper boom McCarthy was a busy place, with hotels, pool halls, restaurants, saloons, dress shops, and even a red light district.

SITKA'S MARY BONG

While some came to Alaska to mine for gold or copper and left quickly afterwards, others found interesting ways to survive in a challenging boom-and-bust economy. Alaska welcomed a diverse group of people in the early American period, but perhaps no one was more multi-talented and hard-working than Sitka's Mary Bong. Mary and Ah Bong arrived in Sitka in October of 1895. She was fifteen years old and had married Ah after leaving China to escape poverty. Sitka was still the capital of Alaska, and Mary was the first Chinese woman registered in the town.

Her husband, Ah, owned a local restaurant and bakery, and it was there that she began to know the people of Sitka and they her. Her nickname "China Mary" was soon her moniker. She became friendly with the Tlingits in Sitka and learned their language. The village had no doctor, and after giving birth to two children of her own, Mary often acted as midwife for the Tlingit women. She never lost a single baby. In return, they taught her how to make bracelets out of silver.

In 1902 Ah Bong died and Mary lost the restaurant. Katherine, her elder daughter, was six and in school, but Anna was only a year old. While Mary did housework, a friendly barber kept Anna in a room at the rear of the store, feeding and changing the baby between customers. At first

Golden Dreams and Real Hardships

Many would-be gold miners left behind vivid accounts of life in the north country as they pursued their dreams of riches. The following first hand accounts, taken from the 1999 PBS program "American Experiences: Gold Fever," reveal some the hardships and rewards of the Gold Rush era:

> … In the night sometime, a snow slide began. I was awakened by the roar, but I could see nothing. Several more occurred, only not as close…. We rushed out and watched a genuine avalanche. It was a grand and beautiful sight. It looked like a great waterfall as the snow came pouring over the rocks. Men came pouring out into the streets of the camp, shouting and shooting their rifles into the air. Moments later a man came running into Joppe and Mueller's restaurant by the Scales, yelling, "For God's sake, come quick! Help dig out Mrs. Maxon and several others! They've been buried alive in their tent." … As far as one could see up the gulch, winding in and out, were men going to the rescue. About five hundred feet beyond, several tents were buried. As I arrived, one tent had been uncovered and three taken out dead. No one knows how many are buried, probably between forty and one hundred.
>
> — *Fred Dewey*

> … You have to get in line and wait your turn to get a chance to go up over the Summit. Though the men are forced to stop for over a half an hour in their place, they are as silent as a grave yard.
>
> —*Clarence McNeil*

Two weeks were consumed in reaching Lake Lindeman, eleven miles further on. Another week had passed before a boat was completed with which we could make our way down the river. While in camp at Lake Lindeman one of the party injured his knee, and three times a hunting knife had to be brought into requisition and incisions made. Only after the most careful nursing was he able to proceed on the journey. Men are often taken with snow-blindness in that country and lie helpless for days in their tents, unable to cook enough to sustain life. If deserted by their companions in this condition their fate is sealed. Many lives have been lost at these various points of danger, and along this section of the river many graves dot the shore where unfortunates have been laid in their last resting place. Niches cut in the frozen ground mark the lonely graves of fathers and sons whose return is waited for in vain by loved ones in the realm of civilization. It is a sad thing indeed to lay your friends away in that desolate region, where only wild beasts congregate to mourn a requiem over their graves. I simply mention these facts in order that any one who thinks of going into that country may know beforehand that the search for gold there is preceded by hardships and privations which they little dream of unless they have penetrated the American land of the midnight sun.

—*J.O. Hestwood*

Gold is as common here in Dawson as iron is in Juneau. Everybody has money. There seems to be no limit to this district, and they are striking new diggings every few days of a hundred miles around, and stampedes are the rage. Men with packs on their backs, breaking for some new creek or new discovery, are met at every turn. Some are leaving good pay bound for something that promises better, and in this way the country is being explored and prospected. I have built a shop 12 by 20 feet, consisting of a tent drawn over a frame of scantling, and am doing well, working sixteen hours a day, and with all the work I can do. For making a half-ounce ring out of Klondike gold they pay me $25. This is the greatest gold camp on record.

—*James Kite*

After leaving Dyea we had a trip full of hair-breadth escapes, and arrived at Dawson on June 9th. We should have started either a month earlier or later, as we struck the worst time.

I start work tomorrow at $1.50 an hour, and will soon have a job which has been promised me at an ounce of gold daily. On the boat which leaves tomorrow for St. Michael's are 50 people who nine months ago were broke, and are now taking out from $10,000 to $100,000 each.

One Montana man took $96,000 out of 45-square feet, and another took $130,000 out of 85-square feet, and other strikes equally rich are reported. Old-timers expect to make big strikes this winter. There are more ways of making money here than in any place I ever saw.

—*Hart Humber*

Mary earned only 25 cents per day, then 50 cents, then finally a dollar. Since the barber refused to charge for the babysitting, Mary was able to manage. After five years, she even paid off her house. A few months later she remarried.

Her new husband, Fred Johnson, was of Swedish-Finnish descent. After their wedding, Mary took the girls to Seattle and enrolled them in boarding school, where she hoped they would receive the education she never had. Then she headed back to Alaska to join her husband at the Chichagof mine where they both worked as wage laborers.

The mine was extremely rich, yielding several million dollars in gold. Mary handled blasting powder and worked underground shoveling ore into cars. When she smashed a finger so that the bone stuck out through the skin, she simply worked the skin over the flesh and bone and sewed up the wound herself. Eventually she allowed the company men to talk her into going back above ground to cook for them.

With their savings, Mary and Fred started a dairy in 1911 at Sawmill Creek, seven miles out of Sitka. They hacked a clearing and built a log cabin for themselves and another one for the cows. The dairy's location, however, was impractical, since the milk had to be taken into town in a small boat. Storms and frequent rough water prevented deliveries, and after a few years of struggling, they sold out. For a while Mary and Fred tried prospecting and trapping, but it was too hard a way to make a living.

In 1917 Sitka gained its first salmon cannery. During the salmon season, canneries brought in gangs of Chinese laborers under contract to work all over Alaska. The laborers gutted the fish and prepared them for canning, often making the cans and weaving the seines for catching the fish as well. Commercial fishing became Sitka's main industry, and Fred bought a cabin troller.

Mary was not one of the Chinese who worked in the canneries; instead, she became the first woman troller in the area. She had an eighteen-foot open boat, and she trolled alone, starting at dawn, fishing all day, and then coming in to sell her catch for three cents a pound. Local legend has it that she went out in weather that kept others in, thus making money when others did not.

In the early twenties, Mary and Fred decided to try fox farming. They purchased an island twenty miles from Sitka and turned several pairs of blue foxes loose on it. Since they could not afford to hire any help, they built their log cabin themselves, and they cooked feed for the foxes from what they caught. Poachers of the foxes drove them out of the business.

At seventy Mary was still working, a matron of the federal jail in Sitka. When the Exclusion Act was repealed in 1943 and Chinese once again had the right to become naturalized citizens, Mary took out citizenship papers so she could vote. In 1958 she was admitted to the Pioneers Home in Sitka, a combination retirement and nursing home for longtime residents of Alaska. She died a few weeks later. Her amazing array of occupations is perhaps unmatched in Alaska: restaurant worker, midwife, Tlingit translator, house worker, miner, fisherwomen, dairy farmer, fox farmer, and jail matron. She certainly exemplified the flexibility needed to live long-term in the boom-and-bust economy of Alaska.

THE ALASKA BOUNDARY DISPUTE

Alaska and Canada share many miles of border and from time to time have run into a few problems. None, however, were as vexing and long-lasting as deciding precisely where the border should be. Although diplomats thought they had it settled in 1825, the issue continued to flare up until 1903, and even now, many Canadians resent the placement of the Alaska boundary.

In the 1820s the Hudson's Bay Company and the Russian American Company were arguing over trading territories. The key document was an agreement between Russia and Great Britain that divided the Northwest American territories of the two powers, signed in 1825. The agreement reduced the territory that Russia claimed and re-opened the Russian colonies to British trading ships for a period of ten years. Russia made a similar ten-year agreement with the United States at approximately the same time, formalizing the activities of independent American trading ships who had been working in the waters of Russian America for decades.

The Hudson's Bay Company claimed that, since they were operating forts west of the Rocky Mountains and the coast had been claimed by British navigators in the previous century, everything between the coast and the Rockies should be theirs. The Russian American Company disputed the Hudson's Bay Company's territorial claim, as they had many trading stations in full operation within that territory.

Negotiations went on between the British and Russian governments for three years, with a great deal of participation by both the Hudson's Bay Company and the Russian American Company. The part of the agreement that eventually set the boundary is quite simple. The British were not to be given access to the coast, though they were allowed access to the rivers that ran to the coast.

Although not a signatory to either of those agreements, one of the people most affected by them was Captain Matvei Ivanovich Marav'ev, who was in charge of the Russian colonies in North America from September 1820 until November 1825. He had the misfortune to assume his position exactly a year before Alexander I made life in the colonies very difficult by prohibiting any foreign ships from trading in the Russian territory or within 100 miles of shore. At the same time Russia also extended its territorial claim much further south, from fifty-five degrees North latitude to fifty one degrees, just off the northern tip of Vancouver Island.

Although Russia desired its colonies to become self-sufficient, the facts were very different. Throughout most of Captain Marav'ev's stay, food and other goods were in critically short supply, particularly when ships from the Russian American Company post at Fort Ross, California, which had been established to help support Russian settlements in Alaska, did not arrive on time or at all. That critical situation remained until Great Britain and the United States ratified their treaties with Russia in early 1825. Russia signed these treaties despite vigorous opposition from the directors of the Russian American Company, who felt that the agreements violated their monopoly and threatened their business. The directors, of course, did not live in the colonies.

Upon the expiration of the ten-year trading period specified in the 1825 agreements, the colonies were very quickly in difficult straits again. Not until Russia signed another agreement with the Hudson's Bay Company in 1839 did they receive proper supplies, in exchange for leasing what is now the mainland of Southeast Alaska.

One aspect of the boundary agreement is often overlooked: The Tlingits, who traded with the Russians, already had an extensive trade network in what became British territory. The Hudson's Bay Company attempted, in 1833, to establish a post on the Stikine River to intercept that trade, but were stopped from passing through Russian territory to do so, even though the 1825 Convention allowed such passage. The professed monopoly trading rights of the Hudson's Bay Company, in any case, did not impress the Tlingit who made that point by sacking Fort Selkirk in August 1852. The boundary was clearly a European convention.

In the wilderness of northwest America, setting a boundary on paper was the easy part; marking its location on the ground got very complicated. Due to the difficulties and cost, sections of the border were surveyed as economic considerations dictated, and no major surveys were undertaken until after the United States purchased Alaska in 1867.

Boat at Grand Pacific Glacier

In December 1872, following the discovery of gold in British Columbia's Cassiar region, President Grant ordered that the entire coastal fringe be studied. Canada surveyed the boundary at the Stikine River in 1877 so they could set up a customs post to collect duty on goods headed to the Cassiar gold fields. In 1887–1888 and again in 1895, Canadians surveyed the region around the Fortymile gold discoveries. In 1889 an American survey party discovered that the Hudson's Bay Company trading post of Rampart House was 30 miles west of the 141st Meridian, well inside Alaskan territory, and the company was forced to retreat up the Porcupine River and build a new post. And so the surveying went a section at a time.

It was the discovery of gold in the Klondike, within Canada, that brought the boundary issue into critical focus. When every square foot of land could yield enormous wealth, the precise location of a border must be known. An important question reared its head: What exactly did the 72-year-old description of the border that ran through the coastal mountains and around or across the deep fjords mean?

The head of Lynn Canal was one of the main gateways to the Yukon. The Northwest Mounted Police sent a detachment to secure the location for Canada, basing the decision on Canada's assertion that the location was more than ten marine leagues from the sea, which was part of the 1825 boundary definition.

A massive influx of prospectors to what became the town of Skagway very quickly made a retreat advisable. Stories tell of a group of heavily armed Americans who demanded that Canada take down its flag on a police post or they would shoot it down. Semi-permanent posts were then set up on the summits of Chilkoot and White Passes, complete with a mounted Gatling gun at each. This was still disputed territory, as many Americans believed that the head of Lake Bennett, another 12 miles north, should be the location of the border. To back up the police in their sovereignty claim, the Canadian government also sent the Yukon Field Force, a 200-man Army unit, to the territory. The soldiers set up camp at Fort Selkirk so that they could be fairly quickly dispatched to deal with problems at either the coastal passes or the 141st meridian.

The posts set up on the passes by the Mounties were effective in the short term; the provisional boundary was accepted, if grudgingly. In September 1898, serious negotiations began in Quebec City between the United States and Canada to settle the issue beyond further dispute. Those meetings failed, and a representative from Great Britain was finally brought in as part of a six-man tribunal. Theodore Roosevelt took over the Presidency in 1901 when an anarchist fatally shot William McKinley in Buffalo, New York. Roosevelt claimed that the "Canadians do not have a leg to stand on."

The problem festered until 1903 when a tribunal of "six impartial jurists of repute" assembled in London to formally decide the matter. Roosevelt appointed the ex-senator of Washington state; George Turner, secretary of war; Elihu Root; and Senator Henry Cabot Lodge. The latter had already publicly denounced the claim before the tribunal.

The Canadians appointed two judges, and Lord Alverstone and the British selection of the Lord Chief Justice of England rounded out the six appointments. The vote came out four to two in favor of the United States. Roosevelt made it clear to English officials during the tribunal that it would be his way or no way at all, and that if the vote did not go his way he would send in the U.S. marines to enforce the American claim. Noted historian Thomas Bailey called it an ideal example of TR shaking the big stick to achieve his ends. This incident, however, would not be the last time Alaska would become an issue for TR.

THE BALLINGER–PINCHOT AFFAIR

Theodore Roosevelt's presidency was marked by a strong commitment to the conservation of public lands. To promote this goal, he surrounded himself with like-minded men, such as Secretary of the Interior James R. Garfield and Chief Forester Gifford Pinchot. Also working in the Interior Department were Richard A. Ballinger, who was the general land office commissioner, and Louis R. Glavis, chief of the Portland Field Division.

In 1906 Congress passed a law restricting the ownership of Alaskan lands in an effort to protect them from commercial exploitation. The law stated that the government would no longer give land away; however, the U.S. would honor claims filed before 1906 once their legitimacy had been established.

Clarence Cunningham had filed 33 claims for land on

behalf of various parties. In July 1907 the Morgan–Guggenheim syndicate purchased a fifty percent interest of the Cunningham claims in the belief that the land was rich in coal. This agreement was illegal, and if it had been discovered, would have been grounds for invalidating the claims.

Glavis heard rumors of the syndicate's involvement in the claims and secured Ballinger's approval to investigate the matter. But before the investigation, Ballinger was visited by Miles C. Moore, a Washington state politician who was one of the Cunningham claimants and a friend of Ballinger. Ballinger then ordered the claims to be "clear-listed," the first step toward granting the deed to the land, without notifying Glavis of his actions. Glavis got wind of it anyway and talked Ballinger into rescinding the order.

Ballinger later resigned from the Department of the Interior and moved back to Seattle. While there he acted as legal counsel to the Cunningham claimants. After Taft became President in 1909, he replaced Garfield with Ballinger as secretary of the interior. While claiming to transfer responsibility of the Cunningham claims to First Assistant Secretary Frank Pierce, Ballinger pressed for a hearing to resolve the matter. When Glavis complained that he could not finish his investigation before the hearing, he was replaced by James M. Sheridan, an inexperienced lawyer.

Glavis appealed to Pinchot for help in delaying the hearing. At Pinchot's suggestion, Glavis presented charges to President Taft accusing Ballinger of negligence and of endangering public lands. Ballinger responded with a hefty 730-page report that defended his actions. Taft claimed to have spent a week studying the facts with Attorney General George Wickersham. On August 22, 1909, Taft wrote a letter, supposedly based on a report drafted by Wickersham, exonerating Ballinger and authorizing Glavis's dismissal for insubordination. Pinchot was later fired as well.

On November 13, *Collier's* magazine published Glavis's account of the incident. The article caused such a sensation that in the following January, Congress created a joint investigative committee to look into the incident.

When rumors reached *Collier's* that the committee was going to exonerate Ballinger, who was then going to sue the magazine for a million dollars, *Collier's* paid for a lawyer, Louis Brandies, to represent the magazine and Glavis. The hearings convened on January 26, 1910. The committee consisted of eight Republicans and four Democrats. Because of its political make-up, the committee was largely hostile toward *Collier's* and Glavis and defeataed nearly every motion brought forward by Brandeis by a 7 to 5 vote. On May 20, 1910, nearly four months after the hearings started, Brandeis and the other lawyers made their closing arguments. No one was surprised when the committee voted to exonerate Ballinger.

The damage had been done, however. Between the attempted cover up of the circumstances surrounding Taft's letter and Ballinger's performance under cross-examination, public opinion shifted against the Taft Administration. There was never a libel case. Ballinger ended up resigning in March 1911, and Roosevelt was so disgusted with the way Taft handled the situation that he ran for President in 1912 on the Bull Moose Party ticket against Taft, thereby ensuring Woodrow Wilson's success in the election. The incident was seen as a vindication for the conservation movement. Ironically, surveys of the Cunningham lands later showed that the lands had little coal. For Alaska the whole affair was great publicity and aided those who claimed Alaska needed more home rule. James Wickersham took the lead in the fight for more government in Alaska. He championed himself as the enemy of monopolies, although Guggenheim had previously turned him down for a job. But home rule was not necessarily an easy sell, despite the Ballinger–Pinchot Affair. Some argued that Big Business would find a territorial legislature even easier to control, and that this would lead to even more misuse of natural resources. President Taft himself was also resentful toward Alaska after the affair.

Finally, on August 24, 1912, Congress passed the Second Organic Act. Alaska now had a territorial legislature, but with limited power. The federal government still controlled use of its natural resources. The Alaska legislature could not alter, amend, modify, or repeal any measures related to fish, game, or soil. Furthermore, matters of divorce, gambling, and liquor were in the hands of the federal government; the Alaska governor was still a federal appointee with veto power over the legislature. Still, Alaskans were gaining a limited say in their own affairs, but Alaska's status as an American colony was far from clear. As we shall see in the following chapters, this status is, perhaps, still in question, even after the achievement of statehood in 1959.

4

Railroads and Planes, Fish and Farms, and Alaska Native Activism

The period from the 1910s through the 1930s was not one of economic boom for Alaska; nevertheless, it saw interesting changes for the new territory. Alaska Natives seeking equal rights and land protection created an important organization and found ways to make their voices heard on the political level. Territorial status won a legislature for Alaska. Plans and construction began for the Alaska Railroad, and the city of Anchorage began to emerge as a construction campsite. Congress created the precursor to the University of Alaska, Fairbanks, with the founding of the Alaska Agricultural College and School of Mines as a land grant college. President Warren Harding came to Alaska to drive the last spike in the Alaska Railroad. Congress extended citizenship to all Alaska Natives and Native Americans in the United States. A Tlingit, William Paul, Sr., became the first Alaska Native elected to the Alaska legislature, though some Alaskans thought the Jones and White Acts conspired to keep Alaska in colonial status. Airmail delivery came to Alaska, along with the advent of the bush pilot. FDR's New Deal brought farmers to the Matanuska Valley and caused the hiring of Tlingits and Haidas through the Civilian Conservation Corps (CCC) to make totem poles. Consequently, this period in Alaska history is worthy of scrutiny.

Alaska Natives: Land and Civil Rights
At the time of the Alaska purchase in 1867, an estimated total of 35,000 Alaska Natives lived in Alaska, comprising approximately 95 percent of the population, but there was little mention in the Treaty of Cession concerning the status

of their citizenship and nothing at all about their property rights. The treaty provided that the inhabitants of the ceded territory, with the "exception of uncivilized native tribes," were to be admitted as citizens of the United States. Those deemed "uncivilized tribes" would be subject to such laws and regulations as the United States might "from time to time, adopt in regard to aboriginal tribes of that country." So, from the beginning of American occupancy of Alaska, the status of Alaska Natives was left in limbo.

Discontent arose among the Alaska Natives of the Southeast as the military governments degenerated into outposts of violence, drunkenness, and poor administration. Alaska Natives felt keenly the disintegration of their people and the deprivation of their lands. After all, the territory had been sold without their consent, and they received none of the proceeds. The Russians had been allowed to occupy the territory partly for mutual benefit, so it seemed logical that the seven and a half million dollars should have been paid to the natives instead of the Russians. Of course, the Russians and Americans did not see it this way.

Importantly, in federal relations with Alaska Natives no treaties were signed. The United States did not officially recognize the tribal relations among Alaska Natives. They could not be citizens until they were "civilized," yet the criteria for determining what civilized meant were ill defined and land rights were left for future consideration.

Alaska remained under military rule until 1884, when Congress finally provided for a measure of civilian government in the First Organic Act. The act also provided the basic protection of lands for the Alaska Natives, but in the same sentence allowed for the development of controversy by leaving this question open for future legislation. It said: "Indians or other persons in said district shall not be disturbed in the possession of any lands actually in their use or occupation or now claimed by them, but the terms under which such persons may acquire title to such lands is reserved for future legislation by Congress." Alaska Natives varied in their use of land, but most were migratory people. In any claims put forward by Alaska Natives, they would have to declare wide areas as being traditionally used lands.

In 1887 Congress passed the General Allotment Act to allow Native Americans to become private, agricultural landowners. Through this act, Congress sought to break up the traditional tribal ownership of lands, to create private ownership, and to assimilate and integrate the Native Americans. In 1906 Congress passed a bill extending the provisions of the General Allotment Act to Alaska Natives. Up to this time, there was no way in which title to land could be obtained unless an Alaska Native was somehow recognized as "civilized" and as a citizen capable of holding property.

The Native Allotment Act provided authority for the Secretary of the Interior "to allot not to exceed 160 acres of vacant, unappropriated, and unreserved nonmineral land in Alaska… to any Indian, Aleut, or Eskimo of full or mixed blood who resides in and is the head of a family, or is twenty-one years of age." This land was to belong to them and their heirs in perpetuity, "except as otherwise provided by the Congress." The Native Allotment Act of 1906 failed miserably. As was typical in the history of Native American policy, failure to appropriate funds for conducting the necessary surveys, investigating claims, and recording the allotments practically destroyed whatever hopes there might have been for Alaska Natives to obtain land after the passage of the legislation. It was left completely up to the Alaska Natives to take the initiative in securing an allotment. With neither a knowledge of English nor a government representative to explain the law, it is no surprise that less than 400 Alaska Native allotments were recorded.

Until Alaska Natives became citizens and until they could organize for their cause, they could do little about civil rights and land claims. Apart from land rights granted through mining claims, the first land rights transferred by Congress went to a group of Tsimshians who had migrated to Alaska from Canada in 1887. Under the leadership of William Duncan, a white lay missionary, they had established a community called New Metlakatla on Annette Island. Although the island was in the territory of the Cape Fox Tlingits, Congress established in 1891 an 86,000-acre reservation for the Metlakatlans.

The continuing movement of whites into interior

Alaska brought about planning for a railroad, which led to what may have been the first conference devoted to Alaska Native land rights, held in July 1915 in Fairbanks. Former Judge James Wickersham, Alaska's delegate to Congress, called for the conference. Wickersham brought the group together because Athabascans in the area had asked him how they could preserve their lands. Fourteen people attended the conference, including six Tanana chiefs. What the chiefs wanted, in the words of Chief Alexander of Tolovana, was that the government "not let the white people come near us. Let us live our own lives in the customs we know."

Through an interpreter, Wickersham explained that the government could not stop the white people, but that Alaska Natives could protect their land by obtaining 160-acre allotments for their homes, or by asking for the establishment of a reservation. After some deliberation, the Athabascan chiefs reported that the two choices offered were not acceptable. The allotments would separate members of the community, and their people lived at many locations throughout the year, not just one. As for a reservation, Chief Ivan of Coskaket noted, "We don't want to go on a reservation, but wish to stay perfectly free just as we are now, and go about just the same as now." Wickersham argued that the reservation would not be a prison, but he could not persuade the chiefs: "I tell you that we are people on the go," said Chief Alexander of Tolovana, "and I believe if we were put in one place, we would just die off." Chief Joe of Salchaket reasoned that "God made Alaska for the Indian people, and all we hope is to be able to live here all the time."

The chiefs expressed the hope that Wickersham could accomplish their request before he sought re-election as delegate. Wickersham said he was pleased at their interest in who would be delegate to Congress. He asked the interpreter to tell the chiefs that "as soon as they have established homes and live like white men, and assume the habits of civilization, they can have a vote." One Alaska Native organization would soon develop with Wickersham's goals in mind.

Alaska Communities: Petersburg, Dillingham, and Craig

Petersburg is located on the northwest end of Mitkof Island, where the Wrangell Narrows meet Frederick Sound. It lies midway between Juneau and Ketchikan, about 120 miles from either community. Tlingit Indians from Kake utilized the north end of Mitkof Island as a summer fish camp. Petersburg got its name from Peter Buschmann, a Norwegian immigrant and pioneer in the cannery business, who arrived in the late 1890s. He built the Icy Strait Packing Company cannery, a sawmill, and a dock by 1900. His family's homesteads grew into this community, populated largely by people of Scandinavian origin. In 1910 a city formed, and by 1920, 600 people lived in Petersburg year round. During this time, residents used glacier ice to pack fresh salmon and halibut for shipment. Alaska gained its first shrimp processor, Alaska Glacier Seafoods, in the area in 1916, and a cold storage plant in 1926. The cannery has operated continuously ever since, though now under the name Petersburg Fisheries, a subsidiary of Icicle Seafoods. Petersburg has developed into one of Alaska's major fishing communities. The community maintains a mixture of Tlingit and Scandinavian history and is known as "Little Norway" for its history and annual Little Norway Festival during May.

Dillingham is located at the extreme northern end of Nushagak Bay in northern Bristol Bay, at the confluence of the Wood and Nushagak Rivers, 327 miles southwest of Anchorage and a 6 hour flight from Seattle. Both Yup'iks and Athabascans inhabited the area around Dillingham and it became a trade center when Russians erected the Alexandrovski Redoubt Post in 1818. Local Alaska Native groups and Alaska Natives from the Kuskokwim Region, the Alaska Peninsula, and Cook Inlet mixed together as they came to visit or live at the post. The community was known as Nushagak by 1837 when the Russian Orthodox church established a mission there. In 1881 the U.S. Signal Corps established a meteorological station at Nushagak. Three years later, the Arctic Packing Company constructed the first salmon cannery in the Bristol Bay region, east of the site of modern-day Dillingham, and established ten more within the next seventeen years. In 1904 the post office at Snag Point and town were named after U.S. Senator Paul Dillingham, who had toured Alaska extensively with his Senate subcommittee during 1903. The 1918–19 influenza epidemic struck the region and left no more than 500 survivors. After the epidemic, the town established a hospital and orphanage in Kanakanak, six miles from the present-day city center. Traditionally a Yup'ik area with Russian influences, Dillingham is now a highly mixed population of non-natives and natives, with the outstanding commercial fishing opportunities in the Bristol Bay area as the focus of the local culture.

Craig is located on a small island off the west coast of Prince of Wales Island and connected by a short causeway as well as to the Alaska Ferry system. It is 31 road miles west of Hollis, 56 air miles northwest of Ketchikan, 750 air miles north of Seattle, and 220 miles south of Juneau. The Tlingit and Haida peoples have historically utilized the area around Craig for its rich resources. With the help of local Haidas, Craig Miller built a fish saltery on nearby Fish Egg Island in 1907. Between 1908 and 1911, Miller also constructed the Lyndenburger Packing Company and cold storage plant at the present site of Craig. In 1912 a post office, school, sawmill, and salmon cannery came to the area. The cannery and sawmill peaked during World War I, and the town formed a city government in 1922. Excellent pink salmon runs contributed to development and growth through the late 1930s—some families from the Dust Bowl relocated to Craig during this time. During the 1950s, the fishing industry collapsed due to depleted salmon runs. In 1972 Ed Head built a large sawmill six miles from Craig near Klawock, which provided year-round jobs and helped to stabilize the economy. Viking Lumber bought Head Mill in the early 1990s.

THE ALASKA NATIVE BROTHERHOOD

In 1912 a group of ten men who had met in Sitka founded the Alaska Native Brotherhood (ANB). The original founders came from various communities and were strongly influenced by the Presbyterian missionaries of Sitka Industrial Training School (later Sheldon Jackson School). This influence was seen in ANB policy on Christian ideals and morality. All of the founders were members of Presbyterian congregations and regarded as outstanding leaders in church work in their respective communities. Certain missionaries at Sitka encouraged the founding of the organization and contributed advice and guidance. Peter Simpson and Alfred Young organized Alaska ANB Camp Number 1 in Sitka in 1912. Camp Number 2 was organized at Juneau and Number 3 at Douglas. In 1913 members of the three camps convened a Grand Camp in Sitka where they elected Simpson president.

Simpson was a Tsimshian raised in Metlakatla, a town that William Duncan, an Anglican missionary, had founded in 1862. Simpson had moved to Alaska in 1887. Sheldon Jackson toured Metlakatla and offered to enroll many Tsimshians in the Sitka Industrial Training School. More than two dozen accepted the offer, including Peter Simpson.

When Simpson finished his studies at the Sitka School, he married and moved into a cottage on the school's grounds. Later he worked as a fisherman and boat builder and gained a reputation as a very religious man who served as an elder at the Sitka Presbyterian Church. For Simpson and other so-called "civilized" Alaska Natives, the key to opportunity in the rapidly changing Alaska was citizenship. Initially the newly formed ANB focused on persuading other Alaska Natives to break their tribal ties and assimilate into Americanism to show their worthiness to become citizens.

In the years immediately following the founding, prominent Alaska Natives of Southeast Alaska joined the ANB. Many were active members of the Presbyterian Church, which at that time was expanding its mission activities throughout Southeast Alaska. Prior to the founding of the ANB, church-affiliated societies organized in nearly every Presbyterian mission. These groups followed the usual pattern of church societies in white Protestant congregations, both in form and function, electing officers and conducting business meetings according to standard rules of parliamentary procedure. They came together to study the Bible, practice church rituals, and assist in charitable and civic acts. Because these organizations were limited to the local mission congregation, only a few survived for more than a few years after the missionaries who had founded them had moved. But the groups did provide a training ground for Alaska Natives to understand how white society worked. At this time, with the Alaska Native way of life threatened to such a large degree, these groups offered a mode for broaching their problems.

Typical of these early church societies was the New Covenant Legion in Sitka which held weekly meetings, drawing its membership from the Alaska Native congregation of the mission church, including both men and women. The society had a full set of elected officers. Bible study constituted one of the major activities; social problems, particularly the desirability of the abolition of both aboriginal customs and the use of alcoholic beverages, were frequent topics of discussion. Most of the founders of the ANB had been members of this society.

The ANB distinguished itself from the previous associations due to its inclusive character. Local chapters, called camps, represented the organization in various communities. The white missionaries did not directly manage local units; therefore, the Alaska Native members took on the responsibility of keeping the groups going. This approach was key to the ANB's survival in its early years. The ANB had been in existence for a few years when the suggestion was made that a woman's auxiliary be formed. Soon the Alaska Native Sisterhood (ANS) paralleled the men's group. As the ANS was introduced in one village after another it usually took over the existing women's societies' functions.

The first chapters or camps of the ANB established themselves in three places: Sitka, Juneau, and Douglas. In the early 1920s camps grew in many other Alaska Native communities in southeast Alaska, except for Metlakatla. Each camp today retains a numeral, or serial number, that indicates the relative time of its establishment. Thus, the Angoon ANB Camp is "Camp No. 7," the seventh chapter to have been chartered. ANB and ANS camps in each community did not necessarily start at the same time and therefore may have different serial numbers.

In Wrangell, an interesting situation developed. Before the Wrangell natives could express serious interest in participating, they had to make a formal settlement with certain Sitka clans. A Wrangell man who had resided at Sitka and who had joined the ANB quite early played a leading part in arranging this settlement and was the principal emissary to Sitka. In an interesting combination of religious and philosophical practices, the Wrangell and Sitka chiefs concerned performed a ceremony and signed a formal treaty of peace, written in English and drawn up largely in terms of Western concepts. Parts of the ancient aboriginal peacemaking ritual also accompanied its signing. A year later the group held its annual convention at Wrangell and organized the Wrangell Camp. Most of the camps have continued to function up to the present day.

Citizenship interested the ANB from the beginning days of the organization. Alaska Natives argued that since they had never assumed the status of wards of the government through treaty, and did not reside on reservations, they were free and equal citizens of the United States. Under the Treaty of Cession the government allowed that only "civilized" Alaska Natives were citizens. Later on, the U.S. made provisions by which a native could become a citizen, holding that the General Allotment Act of 1887 applied to Alaska, so that citizenship was possible for persons who "severed tribal relationship and adopted the habits of civilization." The Territorial Act of 1915 provided a procedure through which Alaska Natives, by proving voter qualifications and demonstrating abandonment of tribal customs, could obtain citizenship. It appears that very few Tlingit took advantage of this method, however. Eventually, of course, the Citizenship Act of June 2, 1924, included Alaska Natives and resolved the problem.

Famous Alaskans: Alfred Hulse Brooks

Brooks was the chief Alaska geologist from 1903 to 1924 of the U.S. Geological Survey, discovering that the biggest mountain range in Arctic Alaska was separate from the Rocky Mountains. The Brooks Range later carried his name. He was noted for having explored many thousands of square miles of the Alaskan interior and was a prolific author of many reports and articles, including an important book, *Blazing Alaska's Trails*, on Alaskan exploration.

William Paul and others regarded an episode that took place in 1922 as of major significance in forcing popular acceptance of Alaska Native rights. Prior to this time, the government had generally barred Alaska Natives from voting in Southeast Alaska. Some, however, had voted regularly in primary and territorial elections since the creation of the territorial legislature.

During the 1922 primaries, Charlie Jones, an elderly Tlingit chief in Wrangell, appeared at the polls to cast his ballot. Jones was a highly respected person and of high status in Tlingit ranks. He apparently had voted in previous elections, but on this occasion an official at the voting place did not permit him to vote. Jones went in search of an educated Stikine woman, Mrs. Tillie Paul Tamaree (the mother of William Paul), to request her assistance, assuming that he had misunderstood because of his rather limited command of English. Mrs. Tamaree returned to the polls with him and insisted that he be given a ballot. When Jones did cast his vote, he was arrested for voting at a time and place where he was not eligible to vote, both of which were a felony; Mrs. Tamaree was also arrested, though released immediately on her own recognizance, for aiding and abetting the commission of a felony.

William Paul came to the aid of the two defendants. In 1894 Sheldon Jackson had begun sending his most promising students to the shining light of acculturation— the Carlisle Indian School in Pennsylvania. In 1897 Paul was one of those students. He spent two and a half years at Carlisle, where he learned to "blaze the way to a political solution to their troubles." Born of part-Alaska Native parents in 1885, William Paul was educated at the Sitka Industrial Training School and later at Carlisle, as well as at Banks Business College in Philadelphia and Whitworth College in Spokane. By the time he returned to Alaska in 1920, he had also earned a law degree through the LaSalle University extension program. He soon gained a reputation as an articulate orator for Alaska Native rights. Paul first attracted territorial attention at the eighth annual convention of the ANB. Its goal prior to 1920 was civilization through assimilation. At the 1920 convention of the ANB held at Wrangell, William Paul and his brother Louis began to politicize the organization, and from then on it became a major force for Alaska Native rights.

The Jones case was perfect for testing the long-standing demands of the ANB for citizenship and voting rights. The case did not revolve around technical points of law but was resolved mainly on the basis of testimony concerning Jones's actions as a member of the community of Wrangell. He testified that he had always been a law-abiding person, paid taxes dutifully, and participated in matters relating to the public welfare. For example, during World War I he purchased war bonds for himself and all members of his family and gave to Red Cross drives. He voted in previous elections, being permitted to do so by election officials who knew he understood that voting was the duty of a good citizen. He was found not guilty of the charge of illegal voting, and the right of Alaska Natives to vote in Alaska therefore won acceptance. Alaska Natives thus gained the franchise before federal legislation allowed all Native Americans to vote in 1924.

Nugget Pond

William Paul's involvement motivated the ANB's participation in the case. The case matched the ANB's campaign for citizenship rights, members of the ANB testified for the defense, and the ANB provided funds to finance the trial. This victory set the stage for the development of the ANB as a political force. Once the right of Alaska Natives to vote was firmly established, natives were in a position to make their influence felt in public matters. The case also established William Paul as a defender of Alaska Native rights and assured his influence in the ANB.

The stage was now set for William Paul's political activities. With the block of several thousand votes could be organized, Alaska Natives in Southeast Alaska could be a potent factor, even to the point of tipping the scales in favor of one or the other of the two major parties. Proof of this power showed itself in 1926, when William Paul, running as a Republican in nominally Democratic Alaska, won election to the territorial legislature. Paul did not, of course, depend entirely on the native vote. He also had important support from the party organization. But the Alaska Native backing, organized through the ANB and through the ANB newspaper, the *Alaska Fisherman*, was a crucial factor.

From its founding, the *Alaska Fisherman* stressed politics and political issues. In addition, the ANB created a political subcommittee of its executive committee. This body had as its principal function consideration of the various candidates and recommended to the membership those considered sympathetic to legislation the ANB desired. ANB political policy stressed voting for the candidate, not the party, and the political committee did not hesitate to recommend crossing party lines.

The ANB also took a position against the exclusion of Alaska Native children from territorial public schools. The group felt strongly that instruction in Alaska Native schools was not up to the standards of territorial public school education. Also, since their children would have to grow up and compete in a "white man's" world, natives needed the opportunity to compete on equal grounds with whites in the public schools. As in the case of voting rights, the exclusion of Alaska Native children from these schools varied. At an early date a test case in Sitka tried to force the acceptance of certain Alaska Native children in the Sitka

Public School, though the case was lost on the grounds that the children's parents "did not lead a civilized type of life." The children's stepfather was, it is said, urged to appeal the case but he did not do so, partly because of the expense and because he was afraid of making enemies among his neighboring whites for whom he often worked.

In 1929 two Alaska Native girls who were attending the public school at Ketchikan were told they could no longer continue there but must enroll in the Alaska Native school at nearby Saxman. The children were good students with fine records. When the father of the youngsters went before the school board and indicated his intention of making an issue of the matter, the school authorities claimed crowded conditions as the source of the decision. William Paul served as attorney for the father, bringing suit against the school board and finally establishing the children's right to attend the school of their choice. The judge ordered that the school accept them and stated in his opinion that if a shortage of space did in fact exist in the school, it was the duty of the school board to provide more space. William Paul and the ANB had succeeded again, and as we shall see, their success set the groundwork for Alaska Native land claims to come.

Jones and White Acts

While William Paul and the ANB were fighting for Alaska Native rights, the federal government passed legislation that adversely impacted the Alaskan Territory. The 1920 Jones Act, sponsored by Washington's Senator Wesley Jones, was a perfect example of the domination of Alaska by outside economic interests. The 1920 act stipulated that commerce between American ports must use American built ships. The clear intent was to prevent Canadian competition for the Alaska and Hawaii steamship trade. The bill effectively eliminated the two Canadian lines serving Alaska, leaving Alaskans at the mercy of the two American lines. American shippers had to be used even if Canadians offered better rates. Alaskans thought the act unfair and in violation of the commerce clause of the Constitution. They brought a suit, eventually leading to a Supreme Court decision. Justice McReynolds recognized the discrimination against Alaska but argued that, since Alaska was not a state, the

Fish Trap circa 1917

Constitution's language of "one state over another" did not apply. The act was of course quite beneficial to Seattle and its shipping industry.

In 1924 the White Act authorized the Bureau of Fisheries to limit catch, seasons, gear, and escapement of fishing (the amount of fish left behind to keep a run healthy) in Alaska. When Congress later took up amendments to the White Act, Alaska's Delegate Sutherland spoke before hearings stating that "the present policy worked to the advantage of the packing interests and to the detriment of the Alaskan fisherman." He strongly criticized the monopolistic practices of the packing industry. Unfortunately, the 1924 White Act bowed to the packers regarding the use of fish traps—large wooden mazes built at the mouth of rivers where salmon came to spawn, thus having the potential to take the entire runs of fish. Despite the potential for destroying the salmon runs, both packers and the Bureau of Fisheries argued that the banning of fish traps would spell the end of the salmon fishing industry in Alaska. The decision once again confirmed Alaska's colonial status while industry and federal forces from outside Alaska overrode the interests of conservation.

Following passage of the amended White Act, Commissioner of Fisheries Henry O'Malley visited Alaska to view conditions for himself. In December 1924, he issued new fishing regulations that prohibited stake net fishing, ordered fish traps to be set a mile and a half apart, placed limits on drift nets, and set dates for open and closed periods for the Copper River and Prince William Sound. These closed periods were to allow salmon an opportunity to move upstream for spawning and people living in the upper Copper River area a chance to fish.

The new regulations touched off a heated controversy, pitting supporters of the packers against resident white fishermen and Alaska Natives. The *Cordova Times* editor immediately ran an article praising the regulations, writing that "There can be no conservation without stepping on somebody's toes." Cordova fishermen protested several points in the regulations but focused their main concern on the prohibition of stake net fishing on the Copper River flats. They noted that the flats were a difficult, storm-prone area to fish by drift boats and that stake net fishing was safer. They also opposed the closed periods on the Copper River claiming that in 1924, without the stringent regulations, sixty percent of the fish made it up the Copper River to spawn.

The Alaska Native community of Cordova sent a petition to Delegate Sutherland to present on their behalf to Commissioner O'Malley. They noted that before the fish traps started operating in the district, they had no trouble going out any day of the year and catching all the halibut and codfish they needed. But now they went out for days and sometimes as long as a week and never caught more than one or two halibut and very few codfish. Clearly the fish traps caught just as many codfish and halibut as they did salmon, and in some areas they practically killed off the halibut. Alaska Natives noted that the companies "either don't care or don't stop to think that fish" was the principal part of their food.

The situation in Cordova revealed the way the White Act could divide Alaskan communities. The *Cordova Times* argued that Alaska Natives had plenty of food:

> The Indians contend that the use of traps interferes with their right to make a living for the entire year during the brief canning season. And when they say this, they mean a living according to the standard of living they have learned from the white race. The fact is that the Indians want a fishing monopoly that will permit them to make enough money in two or three months to live, as whitemen live, for twelve months. They want, in other words, three months of work and nine months of idleness.

Clearly the White Act exacerbated racial divisions.

William Paul intervened and proposed legislation that would tax the canneries' fish traps. The fish trusts' lobbyists complained that such a tax would make it economically unfeasible for them to continue to operate in Alaska. In reaction, the canning industry took out large ads in local newspapers to explain their side of the controversy. According to the ads most of territory's total revenue came from taxes on salmon fisheries. They, of course, neglected to mention that these revenues were small when compared to the profits they were extracting.

Stacks of canned salmon circa 1915

Banning the hated fish traps became one of the rallying cries of Alaskans against the federal government and for statehood. Delegate Dimond, who replaced Sutherland, repeatedly argued for Alaskan control of its fisheries and the gradual phasing out of all fish traps, something Canada's fisheries completed in 1933. Dimond was no more successful than Sutherland. In 1939 the Bureau of Fisheries was transferred to the more conservation-oriented Interior Department, where it eventually became the Fish and Wildlife Service. Two years later the Fish and Wildlife Service reduced the number of fish traps in Alaska but did not eliminate them. It was not until statehood, when Alaska assumed control of its fisheries, that fish traps were finally abolished.

The Alaska Railroad

While Alaskans resented federal control of their resources, the federal treasury was also responsible for bringing important projects to the territory, the most noteworthy of which in this period was the Alaska Railroad. In August of 1912 Congress gave the nod to President Taft to investigate rail transportation in Alaska, and Taft appointed a four-man team to undertake the task. The team explored the region and submitted their report on January 20, of 1913, concluding that railroad connections with ports on the

Pacific were necessary for gaining acess to the fertile regions of the Alaska interior and Alaska's mining resources and that railroads would "open up a large region to the homesteader, the prospector, and the miner." In March 1914, Congress authorized the president to locate, construct, and operate a railroad in the Alaska territory. They also appropriated $35 million and mandated the use of discarded rail equipment from the Panama Canal project. On May 2, President Wilson gave the order to the secretary of the interior to begin surveying railroad routes and also created the Alaska Engineering Commission (AEC) to conduct these surveys, selecting William C. Edes, a man with more than 35 years of experience in building western railroads, as chairman. As part of the commission, Wilson selected Frederick Mears, due to his experience as an engineer on the Panama and Great Northern railroads, and Thomas Riggs, who had spent many years in Alaska, had surveyed the Alaskan/Canadian Boundary, and was very familiar with its weather conditions.

The commission established offices in Seattle in 1914 and began gathering men and supplies for their surveying work. They investigated two routes, one beginning at Valdez or Cordova and the other at Seward or Portage Bay, both ending in Fairbanks. They completed their survey work in little over three months and then headed to Washington, D.C. to assemble the data. They submitted their final report to the president in February 1915, but gave no recommendations as to which route they preferred. In April, the president chose the western route, which began at Seward.

Before the month of April ended, an eager Lt. Frederick Mears returned to Alaska with a crew and began marking the route. In anticipation of future employment, thousands of people arrived in the Anchorage area,

Alaska State Library PCA 20-179

Engine of Alaska Railroad on Eska Creek Spur, March 1917

creating a large tent city. Even though construction labor only paid 37.5 cents per hour, there were more men than jobs. The crews laid the first new rails in April 1915. Large quantities of Panama Canal equipment reached Anchorage in the summer of 1915, including steam shovels, derricks, bridge timbers, structural steel, the AEC's first locomotives, flat cars, wheels, boilers, drills, and shop machinery. Seattle shipped in large quantities of lumber and rail. Steel mills in the lower 48 manufactured seventy-pound rail for the main line and sixty-pound rail for the sidings. A motor car traveled the first 35 miles, charging passengers 12.5 cents per mile and freight $25 per ton.

   In summer, boats and wagons transported equipment, but surprisingly the preferred transportation season was during the winter, when hundreds of horses and sleds carried equipment to construction camps. Although winter could bring an end to laying rail, it was an acceptable time for bridge building in which pile drivers could sink pilings

Alaska Railroad, Denali

and place steel. In 1916 Alaska construction crews laid sixty miles of new track, graded one hundred miles, and cleared the right-of-way for 230 miles. In October 1917 the first train reached the Chickaloon coal mills, which were located seventy-four miles north of Anchorage. Six days later the first shipment of coal arrived in Anchorage.

By March 1919 the end of steel reached mile post 227. 1920 came to a close with 382 miles of new track in Alaska. Only two unfinished bridges, Riley Creek and Tanana River, prevented a connection between Fairbanks and Seward. Crews completed the Riley Creek Bridge in February 1922. The Tanana River Bridge, however, would be another problem entirely, requiring a 701-foot single-span bridge, a record-breaker for its day. By June 1923,

Alaska Communities: Anchorage

Three hours by air from Seattle, Anchorage, the largest city in Alaska with over 269,000 residents, is located in southcentral Alaska at the head of Cook Inlet. To the east the Chugach Mountains serve as the backdrop for the city's skyline. To the west are the waters of Cook Inlet, named after the explorer Captain James Cook who sailed into the area in 1778. Construction began in 1914 on a federal railroad with the construction headquarters in Anchorage. By July of 1915, thousands of job seekers and opportunists had poured into the area, living in a tent city on the banks of Ship Creek near the edge of the present downtown. That July produced the "Great Anchorage Lot Sale," a land auction that shaped the future of the city. Some 655 lots were sold for $148,000 or an average of $225 each. A month later, the town voted to call itself Alaska City, but the federal government refused to change the name. The City of Anchorage was incorporated on Nov. 23, 1920. From 1939 to 1957, major military impacts and government construction of roads, airports and harbors throughout Alaska contributed to Anchorage's growth. Though the city continued to develop steadily, Anchorage remained a relatively small frontier town until the beginning of World War II when the Japanese bombed Pearl Harbor, and Anchorage found itself on the front lines of the conflict. The U.S. constructed airfields, roads, and other infrastructure throughout the war, and the city's population exploded from around 8,000 to more than 43,000. After WWII, the military left this infrastructure behind, creating the framework for Anchorage's development. Anchorage's port followed by the early 1960s as did the Greater Anchorage Area Borough, which formed on Jan. 1, 1964. The Good Friday earthquake in 1964 destroyed a large part of the city, but during the 1970s the development of the Prudhoe Bay oil fields and the Trans-Alaska Pipeline again brought rapid growth, tripling the population, office space, and housing within a ten-year period. Anchorage has a history of cultural diversity, and many residents participate in nearby recreational and subsistence activities. With over 162 parks, including ten large reserves, the city's recreation opportunities include downhill and cross-country skiing, ice hockey, fishing, golf, swimming, hiking, biking, and camping. The George Sullivan Sports Arena, Alaska Performing Arts Center, Egan Convention Center and many other facilities host cultural and entertainment events throughout the year.

crews had broken this record, completing the Tanana River Bridge and converting the last fifty-seven miles of track to Fairbanks to standard gauge.

In July 1923, the railroad was complete, though due to World War I, inflations, and appropriations delays, it was completed behind schedule and had cost almost twice initial estimates.

HARDING'S STRANGE TRIP

On a hot and sunny day near Fairbanks, Territorial Governor Scott Bone inserted a golden spike into the completed Alaska Railroad. President Warren G. Harding missed the spike twice and then drove it home to officially complete the construction. Harding had arrived in Alaska on July 13, 1923, accompanied by his wife and a large entourage, including Herbert Hoover, then secretary of commerce.

The president and his group were advised to outfit themselves in heavy shirts, heavy underwear, sweaters, galoshes, and leggings to protect against the cold and mosquitoes. But Alaska's weather can surprise. In Fairbanks, where Harding made a speech at the local baseball park, the temperature was 95 degrees. Three people collapsed from the heat. This proved to be a poor harbinger for Harding's trip.

President Warren G. Harding driving the "Golden Spike" on the Alaska Railroad at Nenana, Alaska, July 1923

Harding's end is still a mystery. He died on the way home from his Alaska journey on August 2, 1923, and the cause has never been established. The White House said it was food poisoning, and another physician later said it was a cerebral hemorrhage.

Harding had become active in politics more than a decade earlier, serving in the state senate and winning election as lieutenant governor in Ohio. In 1914, with the help of political boss Harry Daugherty, Harding was elected to the U.S. Senate. In his six years in the Senate, Harding missed over two-thirds of all roll calls and votes, compiling one of the all-time worst attendance records in the history of that legislative body. He introduced only 134 bills, none of them significant. As much as he disliked the job, he was a good party man who worked to keep harmony. This was a great help to him in 1920, when a deadlocked Republican convention turned to Harding as a compromise candidate.

Harding made some good appointments in his new administration, like Charles Hughes as secretary of state, Andrew Mellon as secretary of the treasury, and Herbert Hoover as secretary of commerce. But the majority of his appointments were disasters. The Ohio cronies who had helped elect him wanted their share of the spoils, and along with a few others, such as New Mexico Senator Albert Fall, Harding gave them the major offices in his administration. He also named his chief supporter, Harry Daugherty, as attorney general. Daugherty then controlled most of the other appointments. The result was that most of the people in government knew each other well and got along well. They were called the "Ohio Gang."

Warren Harding is consistently ranked very low in presidential polls. Widespread corruption marked his administration. The Navy Department transferred strategic oil reserves to the Interior Department, which then sold the leases to the highest bidder. The newly created Veterans Bureau was looted of millions of dollars that were reserved to support disabled veterans. The Alien Property Custodian also engaged in corruption. Harry Daugherty accepted bribes to decide Justice Department cases. In spite of Prohibition, liquor was served at the nightly poker games in the White House, and Harding continued to have extra-marital affairs.

Rumors circulated about the graft and corruption. Harding began to show the effects of the constant strain, and his health suffered. He was quoted as saying, "I am not worried about my enemies. It is my friends that are keeping me awake nights." As things began to unravel, the head of the Veterans Bureau went to Europe and sent his resignation back to the White House, only to be convicted later and sent to jail. An assistant at the Veterans Bureau committed suicide, leaving a note addressed to President Harding, who refused to open it. An assistant to Attorney General Daugherty either committed suicide or was murdered. He supposedly bought a gun and shot himself with it, but he had an absolute terror of guns. Secretary of the Interior Fall resigned.

The Senate was debating the creation of a special committee to investigate the leases of Navy oil reserve lands to private companies. Harding put all his administration's efforts and resources behind the move to defeat the creation of such a committee, realizing that its members would uncover the poorly kept secrets of his administration and that this would mean certain impeachment.

Famous Alaskans: Big Mike Heney

Known as "Big Mike" to his railroad crews in Washington, Canada, and Alaska, Heney was at home in the front-line construction tents. In the financial and social circles of Seattle, San Francisco, New York, and London, he was called the "Irish Prince." His optimistic vision of the future prompted him to undertake projects often shunned by others. Although he lived for only 45 years, he founded a city, amassed a fortune, and inspired a best selling novel. Without technical training he built two railroads considered imposs-ible by the leading engineers of his day. A ready Irish smile drew people to him and they became friends for life. Wherever "Big Mike" led, his workers followed, each proud to be "one of Heney's men." Heney built two railroads, the White Pass and Yukon Route and the Copper River and Northwestern, considered imposs-ible by leading engineers of his day. He was noted for saying "Give me enough dynamite and snoose and I'll build a road to Hell!"

Needless to say, the time seemed right to escape Washington, D.C. and take an Alaskan vacation. But the goal of buoying Harding's health and spirits was not successful. During the trip, a long coded message reached the presidential train informing Harding that the Senate did in fact vote to establish a special committee to investigate the oil

Plane along the Denali Highway

leases. Reporters traveling with the president later told of a depressed-looking Harding asking them what a president could do when his friends had betrayed him.

During his trip, Harding went to Canada and Alaska, making him the first president to visit the territory. As his train passed through Seattle on the way back, he became ill. On July 27, he went to bed with severe cramps and indigestion. Surgeon General Charles Sawyer diagnosed it as food poisoning. On July 29, his train reached San Francisco, and Harding checked into the Palace Hotel. He developed pneumonia and had a fever of 102 degrees. On August 1, his fever broke, his accelerated pulse had slowed to normal, and his breathing was more comfortable. He was even making plans to go fishing the next day. According to Mrs. Harding, she wanted to cheer him up by reading "A Calm View of a Calm Man," which was a very flattering article about Harding in the *Saturday Evening Post*. Harding supposedly said, "That's good. Go on; read some more." Those were his last words. When Mrs.

Harding finished reading the article, she left him with his eyes closed, assuming him to be asleep. In fact he had died, and doctors concluded that he had suffered a stroke.

Mrs. Harding refused to allow an autopsy. Conveniently, California, where Harding's death took place, did not yet have a mandatory autopsy law. Several rumors began. One said that Harding, already depressed and facing impeachment, committed suicide. Another said that Mrs. Harding poisoned him, to prevent him from suffering the humiliation of impeachment and removal from office or possibly as revenge for his cheating on her. Although the rumors are periodically renewed and reviewed, the lack of an autopsy prevents any definite answer.

AVIATION IN ALASKA

Since the 1920s, Alaska, with its unbridgeable waters, impassable mountains, and tundra and bush country, has employed aircraft. Travel in the far north demands it. Today, one in forty-five Alaskan residents holds a pilot's license, which is six times the national average.

The end of World War I signaled the start for Alaska commercial aviation. Ten-thousand newly made flyers were demobilized, and thousands of military "airships" were dumped on the surplus market. In the 1920s, when Midwestern barnstormers captured the nation's imagination, a handful of adventurers introduced Alaska to aviation.

But Alaska presented special challenges. Engines and oil had to be kept warm in minus 50 degree weather, propellers were lashed to fuselages, and crashes were a part of the aviator's norm. Lacking instruments or reliable maps, aviators followed rivers, railroads, and pack trails when they were visible. Pilots doubled as mechanics and developed strong legs hiking out after their aircraft were downed in the bush.

Alaska Communities: Gustavus

Gustavus lies on the north shore of Icy Passage at the mouth of the Salmon River, 48 air miles northwest of Juneau in the St. Elias Mountains. It is surrounded by Glacier Bay National Park and Preserve on three sides and the waters of Icy Passage on the south. Glacier Bay Park is 3.3 million acres and offers 16 tidewater glaciers. When Capt. George Vancouver sailed through Icy Strait in 1794, the Grand Pacific Glacier completely covered the bay. Over the next century, the glacier retreated some 40 miles, and a spruce-hemlock forest began to develop. By 1916 it had retreated 65 miles from the position observed by Vancouver in 1794. Gustavus is located on a flat area formed by the outwash from the glacier and the area is still growing. It began as an agricultural homestead in 1914 and was once known as Strawberry Point due to the abundant wild strawberries. The current name derives from Point Gustavus, which lies 7 miles to the southwest. President Calvin Coolidge established Glacier Bay National Monument (including Gustavus) in 1925. After many appeals the homesteaders were able to keep their land and planners excluded the Gustavus area from the monument. It became a National Park in 1980 with the passage of the Alaska National Interest Lands Conservation Act and remains a major recreation and tourist attraction in southeast Alaska. Many of the residents who relocated chose Gustavus for its lifestyle, its nearness to natural resources, the beauty of the area, and for the subsistence activities available.

In 1922, Roy Jones made the first trip up the Inside Passage from Seattle to Ketchikan, landing in the Tongass Narrows. Air travel transformed the Alaska bush. River and over-land delivery of mail and cargo, to a large extent, became a thing of the past.

The romance of Arctic flight captured world notice in 1928, when aviators Carl Ben Eielson and Australian-born George Hubert

Polychrome Pass, Denali National Park

Wilkins flew from Barrow to Spitsbergen, Norway, on the first polar flight from America to Europe.

Eielson, who moved to Fairbanks in 1922, inaugurated Alaska mail runs and commercial air service in the Interior region. He received the Distinguished Flying Cross for the first plane flight over the top of the world, to Spitzbergen, Norway. Sadly, in 1929 Eielson disappeared while trying to salvage $1 million in furs from the ice-bound ship *Namuk* off the Siberian coast. His disappearance set off a highly publicized search. Two months later, Joe Crosson and Harold Gillam, two other famous bush pilots, found the downed plane along with the frozen bodies of Eielson and his mechanic. The Fairbanks-area Eielson Air Force Base and the visitor's center in Denali National Park are named for him.

Famous Alaskans: Benny Benson

Thirteen-year-old Benny Benson's fame comes from designing the Alaska flag. Born in Chignik and raised in Unalaska, Benny was the winner of the 1926 contest sponsored by the Alaska Department of the American Legion for Alaska students in grades seven through twelve. The Legion awarded him two prizes in 1927; a gold watch engraved with the flag and a $1000 trip to Washington, D.C. to present the flag to President Coolidge. But Benny never went to Washington. First his father was ill, and then President Coolidge was out of the country, so the $1000 was put toward his education instead. Benny wrote, "The blue in the flag is for the state flower (Forget-me-not) and the Alaskan sky. The gold is for the natural wealth. The Big Dipper and North Star are symbolic for Alaska's position in relation to the heavens." The territorial legislature adopted Benny's design in May 1927 for Alaska's official flag. It is dark blue, with eight five-pointed gold stars in the shape of the constellation Ursa Major (the great bear—also known as the "big dipper") and a larger gold star representing the pole star, Polaris.

Crosson made history by becoming the first pilot to land on a glacier, but he is best known for his grim feats of recovering the bodies of three of his friends and colleagues: Carl Ben Eielson, aviator Wiley Post, and humorist Will Rogers, Jr. But during his life, Crosson was known as an amiable, kind-hearted man who avoided the limelight while risking his life to assist those in distress. Because of its location, Fairbanks was on the route of many record-setting flights. When other pilots pursuing records needed help in Fairbanks, they needed Joe Crosson. In 1926 the Fairbanks Airplane Corporation offered him a pilot's job, and the 23-year-old moved north. Crosson went through it all: catching fire in the air, walking 200 miles to Nenana in minus 40 degree temperatures and, worst of all, the fatal crashes of those dear to him. During his lifetime, he garnered such fame that his marriage was reported in national news-papers and an adventure comic for children featured a fictionalized version of his exploits. As the industry matured, he helped modernize Alaska's fleet and establish regular passenger service. During World War II, he served as a civilian consultant to the armed forces and subsequently became the youngest division manager ever at Pan American

Airways. In 1932, he flew three scientists, plus several hundred pounds of gear, to the 6,000 foot level of Denali's Muldrow Glacier. Gillam exemplified the classic bush pilot's charmed life. While learning to fly he survived a crash that killed his own instructor. He walked away from six crashes in 1931 alone. In 1943, however, his luck ran out when his Lockheed Electra, carrying five passengers, went down in fog near Ketchikan.

Probably the most influential of the Alaska pioneer flyers were the Wien brothers of Minnesota: Noel, Ralph, Fritz, and Sig. Noel first arrived in Alaska in 1924 with 538 hours of barnstorming and aerial circus stunt flying under his belt. Before air charts and radio communication, the navigation of Alaska's rugged terrain depended solely on the use of natural features for check points. Wien was up to the challenge and built up a long list of firsts: he was the first to fly from Fairbanks to Seattle, Fairbanks to Nome, and beyond the Arctic Circle, and was the first to make a round-trip flight between Alaska and Asia. Wien turned a vision of establishing commercial aviation in the north into reality with Wien Alaska Air, which made Fairbanks the hub of Alaskan aviation. Each time he went south he returned with another brother to help manage and build the company. Himself a barnstorming ace, Noel displayed slightly more caution than the others in the flying fraternity. His motto: "Take 'em out and bring 'em back." As a result of flyers like the Wiens, bush pilots became an institution in Alaska. Many residents in remote areas came to rely on these skillful and daring men and women for mail, groceries, supplies, and transportation. In fact, even today, bush pilots make the summer mail run to remote locations throughout the state.

WILEY POST AND WILL ROGERS

In 1935 Wiley Post, one of America's best known pilots, became interested in surveying a mail-and-passenger air route from the west coast to Russia. He planned to add pontoons to his plane to land in Alaska's and Siberia's many lakes. His friend, the famous American humorist Will Rogers, visited him frequently at the Lockheed airport in Burbank, where Post had his plane *Aurora Borealis* built. When the pontoons ordered did not arrive, Post had a set installed that was designed for a much larger plane. Altogether it was a dangerously heavy aircraft, which the two men loaded down further with hunting and fishing equipment.

After a test flight in late July 1935, Post and Rogers left Seattle in the unique plane in early August. Rogers commented on the huge pontoons, but Post dismissed his concerns. Their itinerary was from Seattle to Juneau, Dawson, Fairbanks, the Matanuska Valley, and finally Point Barrow. While Post piloted the plane, Rogers banged out his newspaper columns on his typewriter. On the way to Point Barrow, they became lost in bad weather and landed in a lagoon a few miles from Point Barrow to ask directions. The engine quit when they tried to take off again, and the nose-heavy plane plunged into the lagoon, tearing off the right wing, and killing both men instantly. The Will Rogers and Wiley Post Monument, across from the state-owned Wiley Post–Will Rogers Memorial Airport in Barrow, was dedicated in 1982 to commemorate them and the 1935 plane crash that killed them.

THE MATANUSKA COLONY

The same year of the Post/Rogers crash, President Franklin D. Roosevelt offered 203 families from the hardest-hit areas of Minnesota, Wisconsin, and Michigan the chance to start fresh in the fertile Matanuska Valley. The Matanuska Colony was part of Roosevelt's New Deal, his plan to help Americans recover from the Depression, partly through massive public works projects.

Farming is not the first thing that comes to mind when one thinks of Alaska, but there is a long history of agriculture in the area that dates back to the Russian period. The Russians discovered a couple of important things related to Alaskan farming, namely that grains did poorly in Southeast Alaska and that roots and tubers like potatoes did well.

The Gold Rush era was also an important impetus to Alaskan agriculture. The gold seekers brought food with them but they found that if they had an extended stay, it was much cheaper to grow food than to pay inflated Alaskan prices for it.

In 1897 Walter Evans of the U.S. Department of Agriculture headed a team that surveyed Alaska for agricultural potential. His report was quite optimistic, even glowing, concerning the Tanana valley and the Matanuska/Susitna regions. Evans reported "an abundance of good, nutritious grass and potential for profitable raising of rye, oats, barley and buckwheat." He noted that "there is even hope for hardy apples and six-week corn" and that "these areas may be safely regarded as the garden spots of Alaska." As a result of Evans's report, the federal government established Agricultural Experiment Stations throughout the territory.

Eventually stations existed in such areas as Kodiak, Sitka, Kenai, and Fairbanks, and in the Matanuska valley. These stations tested out what crops and livestock would fare well in their region of Alaska. Local homesteaders were given free seeds in return for information on what worked and what did not. Strawberries, Siberian wheat, Holstein cattle, honeybees, and Jerusalem artichokes were among the experiments tried at the various stations.

Gardens soon became a way for miners and homesteaders to battle the high costs of goods from the south. One miner, James Calbreath, explained when writing back to an experiment station in 1917: "I wish to say that all the seeds were good, especially the turnips. I sowed all I had and had a great crop—roots weighing over two pounds! I never witnessed anything like it! And best of all the dogs are fond of them." James Minano, a Japanese miner near the Brooks Range in 1918, wrote that "we have to dig gardens in order to prospect. Last year we raised close to four tons of potatoes besides turnips, cabbage, and celery. I can truthfully say I found mining potatoes more fruitful than mining gold."

What about commercial agriculture beyond the subsistence farmers? Paul Rickert was a commercial agricultural pioneer in Alaska. He made a good living with about one hundred acres of vegetables under cultivation. He also produced milk, eggs, and raised pork. Fairbanks residents would pay top dollar for these fresh products. C.C. Georgeson was known as the "father of Alaskan agriculture." He headed the Alaska experiment stations in the early 1900s and predicted, based on Rickert's success, that Alaska's farms would "one day support a population of three to six million!" He did point out, however, that in order to get to that population, Alaskan farmers would have to "get married as most are broken down prospectors" who were single. He thought Alaska needed more than just what he termed "bachelor farms."

Rickert and Georgeson tried to solve this dilemma at the 1924 First Annual Tanana Valley Fair. The fair contained the usual exhibits one would find at any agricultural exhibition: livestock, vegetable stands, and arts and crafts. However, there was also an unusual booth that sported a sign above it that proclaimed, "Get Married at the Tanana Valley Fair." An advertisement before the fair promised women who married Alaskan farmers that "we will furnish the license, the preacher, the ring, the music and the flowers." There was also an added bonus of a "free honeymoon trip by airship." Unfortunately for Georgeson and Rickert, the scheme was a bust and there was not one taker.

How did the agricultural focus shift from the Tanana Valley to the Matanuska/Susitna region? First, the Alaska Railroad, built from 1915 to 1923, passed through the Matanuska valley and brought renewed attention to the region's agricultural potential. A few farming homesteads already existed as well as the small community of Palmer, established in 1916, but it was not until the Great Depression that the region became Alaska's major farm belt.

In the early 1930s the United States was in the midst of its worst-ever economic crisis. Staggering unemployment, drought and dust, banking and business in disarray, and long lines for relief shocked the nation. FDR promised a "New Deal" for the American people to resolve the national crisis. He was an experimenter and was willing to use the powers of the government to try almost anything to ease the Depression. The massive government intervention and vast array of so-called alphabet agencies did not leave Alaska out of the plans.

One of FDR's plans called for relocating people from hard hit areas to establish new agricultural colonies. For example, Cherry Lake Farms in Florida, Dyess Colony in Arkansas, Pine Mountain Rural Community in Georgia, and—most controversial of all—the Matanuska Valley Colony in Alaska were part of FDR's relocation plans.

The administration chose Minnesota, Wisconsin, and Michigan as states to supply the people for a new colony in Alaska. The demise of farming and logging had left many there on assistance. The upper Midwest also most closely resembled Alaska's climate. Local aid workers in the Midwest were to find suitable colonists based on the following guidelines: "As far as possible, families should be selected first on their farming ability and secondly, those who may have secondary skills and who may adjust themselves to a diversified farming activity and can assist with carpentry on their homes and then those who may know something about machinery and blacksmithing and who have leadership qualities."

Some mistakes were made. One man arrived in Alaska and was found to have a wooden leg which he had covered up. Eight of the colonists had active tuberculosis and one was committed to a mental institution even before reaching Alaska. A joke spread that the Midwest had sent their problems to Alaska.

In the end, two hundred and three families were chosen for the Alaskan experiment. The Federal Emergency Relief Administration (FERA) would be in charge of the relocation, setting aside two hundred sixty thousand acres in the

Alaska Communities: Wasilla

Wasilla is located midway between the Matanuska and Susitna Valleys, on the George Parks Highway. It lies between Wasilla and Lucille Lakes, 43 miles north of Anchorage, about one hour's drive. Wasilla was named after the respected local Dena'ina Indian, Chief Wasilla (also known as Chief Vasili). In the Dena'ina Athabascan dialect, "Wasilla" is said to mean "breath of air." Other sources claim the Chief derived his name from the Russian language, and that "Vasili" is a variation of the Russian name "William." The town was established in 1917 at the intersection of the Carle Wagon Road (now Wasilla-Fishhook Road) and the newly-constructed Alaska Railroad. It was a supply base for gold and coal mining in the region through World War II. Construction of the George Parks Highway through Wasilla in the early 1970s provided direct access to Anchorage. This enabled families to live in Wasilla and commute to Anchorage for employment. Today residents remain close to the urban amenities of Anchorage, yet enjoy a rural lifestyle.

Matanuska valley for the project and choosing Palmer as the operation's headquarters.

The deal for the Matanuska pioneers was that they would receive a forty to eighty acre plot for five dollars an acre, which they could pay off over thirty years at three percent interest. The government would build houses and barns and provide free transportation to Alaska. Farm machinery, livestock and supplies could be purchased at cost and on credit. The government would also build schools, a hospital, and churches and allow that the farms and dairy run as a co-operative.

The press followed the Alaskans as they made their journey from the Midwest to San Francisco, Seattle, and Anchorage, where a holiday was declared in their honor, and finally to Palmer. Not all went smoothly after their arrival on May 10, 1935. There was a spate of heavy rain that turned the tent city of Palmer into a giant mud field. Supplies were short and housing was not yet inhabitable. Some colonists quickly gave up and left for the lower forty-eight. Other colonists could bear the environment but found journalists to be more of a bother. These journalists labeled them "cream puff pioneers" and searched for incriminating stories to embarrass FDR's administration. Mrs. Johnson noted that "mosquitoes were less formidable than the swarms of journalists" who kept "popping pictures of us in the washtub."

Food that did arrive was not properly refrigerated and went bad. School desks arrived but not the lumber to build a school. Grindstones made their way to Palmer but the axes had yet to come. Even electric meat slicers were unloaded for a town without electricity. The journalists of course logged all of the blunders. Political enemies of FDR also found fertile ground in the Palmer experiment for political satire. Iowa Republican Senator Cyrus Cole wove the Palmer colony into a scathing indictment of FDR's experimentation. He noted that "Semi-Sovietized America is emulating Russia in sending victims of its professional dreamers to a deluxe Siberia called Alaska. Those dreamers should be compelled to go hibernate with their Alaskan farmers."

Despite or perhaps because of the criticism, FDR was determined to see the colony work, spending five million dollars over the next few years to build houses, stores, a community hall, a power plant, a cannery, a creamery, a chicken hatchery, a hospital, schools, and two churches.

Was this enough to guarantee success for the colony? Yes and no. By 1940 only forty percent of the original families had stayed in the valley. Some left for other parts of Alaska but most went back south. Those who stayed came to realize that they needed to take up subsistence activities of hunting and fishing to get by. The short growing season left little room for error or acts of god, and the freight prices to small markets were high. The co-operative was not helpful enough and farmers were going more and more into debt.

But there were a few positives. World War II and the massive military influx provided sustained nearby markets for potatoes, cabbage, and dairy products, and the growth of Anchorage also kept agriculture alive the Matanuska valley.

By 1965 only twenty of the original families were still farming in the valley, but agriculture is still practiced in the area as others carry on the farming practices. Eighty-pound cabbages still appear at the State Fair in Palmer, million of dollars worth of potatoes grow, farmers' markets open during the summer, and valley produce is a regular sight in Anchorage stores. There is no question that the project gave Alaska a profile it had not enjoyed for many years, and it would be difficult to measure the impact this experiment had not only on the colonists but on others who chose to come north as a result of the excitement the project caused and the dreams that it sparked in others.

The Indian Civilian Conservation Corps and Totem Poles

By 1934, as part of the Roosevelt Administration's new pro-ethnic policy, native arts and crafts enjoyed more widespread support. Early that year, Secretary of the Interior Harold Ickes appointed a committee to study and make recommendations concerning the whole problem of native arts and crafts in their relation to the economic and cultural welfare of the Native Americans. Ickes himself made clear his appreciation of the qualities and merits of Native American arts as well as their potential for providing the natives with income and the ability to "live in the modern world without sacrifice of their cultural and racial integrity."

The Committee's report ultimately led to the foundation of the Indian Arts and Crafts Board, created by a legislative act in the summer of 1935 and in full operation

in July 1936. The board's intention was to promote native arts and crafts, ensure authenticity by using a government trademark for works created by natives, and expand their market. The board became doubly active after June 1937, when the artist, writer, and university professor Rene d'Harnoncourt assumed the position of General Manager. D'Harnoncourt, a native of Vienna, had lived in Mexico between 1925 and 1929, where the captivating local popular arts and crafts had inspired him. In 1929 he was asked to organize an exhibit of Mexican art in the United States, where he also assumed teaching positions at the New School for Social Research and Sarah Lawrence College.

In January 1937, *Indians at Work*, Collier's publication intended to stimulate public interest in and support of government-funded projects designed to improve Native American life, had an issue almost totally devoted to the natives of Alaska. An article entitled "Alaskan Arts and Crafts Fund Increasing Market" described the considerable amount of artwork Alaskans were making, including the carving of wooden potlatch bowls and model totem poles for the tourist market. The article cited both the U.S. Indian School at Ketchikan and the Sheldon Jackson School at Sitka for helping improve the quality of the work and its marketing. In 1939 Sitka developed plans to establish an Indian Arts and Crafts store in the form of a replica of an aboriginal communal house to improve the distribution of the moccasins, totem poles, and metal work made by Alaska Natives.

In 1938 Rene d'Harnoncourt traveled to Alaska and visited Ketchikan as well as Klukwan, Sitka, and Hydaburg in order to study conditions among the Alaska Natives and assess market possibilities for their crafts. He noted that in Ketchikan, a city second only to Juneau in size among the southeast communities, highly acculturated natives made relatively poor carvings for the tourists who came in considerable numbers during the summer. In his report, D'Harnoncourt expressed the belief that his role should be to encourage the manufacture of finer quality work among these natives in order to attract the more affluent segment of the market. This would, he thought, result in greater prosperity for the Tlingits of the area.

Wooden statue at an Alaskan harbor

In Hydaburg, d'Harnoncourt met an older Haida, John Wallace, who during his youth had worked on traditional carving with his father, a noted artist. Because of his skill, Wallace had recently been asked to make a forty-five foot pole for the local cannery. So impressed was d'Harnoncourt with Wallace's artistry and interest in traditional art that he invited the Haida to come to San Francisco the following year to carve totem poles for an exhibition. This show was to become a major stimulus in the revival of public interest in, and appreciation of, Native American art in general and totem poles in particular.

As director of the Indian Arts and Crafts Board, d'Harnoncourt organized two major exhibitions of Native American art, the first at the San Francisco Golden Gate International Exposition in 1939, the other at the Museum of Modern Art in 1941.

Totem poles held center stage in each exhibit, both within and outside the buildings. During the exhibit, two Haida from Alaska, John Wallace and his son Fred, carved two poles which were erected in a courtyard. Two years later, one of these poles, thirty feet high, depicting raven, killer whale, devilfish, sea lion and shark, was transported to New York and erected outside the Museum of Modern Art.

In April 1933, President Roosevelt, urged on by John Collier and Secretary Ickes, had approved the establishment of the Indian Civilian Conservation Corps, the initial intention of which was to improve reservation lands. Projects in Alaska included draining sections of Saxman village for gardens, building new quarters for teachers and nurses in Hoonah, and repairing water damage around the Juneau government hospital. By 1938 the projects under the Indian CCC had expanded beyond conservation and rehabilitation to include more aesthetically oriented activities such as the Alaskan totem pole project coordinated by the Forest Service.

Most Tlingit and Haida had stopped making poles by the turn of the century, and those which remained standing were subjected to the moist rot of this humid rainy region. Of the hundreds known to have been standing at the end of the nineteenth century, two hundred remained salvageable for this project. The Indian Civilian Conservation Corps Funds allocated, managed by the Forest Service, to support

Alaska Native craftsmen by retrieving, restoring, and finally erecting totem poles from various villages in southeast Alaska. The intention of the project was to have totem poles displayed along the Alaskan ferry route and to promote Alaska Native art for sale.

The project encountered problems created by the very abandonment of Tlingit poles. Whenever the Tlingit left a village in order to find work in a larger community, American law dictated that their property revert to the jurisdiction of the Forest Service. Thus the Forest Service felt it had the right to remove whatever totem poles it wished and place them in its parks; the Tlingit, however, did not believe that leaving their villages meant abandonment of title to their monuments, and they argued for compensation. As a result, written agreements between Tlingit leaders and Forest Service officials became neccessary. Although many poles ended up in Ketchikan where tourists could see them, some residents wanted their poles to remain closer to the old village; the solution was to establish the Klawock Totem Park.

The final products of this project were installed in several totem parks: the Klawock Totem Park mentioned above, and three in the Ketchikan area, one in the city center, one in the Saxman Park, and one in Mud Bight Village. Boats approaching the city can easily see Saxman Totem Park three miles south of Ketchikan. Standing on the slopes of the park grounds are about twenty-five poles salvaged from a variety of villages.

In all, the CCC project employed about 250 Alaska Natives and restored 48 poles, copied 54 that were beyond salvage, and created 19 anew. Because of this project, Ketchikan now has the largest number of totem poles of any easily-accessible northwest coast community. Virtually all the ferries and cruise ships sailing the Inside Passage stop at Ketchikan; Saxman and Mud Bight are frequently-selected land tours for passengers on these vessels.

New Deal activities in Alaska, while important, were of a much smaller consequence compared to the next force from outside Alaska to impact the Territory. By 1939 Alaskans and its representatives were worriedly following events in an escalating World War and wondering if Alaska's vulnerability to attack from Asia would be exploited.

5

The Impact of World War II

"Operation M 1," the Invasion of the Aleutian Islands

As global conflict spread during 1940, U.S. military leaders directed their attention to preventing attacks on the Pacific frontier and strengthened their defense of the United States' western outposts of Alaska, Hawaii, and the Panama Canal. Although Alaska was low on the priority list, by June 30, 1940 the Army had committed at least 5,000 troops to its defense.

Prior to American involvement in the Pacific War, the United States began to plan for the defense of Alaska against a possible Japanese attack. Alaska's relative geographical proximity and its rich seas for salmon and fur seals had long attracted the Japanese. In fact by treaty, voided in 1941, the Japanese government was receiving a percentage of the profits from the Pribilof fur seal harvest, on the grounds that the range of the seal included Japanese territorial waters.

By the beginning of 1941, the approaching Pacific war increased the strategic value of the Aleutians. The westernmost Aleutian island, Attu, lay only 600 miles from Japan's northern flank in the Kurile Islands. The Boeing airplane plant and the Bremerton Navy Yard in Seattle were only an eight hours' bomber-flight from the Aleutians. The Aleutians were stepping stones which either the United States or Japan could use offensively. They were also important to the United States as passage points on the shipping route for Lend-Lease traffic to the Soviet Union.

With the above in mind, the military created the Alaska Defense Command (ADC), with Brigadier General Simon B. Buckner in the lead, in February 1941 as part of the recently formed Western Defense Command to raise Alaska's priority in military operations. Earlier the Navy had established the Alaska Sector under the Thirteenth Naval District commanded by Rear Admiral Charles S. Freeman. Throughout the summer of 1941, garrisoning accelerated. The Army constructed fortifications on Unalaska Island to defend the naval installations at Dutch Harbor and sent approximately 5,500 troops there.

During the fall of 1941, construction of air bases strategically located at Cold Bay in the Alaska Peninsula and Umnak Island in the Aleutians moved ahead. They were secretly built under the names of fish cannery companies. The Umnak airstrip was particularly important because it protected Dutch Harbor, which controlled the passage through the Aleutian chain, linking the Pacific Ocean and the Bering Sea. Therefore, strategic use of the Aleutians hinged largely on possession of Dutch Harbor. On June 26, 1941, Army intelligence informed the War Plans Division that Japan might take advantage of the war between the Soviet Union and Germany to move against Alaska. It strongly urged the War Department to bring the Alaska garrisons to full strength as soon as possible. Thereafter, 225 more officers and 5,200 enlisted men moved into Alaskan positions.

After an eighteen month effort to strengthen defenses, General Buckner had available by November 1941 "a sizable ground force of 20,000 men, four major airfields in southeastern and central Alaska, Army and Navy posts in Sitka, Kodiak, and Dutch Harbor." The War Department, on November 28, 1941, warned that it expected Japan to begin hostilities soon and directed General Buckner to put the Alaska Defense Command on full alert. The attack 10 days later targeted Hawaii's Pearl Harbor, but the threat to Alaska remained.

Following Pearl Harbor, the ADC bolstered the Aleutian bases in preparation for a future offensive against Japan. Since the Alaskan naval bases were still under construction and lacked adequate air support, the ADC was concerned about a possible attack. The governor of the Alaskan Territory, Ernest Gruening, wrote to Secretary of the Interior Harold Ickes, "It was well known to the Japanese that the Alaskan bases, while designed ultimately to be used offensively, are still far from complete, and that if they attacked soon would probably be unable to defend themselves adequately." He lamented that "Dutch Harbor is the base at which the Japanese can strike most easily and which they will probably select first since it is the most difficult of all to defend." In the five months after Pearl Harbor the Army nearly doubled its Alaska garrison to 40,424 men. In mid-March, Army intelligence reported that a Japanese offensive could be expected at any time.

In late April Colonel Jimmy Doolittle bombed Tokyo. The Japanese Imperial Staff was acting to rapidly leverage its newly-acquired possessions and resources in the South Pacific. The Japanese believed, erroneously, that Doolittle had launched his highly symbolic attack from the Aleutians and they acted to protect their exposed northern flank.

On May 5, 1942 in an effort to intercept Lend-Lease traffic to Siberia and to cripple U.S. naval forces in the Pacific, Japan authorized "Operation M I." This two-phase operation involved establishing both defensive and offensive strategic positions in the Pacific. The Japanese planned to attack the Aleutian Islands as a diversion while simultaneously attacking the more strategically valuable Midway Island. They believed U.S. forces would concentrate in defense of the Aleutians while their main thrust hit Midway and the U.S. fleet divided between the Aleutians and Midway. If victorious, Japan would control the Pacific from the western Aleutians south to Midway.

The attack against the U.S. Pacific Fleet was the largest naval operation in Japanese history. Having broken the secret Japanese code, the U.S. Navy knew the details of their plan and knew an attack force would be launched from Japan around May 20. The Japanese planned to attack the Aleutians and Midway sometime after May 24. The commander-in-chief of the Pacific Fleet, Admiral Chester Nimitz, decided not to split his forces and instead dispatched a small nine-ship force to Alaska. In essence, Nimitz left Attu and Kiska undefended. On May 25, 1942 Nimitz warned Rear Admiral Robert A. Theobald, Commander of that North Pacific Force that the "Japanese have completed plans for an operation to secure an advanced base in the Aleutian Islands." Intercepted Japanese messages enabled the U.S. to predict even more precisely when the attack would occur. Military historian Stetson Conn observed that "by May 21 the United States

Bombing of Dutch Harbor

knew fairly accurately what the strength of the Japanese Northern Area Force would be and when it would strike." Even so, poor weather made it impossible to locate the enemy attack force until a Navy patrol plane spotted the Japanese on June 2, 400 miles south of Kiska Island.

On the morning of June 3, 1942 the Japanese bombed Dutch Harbor naval installations and the following day attacked army facilities at Fort Mears. Nearby Unalaska's air defenses were unable to hold off the enemy attack. Squadrons coming from Cold Bay arrived too late, and the radio communication systems were so inadequate that the secret airfields at Umnak never received word of the Japanese attack. Even though the Japanese were suffering a decisive defeat at Midway, their commander, the well known strategist Admiral Yamamoto, ordered the Aleutian campaign to continue, presumably to secure a defensive position in the northern Pacific.

Foggy weather and the usual poor radio communications continued to make the roving Japanese fleet difficult for U.S. vessels to find. On June 7 and 8, while Admiral Theobald was searching for it in the Bering Sea near the Pribilof Islands, the Japanese Northern Force landed approximately 2,500 soldiers on Kiska and Attu without opposition. Japan took ten U.S. weather crewmen on Kiska prisoner, and on the following day in Chigarof village on Attu, captured 42 Aleuts and two non-Aleut Indian Service employees. The radio silence from the two islands made headquarters fear the worst, and these fears were confirmed on June 10 when a break in the weather allowed an American scouting plane to sight the Japanese occupation forces on Kiska.

Long-distance bombings proved ineffective in dislodging the Japanese so an airstrip and command post were constructed on Adak Island in the western Aleutians. Throughout the fall of 1942, continuous bombing of Japanese installations on Kiska kept the Japanese on the defensive. Secret U.S. airfields on Umnak prevented the Japanese from patrolling the waters of the north Pacific from the Aleutians. Historian Stetson Conn noted that "while enemy orders referred to Kiska as the key position on the northern attacking route against the U.S. in the future it is fairly evident that the Japanese had no such design and were attempting only to block the American advance."

That fall General Buckner landed small forces on Atka and other islands, including St. Paul in the Pribilofs. Among the advance scouts were Aleuts from villages on the Pribilofs and along the Aleutian chain. To Buckner the Japanese occupation of Kiska and Attu was the only obstacle to launching an offensive against Japan from the Aleutians. By December 1942 Buckner had amassed 150,000 troops in the Alaskan theater and in the following month Admiral Nimitz ordered the North Pacific Force to clear the islands of Japanese troops.

During the winter of 1943 the North Pacific Force blockaded Attu and Kiska to force the Japanese to surrender these outposts. The blockade was effective, for the last Japanese supply ship reached Attu in March. Equally devastating, the Japanese had lost the air war to the U.S. by the middle of the spring; losing more than 1,000 airplanes at Guadalcanal, the Japanese had no replacements for the Aleutian campaign. Finally, Japanese naval supremacy in the north Pacific ended in March after the U.S. won the battle for the Komandorski Islands west of Attu.

Fewer than 10,000 Japanese troops on Kiska and Attu awaited the inevitable attack. The first target was Attu to cut off Kiska from potential support. On May 11, 1943, two contingents of U.S. soldiers, numbering approximately 12,500 men in total, landed on the north and south ends of Attu Island and began pressing toward the Japanese strongholds at Holtz Bay and Chichagof Harbor. Progress was slow and costly.

Eight days of heavy fighting passed before the South Landing Force climbed its way out of Massacre Bay. The North Landing Force, amongst their numbers the unorthodox Alaska Scouts, forced the Japanese from Holtz Bay and then continued toward Jarmin Pass and the North Landing Force to complete the pincer movement. The approximately 2,300 Japanese troops that remained had retreated to the wild heights of Fish Hook Ridge above Chichagof Valley, waiting for reinforcements. None arrived. On May 23, U.S. P-38 Lightnings over Attu met a force of sixteen Japanese Betty bombers and downed five. It was the last attempt by the Japanese to support their Aleutian troops by air. On the ground, American forces had increased to 15,000. Air strikes and U.S. ground force assaults up the precipitous Fish Hook Ridge further diminished Japan's hold.

On May 29, Colonel Yamasaki and the remainder of his Attu troops, numbering 750 or less, broke through American lines in a desperate attempt to reach Massacre Bay and needed stockpiles of U.S. supplies. They were finally halted at Engineer Hill, as a hastily organized U.S. defense repelled wave after wave of banzai attacks. Those Japanese troops who were not killed by U.S. fire took their own lives. After a bloody nineteen day battle in May, marked by frenzied suicidal counter attacks, the United States regained possession of the island. Out of a force of 15,000, 549 died on Attu, 1,148 were wounded, and 2,100 were felled by disease and non-battle injuries. The Japanese lost their entire force: 2,350 dead and 29 prisoners.

In July 1943 the U.S. successfully launched a bombing attack from Adak against the Japanese Northern Force on Paramushiro in the Kurile Islands. Intelligently, the Japanese, faced with a weakening northern flank, withdrew their troops from Kiska in late July under the cover of dense fog. When the Americans attacked Kiska in mid-August their only opponent was the fog. After the expulsion of the Japanese from Attu, U.S. naval and aerial bombardment of Kiska increased in fervor. Japanese submarines attempted to evacuate the estimated 5,100 Japanese troops on the island, but the process proved too slow and far too dangerous with a tightened U.S. blockade. On July 28, with the fog still providing cover, Japanese cruisers and destroyers managed to slip through U.S. naval forces and aerial reconnaissance without detection. In thirty minutes, the 5,100 Kiska troops were boarded, and the fleet headed back to the safety of Paramishiro Harbor. The evacuation was so bold and well executed, U.S. commanders refused to believe it had taken place. However, U.S. fighters strafing Kiska no longer received return anti-aircraft fire. In one instance, four U.S. P-40s landed on the shell pocked Kiska airfield. The pilots left their planes and strolled near the runway, seeing no sign of the enemy. In spite of this evidence, U.S. intelligence argued that the Japanese adherence to the Bushido Code forbade them from surrendering Kiska without a fight. The lessons of Attu, America's first experience with Japanese suicide attacks, had been too well learned. The invasion of Kiska proceeded as planned. On August 15, 1943, U.S. and Canadian troops landed. In the three day operation that ensued, over 313 allied soldiers died from "friendly fire," booby traps, and land mines. The Japanese had occupied U.S. territory for over a year before being routed at Attu. Not since the War of 1812 had a foreign battle been fought on American soil.

It was clear at this point that the Japanese no longer challenged the United States in the Aleutians. Although military historian George L. MacGarrigle thought that "in one sense the departure of the Japanese from Kiska without a fight was unfortunate," because it misled American commanders as to the resolve of Japanese troops facing overwhelming

Alaska Communities: Atka

Atka is located on Atka Island, 1,200 air miles southwest from Anchorage and 350 miles west of Unalaska. Aleuts have occupied the island for at least 2,000 years. The first contact with Russians occurred in 1747, and Atka became an important trade site and safe harbor for Russians. In 1787 Russia enslaved and relocated a number of hunters to the Pribilofs to work in the fur seal harvest. The town was settled in the 1860s. After the end of the sea otter hunting era in the late 1800s, Atka had no viable cash economy. Reindeer were introduced to the Island in 1914. During the 1920s, Atka became relatively affluent due to fox farming. After the Japanese attacked Unalaska and seized Attu and Kiska in June 1942, the U.S. government evacuated Atka residents to the Ketchikan area and burned the village to the ground to prevent Japanese forces from using it and advancing. The U.S. Navy rebuilt the community after the war and allowed residents to return. Many Attu villagers, released from imprisonment in Japan in 1945, relocated to Atka. The Aleut language is still spoken in one-fourth of homes. The St. Nicholas Russian Orthodox Church is also a central part of village life. Sea lions and other sea mammals are an important part of the subsistence lifestyle, and meat is shared village-wide on an informal basis.

odds. Attu, not Kiska, was the prototype for the Pacific war. American troops in the Aleutians shifted over to garrison duty and to watching the sporadic bombing raids launched from the islands.

ALEUTS AND WORLD WAR II

In 1913 the Aleutian chain was made into a national wildlife refuge. Aleuts on the islands could take any wildlife for subsistence and could catch foxes to sell the fur. The federal government brought reindeer to Atka, Umnak, and St. Paul during the WWI period. A presidential order created small reserves of land for schools and a hospital, beginning in Unalaska in 1897, but did not introduce the whole reservation system there, as elsewhere in Alaska.

The combined efforts of teachers, missionaries, and traders forced Aleuts into the wage economy. But on the eve of World War II, many still survived on subsistence activities. Until the end of the nineteenth century, Aleuts' income came primarily from sea otter hunting. By then sea otters were disappearing, and Aleuts had to find other sources of employment. Harvesting and preparing seal skins became the major occupation on the Pribilof Islands. The U.S. government ran this hunt and kept Aleut labor under tight control. The government also influenced Aleuts on islands other than the Pribilofs through BIA-run schools and various government-backed projects promoting the use of the sea's resources. The Fish and Wildlife Service had controlled St. Paul and St. George of the Pribilof Islands since 1913. The federal agency managed the fur seal kill and marketing of the pelts. The agency also managed Aleuts' lives through weekly inspections of their homes to insure cleanliness and by paying them in script that was only redeemable locally. One scholar called the Pribilof Aleuts "virtually slaves" to the federal government.

Other Aleut communities experienced cycles of rapid economic development and then severe decline. Outside decisions by various actors, including the federal government, relating to Aleuts' natural resources and the manipulation of them for profit prompted these cycles. Such ventures included a whaling operation run out of Unalaska in 1890, fox farming on Unalaska in the 1920s and 30s, a white-owned and operated sheep-raising

business started on Umnak Island in 1934 that employed some Aleut, and codfish and salmon-packing plants built by whites in the 1880s in the Alaska Peninsula for which some Aleuts worked on a seasonal basis. The seafood industry was later extended westward to Akutan and Unalaska. At Unalaska in the 1930s a herring packing business employed both men and women.

The relationship of Aleuts and other Native Alaskans to the federal government was in many ways separate from the official policy regarding Native Americans living in the continental United States. In Alaska there were no reservations because government officials believed there was no need to separate the aboriginal people from the sparse white population.

American citizens since 1924, the Aleuts suffered both immediate and long term effects from the war. In truth two forces had invaded their homes. The catalyst of these effects was the Japanese invasion, but it was the American forces who made the greatest impact in the Aleutian Islands. From early 1942, they confined the natives to their home towns, which were surrounded by barbed wire. Military police manned checkpoints and enforced curfews, while blackouts and practice alerts were frequent. The army also built bomb shelters and drilled the Aleuts in their use.

With the Aleutians cleared and 144,000 American and Canadian troops stationed in the Alaska/Aleutians area in September 1943, the army reevalued Alaska's role in the War. General John L. DeWitt, head of the Western Defense Command, submitted a plan to the Joint Chiefs of Staff for the invasion of Japan by forces based partially on Attu and Kiska. The plan was never used. Also in September, Admiral Nimitz placed the Aleutians in a "Non-Invasion Status." Presumably such status removed any obstacle to the Aleuts returning home; however, as we will see, such an easy return was not to be the case. While the military continued to discuss strikes against Japan's Kurile Islands from the Western Aleutians, Washington reduced the Alaska garrisons. By the end of 1943, the government had decreased army forces to 113,000 men and instructed General Buckner to prepare for further cuts to 50,000 men. Possible use of the islands as an offensive base appears to be the rationale for keeping Aleuts away. But military historian Stetson Conn concluded that by then "any danger to Alaska and the Western Hemisphere had long since disappeared."

Clearing the Japanese from the Aleutians eliminated both a military and psychological threat. Japan lost its toe hold in the Western Hemisphere. In June of 1942 Japan had threatened America's northern flank; fourteen months later the threat was against Japan.

It is important to evaluate the Aleuts' treatment during the war in light of the military situation. American commanders almost immediately recognized that the Japanese purpose in occupying Attu and Kiska was to prevent their use as bases for Allied air strikes against the home islands. The military conclusively established the purely defensive Japanese objectives in the Western Aleutians by the fall of 1942, as the enemy made no effort to launch air strikes against American military installations to the east. Also, the Japanese sacrificed their entire Attu garrison and afterwards withdrew completely from the Aleutian theater. The war in Alaska was over in late August 1943—only 14 months after the Aleuts had been evacuated from their homes.

As we shall see, the longer the government kept the Aleuts in the unsafe conditions of the camps, the more deaths would occur. Return to the islands was possible in 1943, and indeed some Aleuts did return for a few months to conduct sealing operations, and yet no arrangements were made for the return of other Aleuts. The Navy argued that the Aleuts had to be moved for their own safety, but after August 1943, their safety was in more jeopardy in southeastern Alaska than it would have been on the Aleutians.

THE RELOCATION OF ALEUTIAN VILLAGERS

While global military events were conspiring to bring Japanese and Americans into conflict on the treeless tundra of the Aleutian Islands, the bureaucratic organizations that controlled Aleuts' lives engaged in debate over the fate of the indigenous peoples. The outcome of that debate was the removal of the Aleuts for their own safety. Unhappily, these organizations did not give the Aleuts proper warning that they would be moved, did not allow them to take valued possessions that would have improved their psychological

Attu Village, Attu, Aleutian Islands, 1937.
Courtesy National Marine Fisheries Service

well being, and never offered them a voice regarding
transportation or camp locations. These actions only
continued the unilateral policymaking in native affairs
despite the recent Indian New Deal emphasis on sovereignty.

Interestingly, government officials had rejected the
possibility of relocating Aleuts before the Japanese
attacked, even though they thought an attack could come.
Governor Ernest Gruening opposed the evacuation of the
Aleutian Island villages on the grounds that
"bombardment of non-military areas is unlikely" and that
the dislocation from a forced evacuation "would be a
greater damage and involve greater risks to the ultimate
welfare of the people than the probable risks if they
remain." Office of Indian Affairs Commissioner John
Collier, the author of the Indian New Deal, thought that
the military should "leave the Natives where they are,

unless the navy insists that they be moved out." John Collier's goal was to encourage native tribalism and independence. This could, in part, explain why there was an insistence that Aleuts from different islands be held in different camps. Collier's memorandum appears consistent with his goal of keeping native societies on their land, but in no way were the Aleut given the "status, responsibility and power" the New Deal policy supposedly granted to Native Americans. The final decision over the Aleuts' fate would rest with the Navy.

Major General Simon B. Buckner, commander of the Alaska Defense Command (ADC), also argued against relocating Aleut villagers. Characterizing Buckner's position in a June 4th letter to Secretary of the Interior Ickes, Governor Gruening wrote "... that it would be a great mistake to evacuate these natives... [it would be]... pretty close to destroying them." According to Gruening, Buckner feared "that if they were removed they would be subject to the deterioration of contact with the white men, would likely fall prey to drink and disease, and that probably they would never get back to their historic habitat." Unfortunately, Buckner's fears were prophetic; ironically, he would be the one to order the Aleuts relocation in the end.

Out of consideration for the Aleuts, Gruening recommended that they be consulted before evacuation, but the actions of the Japanese precluded this well-intentioned plan. Despite the officials' reservations, the Navy proceeded to evacuate Aleuts. The officials understood the probable effects on Aleuts, but bowed to the Navy's decision as a priority of wartime. Each island had its particular problems with the relocation; all suffered from the lack of warning and severe restrictions upon the goods Aleuts could take with them.

On the more geographically isolated Pribilof Islands, located about two hundred miles north of Dutch Harbor in the Bering Sea, the circumstances of evacuation were to be unique. In 1942 St. Paul and St. George were among the largest Aleut communities. The islands were the principal breeding grounds for the North Pacific fur seal and were a federal preserve administered by the FWS, which employed the Aleuts who lived on the Pribilofs to conduct the annual fur seal harvest.

On June 14, 1942, two days after the evacuation of Atka, officers from a navy patrol craft went ashore to St. Paul to notify FWS personnel and the Pribilovians that their communities would be evacuated in the immediate future. The St. Paul community, consisting of 294 Aleuts and 15 non-Aleut FWS employees, was loaded aboard the *USAT Delarof* on June 15. The next day the *Delarof* anchored off St. George Island and evacuated 183 Aleuts and 7 non-Aleut FWS employees. Dan Benson, the caretaker on St. George Island, wrote the superintendent of the FWS in Seattle that initially the military came to the island to remove all the "whites who wished to leave." All decided to leave except Father Theodosy, who "elected to remain with the natives." Later that day a radio message informed them "that the entire population of the Pribilofs was to be evacuated immediately." The navy instructed Benson to "prepare the village for destruction... by placing a pail of gasoline in each house and building and a charge of dynamite for each other installation such as storage tanks, light plants, trucks, radio transmitters, etc." And, as was to become the rule, everyone was limited to "the packing of absolutely nothing but one suitcase per person and a roll of blankets." It was a dramatic scene as they hauled all the baggage and blankets, as allowed, down to the beach and loaded the Aleuts. Some Aleuts would, unknowingly, be taking their last look at their home island.

When the *Delarof* arrived at Dutch Harbor on the island of Unalaska on Wednesday afternoon, it took the Atka population aboard and headed out early the next morning for an unknown destination. The military reported sending the boat to Seattle, Cook Inlet, or Wrangell. Finally on June 23 the ship met a patrol boat which was carrying orders for the *Delarof* to proceed to Funter Bay to leave the Pribilof group and then on to Killisnoo to drop the Atka people. The Atkans, who the *Delarof* picked up at Unalaska, were also in the first group of Aleuts to be relocated.

By the end of June 1942, the Japanese were only beginning their occupation of the Aleutians. Governor Gruening, as chairman of the Alaska War Council, telegraphed Secretary Ickes on June 20 that the Council feared the Japanese planned to invade the U.S. mainland, using the Aleutians as a base. General Buckner advised the

Alaska Communities: St. George and St. Paul

St. George is located on the northeast shore of St. George Island, the southern-most of five islands in the Pribilofs. Over 210 species of birds nest on the cliffs of St. George Island. It lies 47 miles south of St. Paul Island, 750 air miles west of Anchorage, and 250 miles northwest of Unalaska. St. Paul is located on a narrow peninsula on the southern tip of St. Paul Island, the largest of five islands in the Pribilofs, and only 47 miles north of St. George Island. Gavrill Pribilof of the Russian Lebedov Lastochkin Company discovered the Pribilofs in 1786 while looking for the famed northern fur seal breeding grounds. The island of St. George was named Sveti Georgiy, and its larger neighbor to the north was originally called St. Peter and St. Paul Island. In 1788 the Russian American Company enslaved Aleut hunters from Siberia, Unalaska, and Atka and relocated them to St. George and St. Paul to harvest the fur seal; their descendants live on the two islands today. In 1870 the U.S. government awarded the Alaska Commercial Company a 20-year sealing lease and provided housing, food, and medical care to the Aleuts in exchange for seal harvesting. In 1890 the North American Commercial Company received another 20-year lease; however, the fur seals had been severely over-harvested and poverty ensued. In 1910 the U.S. Bureau of Fisheries took control of the islands, but poverty conditions continued due to the over-harvesting of the seals: food and clothing were scarce, social and racial segregation continued, and working conditions were poor. As part of the area wide evacuation during World War II, the U.S. military moved residents of both islands to Funter Bay on Admiralty Island in Southeast Alaska, where they were confined in an abandoned cannery and mine camp at Funter Bay. In 1979 the Pribilof Aleuts received $8.5 million in partial compensation for the unfair and unjust treatment the federal administration had subjected them to between 1870 and 1946. In 1983 the U.S. government ended the commercial seal harvest and withdrew from the islands, providing $20 million to help develop and diversify the local economy—$8 million for St. George and $12 million for St. Paul. The city of St. George incorporated in 1983. Today, residents are working to develop commercial fisheries, bird watching, and tourism. Although subsistence has not historically been the focus of the local culture, residents share halibut and seal with relatives living in other communities for salmon and reindeer. The Pribilof Island seal population and the community's dependence on it has been a major influence on the local culture as more than a million fur seals congregate on the islands every summer. The Russian Orthodox Church also plays a strong role in community cohesiveness.

OIA that no more villages in the Aleutian Islands should be evacuated, but Admiral Freeman felt that other Aleutian villages were in danger. Freeman prevailed and issued orders directing the evacuation of all Aleuts from the Aleutian Islands.

The navy evacuated the islands in a sweep eastward from Atka to Akutan, the Aleut villages of Nikolski on Umnak Island, Makushin, Biorka, Chernofski, and Kashega on Unalaska Island, and Akutan on Akutan Island. Nikolski was the first, one week after Freeman issued his order. The Aleuts of Nikolski were not warned of their impending evacuation, and when the time came they, like the Atkans and Pribilovians, were given only a few hours notice. On July 5, two navy and army ships arrived at Nikolski and removed the entire village of 70 Aleuts plus the teacher in the village, her husband, and the non-Aleut foreman of the Aleutian Livestock Company, a sheep ranch on Umnak.

Commander William N. Updegraf, captain of the naval station at Dutch Harbor, issued orders that "all natives or persons with as much as one eighth native blood were compelled to go." This order had a divisionary effect among Aleuts. For example, Charles Hope, a white man, remained in Unalaska while his Aleut wife was required to evacuate. The navy removed a total of 881 Aleuts. But American military forces were not the only military groups to remove Aleuts from their homeland. The Japanese military, after occupying Attu, also had to decide how to deal with their Aleut captives.

In May 1942 the U.S. Navy had attempted to evacuate the Attu islanders, but adverse seas made it impossible to land on shore. The Japanese invaded on June 8, 1942. As soon as they occupied the village, the Japanese gathered all the inhabitants in the schoolhouse for interrogation and also interrogated two non-natives, Foster Jones, an OIA radio operator, and his wife Etta Jones. Following the questioning, the Japanese put all of the islanders into one of the Aleut homes while the troops searched the village for weapons and other threatening items. Later in the day, after the army had established headquarters in the Jones' house (the schoolhouse), they confined the Aleuts to their homes. The second day of the occupation, the Joneses cut their wrists. Foster Jones bled to death, but Etta's cut was

Harbor at Dutch Harbor. Courtesy NOAA Corps Collection

superficial and she lived. There are conflicting accounts of the death of Foster Jones. The *Polar Times* of Juneau asserted that the Japanese killed him, but Aleut survivors think that Jones killed himself rather than submit to capture. Shortly after the incident, the Japanese sent Etta to Yokohama and detained her there with other non-combat civilians captured in the Pacific theater.

The Japanese began immediately to garrison the island and construct housing for their troops. Shortly thereafter they eased restraints on Aleut movement allowing them to fish and go about their routine. In September 1942 the Japanese temporarily changed their Aleutian strategy and decided to abandon Attu (only to return in October), moving their troops to Kiska. On September 17 at 9:00 in the morning, Japanese forces ordered the forty-one Aleuts onto the *Yoko-maru* with whatever possessions they could carry, and burned or destroyed everything that remained on the island. The invaders took the Aleuts to Kiska and then transferred them to the *Osada-maru* for shipment to Japan. The Japanese feared the Attuans would reveal their military strength to American forces so the forty-one Aleuts were taken to Otaru on Japan's northernmost island of Hokkaido.

Secretary Ickes wrote an angry letter to Secretary of War Henry L. Stimson when he heard of the Aleut relocation. He was concerned about "the loss of more than a million dollars by reason of the discontinuance of operations at the Pribilof Islands, where 95,013 fur-seal skins were taken in the summer of 1941 and 834 fox skins were obtained during the preceding winter. In addition, the byproducts plant produced oil and meal of considerable value." He demanded that arrangements be made to return the Aleuts and supervisory personnel by naval transport to the Pribilof Islands the next April or May to resume sealing and other operations. Stimson defended the "military necessity" behind the Pribilovian's evacuation and asserted that they could not be returned immediately.

Because the evacuation was so poorly planned, the Aleuts lost the possessions they had reluctantly left behind. Testimony from the evacuees established that in most cases they were given unnecessarily short notice, forcing them to abandon most personal belongings—including clothing, family albums, musical instruments, highly prized icons, craftwork, boats and essential hunting and fishing equipment. Neither the OIA nor the military made provisions to care for these possessions. They were left, in most cases, unpacked and secured only by a lock on the front door, quite vulnerable to the theft and deterioration that followed. The invasion by the Japanese and the evacuation of the islands exposed the racism against Aleuts that had long existed on the part of whites who inhabited or visited the islands and in general throughout the territory of Alaska. Racial segregation and Jim Crow policies were standard practice throughout much of Alaska, and the manner in which Aleuts were evacuated showed that those Jim Crow attitudes were alive and well. The condescension, the application of unilateral policy, so typical in U.S. native relations in the past, manifested itself throughout the entire relocation process. The hasty evacuation also revealed a lack of planning even though the need for safe and adequate relocation facilities had been recognized for months prior to the bombing of Dutch Harbor and the conquest of Attu.

Aleut Relocation Camps

> Some called the ordeal suffered by… Aleut-Americans the "craziness of war," and dismissed that ugly portion of our history with that excuse. Not many of our people… realized the ultimate insult of the entire story. The evacuations were not necessary; the Aleuts suffered for nothing.
>
> —*Agafon Krukoff, Jr., St. Paul Aleut*

Anyone who saw pictures of the *Exxon-Valdez* oil spill or who has taken an Alaskan cruise knows that the coast of southeastern Alaska is intimidating and beautiful. Large snowcapped mountains soar above dense forests that seem to flow into the ocean. The rocky beaches are narrow and the forests appear as walls behind them. It was into this setting that Aleuts from a world of treeless tundra would be forced to live for three years during World War II.

General problems of survival, adequate shelter, decent food, and proper medical care would need to be solved for Aleuts to subsist in that new environment. Unfortunately, for Aleuts these basics were for the most part unmet. Apart from fundamental needs, Aleuts also had to deal with negative psychological reactions to the new environment, hostile relations with government officials and other whites in southeastern Alaska, and adjustments to camp life. By exploring all of these aspects of the various relocation camps, a picture of Aleut life during this time emerges, showing the genuine failure of the government's attempt to protect them.

As the Aleuts were sailing across the Gulf of Alaska on the *Delarof*, officials made frantic efforts to determine where the people could be relocated. The hardships suffered by the Aleuts during relocation began on the voyage of the *Delarof* across the Bering Sea and into the Gulf of Alaska with the combined populations of Atka, St. George, and St. Paul. The transport vessel initially proceeded to Dutch Harbor, where cargo was transferred, and the Aleuts from the burned-out village of Atka became additional passengers on a voyage to an as-yet unknown destination.

One account of events aboard the *Delarof*, written by F. Martin March, wife of a doctor on a temporary visit to the Pribilofs when the evacuation occurred, gives some of the tragic details:

Since once aboard the ship the St. George doctor felt completely free of responsibility for his islanders and had no personal interest in any of these patients of his, he could not be coaxed into the disagreeable crowded hold even before all the Aleuts and many non-Aleuts came down, after our stay-over at Dutch Harbor, with "ships cold," a serious grippe infection. He did not come to assist even at the birth of a St. George baby or its subsequent death of bronchial pneumonia because of our inability (Dr. S.R.B. and mine) to separate mother and child from the other grippe sufferers, and the mother herself was ill. I think I recall this doctor attending the midnight or after funeral of the poor little mite, such a tiny weighted parcel being let down into the deep waters of the Gulf of Alaska against a shoreline of dramatic peaks and blazing sunset sky.

At the age of three days, the infant became the first casualty of the Aleut's dislocation.

Ultimately the decision to keep the Aleuts in Alaska was made at the federal level, where it was determined that Aleuts should be "housed so that each village keeps its individuality." The OIA chose not to relocate the Aleuts to the eastern part of the Aleutian chain or the Alaska Peninsula. The rational was unclear, but perhaps those in the agencies wanted the Aleuts as far from the war zone as possible and yet still in Alaska. Instead, Assistant Indian Affairs Commissioner William Zimmerman made the fateful suggestion that abandoned fish canneries in southeastern Alaska would be the best location for the refugees. However, the selection of specific sites was left to local FWS and OIA officials.

Perhaps the lack of coordination among agencies in Alaska can partially explain this unpreparedness. Their headquarters were 300 miles apart, and the exchange of intelligence information was sometimes slow and inaccurate. The evacuation of Aleuts began without a clear policy to define the divisions of responsibilities between the military and civilian branches of government. The Navy passed decision-making responsibilities to Interior; the Department of the Interior was unable to reach an internal consensus on what to do with the Aleuts; and the Army, despite its knowledge of an inevitable Japanese attack, took a position which they, like the others, would reverse once the Japanese invasion became a reality. Eventually the OIA and FWS decided to house the relocated Aleuts in camps at Funter Bay, Killisnoo, Ward Cove, and Burnett Inlet all in southeastern Alaska. Funter Bay would hold the Pribilovians, Killisnoo the Atkans, Ward Cove and Burnett Inlet the Unalaskans.

On the morning of June 24, 1942, the *Delarof* arrived at Funter Bay and immediately disembarked the St. George and St. Paul Aleuts. The ship's captain and FWS officials aboard the boat held a conference. The captain agreed to leave enough mattresses, blankets, and food supplies to maintain the Aleuts until a supply ship arrived from Seattle.

In the meeting the original plan to take all the white FWS personnel to Seattle and leave the natives to shift for themselves was modified, leaving eight whites to assist with the work. But both doctors decided to resign rather than stay at the camp.

A high-level member of the Alaska Indian Service and FWS officials arrived at Funter Bay aboard the fisheries patrol boat *Brant* not long after the *Delarof* had anchored there on June 24. They all met aboard the *Delarof* and decided that the St. Paul Aleuts would be established in the abandoned cannery facilities at Funter Bay; the St. George people would be located across Funter Bay in the abandoned gold mine; and the Atkans would be taken to Killisnoo's abandoned herring plant. No Aleuts were at the meeting. The conferees decided that Lee McMillin would be placed in charge of the Pribilof group at Funter Bay and that C. Ralph Magee would be in charge of the Atkans at Killisnoo. Both men had worked on the Pribilof.

Aleuts and on-site officials were shocked at the camps Aleuts were to inhabit. Flore Lekanof, from St. George, remembered that "no one really knew until we arrived at Funter Bay that that's where we were going." He could see that "the Federal Government did not make preparations for us to move to a decent place." In one particular case, an elderly woman attempted to commit suicide. She could not face the camps, calling them a "horrible thing." Lekanof saw that "the elderly were hurt, they didn't want to leave the island, and they were forced."

The Atkan people were also apprehensive and angry when they landed at Killisnoo because they were not sure where they were going. Alice Petrevilli recalled that their arrival on "a beautiful morning" which was "warm and you could smell the wild roses" did not foreshadow the following years. For many, Killisnoo was a relief after the rough trip aboard the *Delarof*, but when Petrevilli saw the camp she came to realize that it "was just a run down old thing."

The Magees, the BIA school teachers who accompanied the Atkans, could feel that "the people were plenty sick for Atka, where there were no trees to hem them in." The presence of a large forest was for the Aleuts particularly disconcerting. George McGlashan of Akutan recalled that his arrival in southeastern Alaska was "a dark day to me. There was no light. Too many trees. People weren't used to it."

The most immediate and life threatening problem at the camps was the lack of acceptable shelter. Funter Bay, the site of two internment camps, was situated on the west coast of Admiralty Island, about sixty miles from Juneau and had few buildings suitable for human habitation. An abandoned cannery and a gold mine across a bay from the cannery were selected as camps for the Pribilovian Aleuts from St. Paul and St. George islands. These camps were the largest and best documented camps run by the FWS and the OIA.

On site officials noted that the cannery's water supply came from about one mile above the camp. Water pressure in the deteriorated system was too weak for use in fire fighting, and sanitary facilities were no better. There was no sewage disposal system, and the three outdoor toilets depended "on the action of the tide to remove the sewage." Juneau OIA representatives reported that the "toilets are entirely open, and a probable source of insect-borne contamination.

Across the bay, on the gold mine side of Funter Bay, officials knew the dangers of "the establishment of a large number of people in these facilities" and pointed out that it "would immediately create danger of water pollution." In their report, the Juneau officials noted that the water supply was "two small streams so situated that none of the living quarters are more than 100 yards from a stream." They thought that the "water from the stream has been used for domestic purposes, although it is not known if a sanitary inspection has been made." Finally, they concluded that "all water supplied to the various living quarters would have to be carried, and the establishment of a large number of people in these facilities would immediately create danger of water pollution unless adequate precautions were taken to prevent contamination of these streams." The sewage disposal was reported to be two "somewhat dilapidated pit-type toilets which are mounted on pilings over the beach." A small shack near the mess hall had been converted into a bathing facility, with a single shower unit of crude construction.

Despite the acknowledged problems with the sites, the officials leased and adopted them for use, reaching an agreement with the P.E. Harris Company for the use of its cannery at Funter Bay "providing that the company will not assume any responsibility for injury received on the premises." And the Admiralty Alaska Gold Mining Company made its abandoned facilities, located across Funter Bay from the P.E. Harris Company cannery, available as well. The cannery owners received $60.00 per month for the use of their property. These locations became mandatory living quarters for the majority of Pribilovians for most of the war's duration.

After two weeks the problems with the camps were clear. Agent McMillin noted that "the sanitary engineer that was here said this water system can not under any conditions be made usable for winter and if these people are going to stay here then some other arrangements will have to be made and that should be quick." He went on to tell his superior "if you think this is any fun you should be here." McMillin begged for "some of the portable houses that are piled up around the coast" that "could be made into fairly good places to live." A visiting engineer said they "would have to put in flush toilets if we stay here and hot water for washing and baths…. We cannot dig clams nearer than a mile from the cannery because of the dumping of all garbage and toilets into the bay." They discovered that they could not "build outdoor privies" because at high tide "sewage washes back onto the beach for the flies to walk on and the children to track around." McMillin added: "There wasn't much left to say except they (the buildings) are so old and rotten it is impossible to do any repairing whatsoever." The only buildings that were capable of being repaired were the two structures where Aleuts slept. All the other houses were absolutely "gone from rot." The result was that "as many as ten and thirteen persons, large and small," were sleeping, "or trying to sleep, in one room."

McMillin knew that the novelty had worn off long ago. Without brooms, soap, mops, or brushes they could not "keep the place suitable for pigs to stay in." McMillin's final analysis was that "it seems funny if our government can drop so many people in a place like this then forget about them altogether."

Dr. N. Bernta Block wrote the most extensive report on Funter Bay conditions. Her report chronicles a visit from October 2 to 6, 1943. She went to the Bay initially to see if she could help control an outbreak of measles. In her report she noted the horrid health conditions, but with a twinge of ethnocentrism. "I expected to find a group of people interested in their own health and welfare, thrifty and adept in managing their own affairs. I am sorry to say I was a bit disappointed. I am sure that much effort has been expended in order to provide adequate quarters for these people but it goes without saying that there is still room for much improvement." Despite her critical paternalism she seemed sincerely to want to help the Aleuts. For Block the situation was a paradox for which she laid blame not only on the Aleuts themselves but also the public health institutions. She had been to the Aleutians and thought it was "strange that they could have reverted from a state of thrift and cleanliness on the islands to the present state of filth, despair, and complete lack of civic pride."

After the Pribilovians landed at Funter Bay, the *Delarof* proceeded to Killisnoo to discharge the members of the Atka community on the morning of June 25. Along with the OIA teachers (the Magees), eight-two Atkans were taken ashore. The *Delarof* with its escort cutter departed without delay after completing its task.

Located on a small island of the same name in southeastern Alaska, Killisnoo was about three miles from the Tlingit village of Angoon. Killisnoo was the location of a village that had burned in 1928 and never been rebuilt. Those who lived in Killisnoo before the fire moved to Angoon. Because of the declining herring catch, the fish cannery at Killisnoo had been shut for ten years prior to the Aleuts' arrival, occupied only by a caretaker. V.R. Farrell, Education Director of the Alaska Indian Service, concluded in a Memorandum to FWS Superintendent Hirst that "approximately 75 to 80 people" could be accommodated at the Killisnoo location.

Farrell's own report shows the sadly inadequate state of the facility. The sanitary facilities consisted of three outdoor pit toilets and one bathtub. The electrical wiring presented a fire hazard. It was doubtful if the dilapidated old generator "could be put back in working order." Among the buildings at the Killisnoo cannery were five one- or two-room cabins, three small houses, a bunkhouse, laundry building, carpenter shop, wood storage shed, cold storage building, mess hall, and warehouse. There was also a storage building and an unusable structure that had been an office when the cannery operated. When the Aleuts were settled there, the Killisnoo water supply was limited to a small spring with a maximum capacity of about twenty-four barrels per day.

After the first wave of Aleut relocations and resettlement in June, evacuations continued along the chain. In July, the Aleut people of Nikolski, Akutan, and three small Unalaska Island villages arrived at the Wrangell Institute, the Indian Service boarding school. They remained there for some weeks as materials were assembled for the construction of shelters in which they would later live at Ward Cove. While at Wrangell they lived in tents and school buildings.

The Russian Orthodox graveyard at Unalaska.
Courtesy NOAA Corps Collection

After building a barge to transport construction materials and their personal effects, the Aleuts were shipped to Ward Cove, a CCC constructed facility near Ketchikan, where they were to remain for nearly three years. At Ward Cove the villagers assembled "ten 16 x 16 feet buildings for the small families" and occupied some of the abandoned houses nearby.

The Aleut community of Unalaska was interned from August 1942 until April 1945 in an abandoned cannery facility located at Burnett Inlet on Etolin Island, near Wrangell in Southeastern Alaska. There were similar stories of poor housing and unclean water at these camps as well.

As noted in several of the reports, the sanitation, or lack thereof, and the shoddy shelter made Aleuts vulnerable to disease. As predicted, these diseases soon became rampant and caused many deaths. Influenza was widespread, and tuberculosis, already a problem on the Aleutian Islands, quickly spread.

Inspectors noted that, "coughs are numerous" and that "this is an ideal set-up for the spread of tuberculosis but the results may not be evident for some time." FWS employees themselves thought that "there is more than a possibility that the death toll from tuberculosis, pneumonia, influenza and other diseases will so decimate the ranks of the natives that few will survive to return to the islands." With the onset of disease the FWS officials found it "more and more difficult to defend our position." Scarcely a day passed when a well meaning person did not descend upon the FWS "with recrimination" for its "heartless methods." Censorship kept the press off the FWS's "necks," but they feared that "line of defense" was "weakening rapidly."

To illustrate the dilemma, one FWA official related the events of two days hence when he was "advised by one of the physicians who had inspected the camps and aided in emergency work there," that he was preparing a report to the Surgeon General of the United States and also to Secretary Ickes and had no intention of "pulling any punches." The official feared that "it was only a matter of time until some publication, such as *Life* magazine, would get hold of the story and play it up, much to the disadvantage of the Service and the Department of the Interior as a whole."

The Aleuts themselves tried to manage with the epidemics. Every time one of the St. George side got sick, they were taken "across over the water in an open dory to the St. Paul side" where the medical facility, such as it was, existed. Then all they could do was wait and hope that they would not be notified of another death.

The climate of southeastern Alaska, colder and wetter than the Aleutian Islands, exacerbated the tubercular condition suffered by many interned Aleuts. Poor drinking water also played a role in spreading disease. William Dirks remembered that at Killisnoo a dead lake supplied the water; it "had bugs and people died from it." At Killisnoo, there was no medical care except for a visiting nurse. Petrevilli remembers that "we all got measles and God, we got lice, we got sores, we got everything, and some people got TB." For her it seemed as though "they dropped us there and forgot about us."

Lavera Dushkin from Nikolski was 15 years old when she was evacuated and has vivid memories of the experience. She recalled that in the first week, everyone from the villages had to have a medical checkup by the Army, Navy, and civilian doctors. They were sick already from tuberculosis, virus, pneumonia, and shock, but despite diagnosis, they received no medical treatment. Appointed as interpreter and helper to the medical group, Dushkin remembers the humiliation and disorientation of the children and some adults when the medical staff cut their hair short to the scalp because of lice and rubbed kerosene onto their heads, leaving it on for 12 hours before washing their hair. For the Aleut even taking a shower was a shock, as many had never taken one before. At Nikolski they had bathed in a small tub and had taken steam baths in "banyas." At Burnett Inlet medical care was limited to the service of midwives, augmented by one doctor who removed tonsils and adenoids and gave cursory examinations.

Martha Krukoff was 31 at the time of the relocation and she remembered that "it was in that cold, heatless place that I gave birth to my son Harry. All my family was sick in bed with measles including myself." In all the time she was pregnant, she never received a checkup. Only once did a "lady doctor from Juneau" come to help the people who were sick with the measles. She remembered that "it was terrible being sick and not having any kind of heat in the room."

The inevitable result of untreated disease and poor shelter was an early death for many Aleuts. When Inspector Hall ended his report on the cannery side of the Funter Bay camp he noted, with a touch of irony, "only 8 deaths have occurred which seems to be a good record. (Compared to 20 among 184 people at Ward Cove)."

Part of Father Lestenkoff's duties when he was at Funter Bay, for $20 dollars a month, was the grisly task of burying the dead. The gravesite was "next to a creek, if someone died, you started to dig the grave, you cut into roots of trees, and when you got down three feet or less water started to come up. When you put the body in there a couple of guys would get down there and bail it out as quickly as they can bail."

The Indian Service schoolteacher, Ruby J. Magee, and her husband, C. Ralph Magee, wrote to a friend in Greenbelt,

St. Paul village on the island of St. Paul. The Native Americans here carried on the fur seal industry under the supervision of the Fish and Wildlife Service at the time of this photo. Today the National Marine Fisheries Service monitors the fur seal industry.
Courtesy National Marine Fisheries Service

Maryland, describing the situation up to June 1943 at Killisnoo. One of the first to die at Killisnoo was Larry Nevzoroff. The Magees called him "the boat builder, who was the best and oldest man of the village. He was buried the very day we left." They thought he died because "he took some Angoon Indian medicine which we think poisoned him." They were saddened "to think he wasn't able to return to Atka to spend his last days." Another man who died of tuberculosis was buried the same day. For the Atkans it was already "the worst winter in fifty years" in terms of deaths.

Alice Petrevilli testified that of the 82 people moved to Killisnoo, seventeen passed away. "Some of it was due to pneumonia. Mostly we do not know why a lot of them died but I think it was due to bad water. Some elderly people died I think of shock or something." Leonty Savoroff was thirty when he was evacuated. He remembers seeing one of his friends John Krukoff one morning before he went to work looking well, but by the time Savoroff came home from work in the afternoon Krukoff was dead from an unknown cause. Savoroff himself lay in a bed at Ward Cove for six months with double pneumonia, but he was never taken to the city hospital. In fact, despite the deaths and disease in the camp, he recalled only one visit by a doctor during the three year span.

The Aleutian/Pribilof Islands Association has compiled an incomplete list of those Aleuts assigned to the Funter Bay camps who died during the internment years. They have identified by name forty persons from the St. George and St. Paul communities who perished following the evacuation. The death rate is in part corroborated by FWS official records that report twenty-five deaths in the calendar year 1943 alone. Almost all those who died are buried at Funter Bay in a cemetery near the cannery.

In the case of Killisnoo, the depositions of survivors document at least ten deaths among the Atkans assigned to the camp. The records of the Nikolski community are more extensive, and are drawn primarily from Russian Orthodox Church records. At least nineteen Nikolski people died while assigned to the Ward Cove Camp. The Ketchikan newspaper reported in May of 1943 that twenty Aleuts had already perished at Ward Cove. Those who survived recalled at least two Aleuts from Akutan who died there, along with five from Kashega and two from Makushin.

Burnett Inlet was the least life threatening. Still, there were four deaths recorded there during the internment years.

Relocation meant a drastic change in the diet of Aleuts. Not only was the food different but many basic facilities for boiling and cooling water were not available. Mike Lekanof recalled that "the eating facilities were inadequate and unorganized." They ate mostly "beans and clams." At Ward Cove, some food and a few pots and pans were issued to the Aleuts, but only for a while. Then they were left on their own.

Flore Lekanof was bitter that "the white people who were at Funter Bay with us got much better food than the native people." Father Michael Lestenkof remembered that while they were in Funter Bay, "the food situation was very poor. Clams, clams every day." He had an infant who was about "six months old." One night his wife went to the kitchen to fill a nursing bottle with hot water. On the way one of the "government leaders" sent her home because "he said you could not walk in this time of the night, so the baby was not fed."

Natalie Misikian, who was six-years old at the time of the relocation, remembered the food: "What they would feed us wasn't worth eating. You could feed it to the rats for all I cared. You know, scrambled powdered eggs, scrambled eggs. I hate it." Toward the end many remember the food getting worse instead of better. The eggs seemed to be a strong memory for many Aleuts. At Killisnoo they tried to live off the land, but "food froze solid during the coldest weather. Meat was scarce. Deer were hard to get, and little to them when they were found."

At Killisnoo the people of Angoon came to the aid of the Aleuts. Petrevilli recalled that "every day in the summertime from their fishing village they'd drop by and drop off fish or share meat with us." She thought this help was crucial to those who survived the camps, because "we just couldn't find the goods in wartime. Food was hardest to come by. Because we didn't have any guns, we didn't have any boat, we didn't have any fishing gear."

Coping with camp conditions by the Aleuts met with varying degrees of success. For some, relocation was an adventure, for others a nightmare. Most Aleuts assumed the situation was temporary, but that assumption was uncertain. Examples from Killisnoo and Burnett Inlet illustrate Aleuts' adaptations. At Killisnoo after the first year, the people pulled together and made two boats and bought a net and the government sent some guns. The Angoon people showed Aleuts where to go salmon fishing and deer hunting. Alice Petrevilli remembered Killisnoo after the first year "still had bad homes, bad drinking water, bad medicine, but we did have enough food to eat." They "ate off the land," once they learned where everything was. Also, Angoon had a small Russian Orthodox Church. On holidays Aleuts could go there and visit the "one room with a few icons." But it served as a reminder of their home church and reinforced their religious feelings.

The Magees could also see that with time the Aleuts "were reconciled to the change." But that adjustment was not easy or always successful. A crucial element of Aleut culture was the making of grass woven baskets of intricate design and great detail. At Killisnoo according to the Magees "a few women tried making baskets from the grass, but it was of a different quality, harder to work with so they soon gave up." The Magee also noted that a "few of the girls went 'wild'—especially Martha, the one who made such pretty baskets." Her husband had fallen off a Juneau dock while intoxicated the previous spring and drowned. Martha's experience demonstrates the depths of frustration, anxiety, and displacement suffered by many Aleuts. Not making baskets may seem inconsequential, but it was a task that was important to Aleut women and their identity as Aleuts. For women like Martha, who made the "pretty baskets," that Aleut identity was shaken.

One crucial aspect of the relocation experience for Aleuts was their new relationship with other Alaskans. Pribilovians had long interacted with government officials, but for Aleuts from the other islands, the experience was new. Paternalism toward Aleuts, mostly outright rascism and some empathy, dominated the relations with other Alaskans and government officials. The experience of the Ward Cove Aleuts is a striking example of these trends. The majority of these Aleuts had never been far from their isolated island homes. Although adept at survival in a rugged environment, they were unprepared for life in the "wilderness" they found in Ketchikan. A frontier town of fishermen and lumberjacks, it had a population of roughly 5,000 whites and natives. The

Aleuts were coming from villages that for the most part consisted of a few dozen friends and family.

With the exception of tuberculosis, the Aleuts arrived in Ketchikan in good health. Soon, however, they became, in the words of the Chief of the Akutan Village Mark Petikoff, victims of "bootleggers and white exploiters." The sad result was that the Ward Cove Aleuts were struck with epidemics of venereal disease and alcohol abuse. Although the Aleuts were "free from venereal disease when they left Wrangell for Ward Cove," within months the camp was ravaged by gonorrhea.

The Police of Ketchikan were not happy with the selection of a site near their town for the relocated Aleuts, which Harry McCain, Chairman of Police, Health and Sanitation, made clear in a strident letter to Governor Ernest Gruening. McCain thought that the Aleuts "were rotten with gonorrhea especially, and also syphilis." When the quarantine lifted, McCain thought "they would immediately flock to town in droves and infest the public places." McCain used as an example: "One girl who had been suffering from a virulent case of gonorrhea immediately disappeared in town and up to an hour ago had not been located. As a result of her activities, it is probable that twelve to fifteen people have already been infected." McCain also noted that Aleuts were "badly honeycombed with tuberculosis, from which a considerable number have died since they were placed at Ward Cove." He could not "conceive how they could be located in a worse place than at Ward Cove, in the very heart of the Ward Cove Recreation Area."

As McCain's letter continues, it becomes apparent that his motive for writing is not the health of the Aleuts, but rather to remove what he deemed a menace from his town. McCain's hostile attitude, if shared by the rest of the police department, explains the constant arrests of Aleuts without provocation.

McCain thought sending "people rotten" with disease into one of the most beautiful natural recreation areas in Alaska was a waste of "many, many thousands of dollars" the government spent improving the area. In his mind, it would be impossible "to expect them [the Aleuts] to last... as a part of the community." One story summed up community relations for McCain. The proprietor of the

Totem Lunch asked McCain whether or not she could refuse their patronage to the Aleuts "for the reason that they were unsanitary and diseased and thus obnoxious to her regular customers besides requiring an unusual amount of trouble in sterilizing of their dishes." McCain noted that the same attitude existed in other business places: "even the bars would prefer not to have their patronage."

McCain's solution was not to call for an upgrade in camp conditions but instead to relocate the Aleuts yet again, preferably to "some suitable location where they would not have immediate contacts with large numbers of people." Toward the end of his letter, he finally states what was obvious: "There should be some way in which the welfare of the Aleuts can be properly cared for without menacing established communities of white people. We shall sincerely appreciate any assistance that you can lend us in ridding Ketchikan of this dangerous menace." McCain ended his letter by notifying the governor that he was about to present his suggestion to the city council.

The council meeting and McCain's letter created a heated debate among townspeople that McCain would lose. In fact, after the council meeting, he penned a very different letter to Governor Gruening.

In an amazing change of heart, McCain told the governor that he "realized that my suggestions were too harsh and give a color that I did not want to lend to my feelings." He now knew that "these people are not here at their request and are unwilling victims of a condition which they cannot prevent. As a matter of fact, they desire to return to their homes." McCain learned that "20 of them have died since they came to Ward Cove while six others have been sent out for TB care. That is a terrible toll out of about 150 and shows a condition that should be cared for." His sudden revelations caused him to tell the governor that "we do not desire to shirk our duty in regard to such evacuees nor place undue burden upon them."

Despite McCain's change of heart, his initial suggestions made at the city council meeting filtered back to the Aleuts. The chief of Akutan village wrote a letter that appeared in the Ketchikan paper on May 21, 1943, in which he pondered "why we as American citizens were moved to Ward Cove by the military, for war safety measures, should be made a football of and kicked around is not quite clear." The Aleuts were told that they were "undesirable" because some of their "people are said to have venereal diseases." The Aleut chief asked the Ketchikan people: "Are we the only group of Alaska citizens so affected? Are the other groups kicked about for that reason?" Many of the Aleut men were already in the armed forces. Others were employed in and around Ketchikan and buying their share of war bonds. The Aleuts "did not come to Ward Cove" of their own will, but "fell in readily with war plans of those over us." The Chief now demanded "the same treatment as any other group of citizens," "not asking any special favors."

For the Aleut Chief the problem was that those who were "so anxious now to kick us out of our homes at Ward Cove" had not shown the same "zeal in keeping away the whiskey bootleggers and white exploiters when our men, women, and children first landed there, from greatly changed environments." Speaking for his people, the Aleut Chief resented "any un-American efforts to kick us about from pillar to post."

Harassment of Aleuts did not end, however, after those initial confrontations. Dorofy Chercasen's most vivid memory is of the Ketchikan City Police, who according to him, "many times picked up us Aleuts for no reason." These were times when they "would not even have had a single drink." One time after work he went to the bake shop and bought a pie to take back to the camp. On the way to the bus a policeman picked him up and took him and his pie, which he believes the judge ate, to the city jail. He was there from Friday until Monday morning when the trial came up. He was fined $10.00 for loitering. But since he had no money, his employer came and paid his fine. For Chrecasen, it was immensely frustrating to be "put in jail and fined left and right. It was hard enough earning money to feed ourselves and our families without having it squeezed out of us by the law."

Another aspect of the Aleuts' relocation was their relations with government officials in this time of crisis. Events at Burnett Inlet provide insight into that relationship. Martha Newell, part Aleut and married to a white, wrote from Burnett Inlet on March 18, 1943 to her

A view of Unalaska, circa 1938. Courtesy America's Coastline Collection

husband working in Seattle: "If I am able to go back I'll walk the ocean…. We're all anxious to go home. I can't stand thinking of staying another winter, and most of the folks feel the same as there's no work and we are paying for our food." She pointed out that "the Japs in the States" were not paying for food, and she thought they were "probably treated better than we are."

A week later she wrote again to her husband to ask him to write to Washington and "ask them why we have to pay for our food and other things when we have no way to make a living." She wanted to know why "if it's clear, and not so dangerous in Unalaska," they could not return. She told her husband "we're all fed up here. They practically treat us as if we were so dumb, or as aliens."

Kenneth Newell followed his wife's request and wrote to Anthony Dimond, Alaska Territories Delegate to Congress, in Washington, D.C. His letter pointed out that there was no need to keep the Aleuts away from Unalaska for military security and that it was unfair for the Japanese internees to receive housing and food while "our own citizens must take what they can get... this really smells rotten.... At least treat our own citizens with as much respect as we show the Japs—at least that much." Of course, Newell was overlooking the fact that the majority of interned Japanese were American citizens.

Edythe Long, the OIA representative at Burnett Inlet, shared the condescending attitude of many OIA bureaucrats. She resented Martha Newell's complaints and tried to make sure they would be ignored. She wrote to the Alaska Indian Service:

> Mrs. Newell has a firm conviction that the more complaints she registers and the more dissatisfaction and discontent she can arouse amongst the evacuees here the sooner the Authorities will be obliged to move her back to Unalaska. Her entire being is centered on that one purpose—to go back to her home this spring, and it seems she will go to any lengths even gross misrepresentation to attain this end. She turns deaf ears to any account of reasoning and refuses to face the fact that Unalaska is a war zone and that no women and children can be returned there at present. She not only complains for herself but goes from house to house spreading discontent; she ridicules anyone who tries to make their homes attractive and livable for the duration, criticizes everything, and even advises others to write to their families that the food and homes are intolerable.

Long went on in the letter to criticize the Chief of Unalaska, Zaharoff, saying that "he has proved himself to be a problem also... with his childish attitude." Apparently the Chief also complained that his people did not have the money to purchase all their food and he thought the continued relocation was unnecessary. Long's solution for the Chief's attitude was to ignore it as "he has suffered personal loss and grief." As for Martha Newell, she was to be given her food at no cost so she could save enough to pay for transportation to some other part of the state "where she may be able to be more content for the duration." But Long suggested no location. Interestingly, she mentions in passing in the letter that in the past she had "held Mrs. Newell in rather high esteem, and felt she was rather a friend." Apparently the separation anxiety of the Unalaska Aleuts such as Martha Newell created a greater rift between the OIA teachers and the Aleuts than had existed on the island. Edythe Long seemed incapable of understanding this anxiety and discontent. Martha Newell died at the Burnett camp. Her final request was that her body be returned to Unalaska for burial was granted.

Philemon M. Tutiakoff, now chairman of the Board of the Aleutian/Pribilof Islands Association, gave a statement in 1980 that summed up relations with government officials: "The most galling and demeaning feature that many of us recall explicitly is that those in charge regarded us as incapable... of any form of decision-making. At no time throughout this entire process were we given the right to make choices of any kind." Sergie Shaishnikoff, who was at Funter Bay, felt that the agents "treated us like children. It was ridiculous."

This examination of the Aleut internment camps shows that Aleuts did not passively accept their fate. In the face of numerous epidemics, the anxiety of displacement, and racism, Aleuts protested the paternalism of on-site government officials and teachers wrote letters to newspapers and relatives, renovated the dilapidated buildings, cared for the sick and dying, and worked when they could find jobs. By bringing together many Aleuts into confined spaces, the Army, Navy, FWS and OIA created ideal conditions for the spread of tuberculoses and other deadly infectious diseases. The situation was further exacerbated by allowing the ill to live in camps without adequate heat, food, water, or medical care. Clearly, as we have seen in the organization of this chapter, the government denied Aleuts the basic necessities of life, and so they died under the government's care. Despite what some officials thought, the cause of failures in the government-run camps was not the Aleuts, but the officials themselves.

Despite their poor treatment at the hands of the U.S. government, Aleuts remained patriotic. Twenty-five Aleut men joined the Armed Forces. Three took part in the U.S. invasion of Attu Island, and all were awarded the Bronze Star. At their camps, Aleuts voted in territorial elections. Through exposure to the outside world they understood the importance of their participation in the democracy and their full rights as citizens.

Aleuts who returned home found their houses ravaged

by the weather and vandalized by U.S. servicemen, the windows smashed, and doors and furniture gone. Also religious icons and subsistence equipment, such as boats and rifles, had been stolen. It would take years to recover, to fashion new communities and a new order for themselves. Politicized by their stay in the camps, the Aleut began the long battle for restitution. The evacuation may have taken place for safety reasons, but racism too had played a role in the abruptness of that evacuation and their poor treatment in the camps.

It would be forty years until restitution would be made, but on August 10, 1988 Public Law 100-383 was signed calling for financial compensation and apology from Congress and the President in behalf of the American people.

THE IMPACT OF WORLD WAR II ON ALASKA

While World War II brought misery for Aleuts and soldiers on the Aleutians, it also brought improvements and development to Alaska. For years, the American and Canadian governments were contemplating building a highway to Alaska. It would take the onset of World War II to give the project the impetus to begin.

The Army Corp of Engineers was given the task to build a road over 1500 miles of difficult terrain. The corp finished the project nine months and six days after the start of construction. The pioneer road was crude but by December of 1943 supplies for Alaska and the Soviet Union headed north via the road.

The Alaska Highway is considered one of the construction triumphs of the world, punching through 1,500 miles of mountains, muskeg, and mosquitoes. It began in the small town of Dawson Creek, with a population of about 600 people. On March 9, 1942, the first train carrying troops arrived and within weeks the town's population boomed to over 10,000.

More than 11,000 American troops, including seven regiments of engineers, 16,000 civilian workmen from Canada and the United States, and 7,000 pieces of equipment were thrown into the Herculean task of creating a road through wilderness. The construction bill for the 1,523 mile route came to about ten million dollars. The route included 133 major bridges and more than 8,000 culverts.

Alaska Communities: Tok

Tok is located at the junction of the Alaska Highway and the Tok Cutoff to the Glenn Highway, at 1,635 feet elevation, 200 miles southeast of Fairbanks. Called the "Gateway to Alaska," it is the first major community upon entering Alaska, 93 miles from the Canadian border. Many believe the name Tok derives from Tokyo Camp, but there are at least three other versions of how the town got its name. Tok began in 1942 as an Alaska Road Commission camp. So much money was spent in the camp's construction and maintenance that it earned the name "Million Dollar Camp" by those working on the highway. In 1944 a branch of the Northern Commercial Company opened, and in 1946 Tok officially became a town. With the completion of the Alcan Highway in 1946, a post office and a roadhouse followed. In 1947 the area earned its the first school, and in 1958 a larger school opened to accommodate the many newcomers. The U.S. Customs Office was located in Tok between 1947 and 1971, when it moved to Alcan at the border. Between 1954 and 1979, a U.S. Army fuel pipeline operated from Haines to Fairbanks, with a pump station in Tok. The Bureau of Land Management purchased the station's facilities for its area headquarters. The U.S. Coast Guard constructed a LORAN (Long Range Aid to Navigation) station in 1976, and today four 700 foot towers, located 6 miles east of Tok Junction, transmit radio navigation signals for air and marine traffic in the Gulf of Alaska. In July of 1990, Tok faced extinction when a lightning-caused forest fire jumped two rivers and the Alaska Highway, putting both residents and buildings in peril. The town soon evacuated, and the efforts of over a thousand firefighters could not stop the fire. At the last minute, a "miracle wind" (so labeled by Tok's residents) came up, diverting the fire just short of the first building. The fire continued to burn the remainder of the summer, eventually burning more than 100,000 acres. Visitors can see evidence of the burn on both sides of the highway just east of Tok. The area was traditionally Athabascan, although the current population is primarily non-native. Tok has also become known as the "Sled Dog Capital of Alaska." Although residents have chosen not to incorporate as a municipality, there are numerous local volunteer committees for various community functions and membership organizations.

On November 20, 1942, 250 soldiers, civilians, and Royal Canadian Mounted Policemen watched as officials from the United States and Canada cut the ribbon at Mile 1061, known as the "Soldier's Summit," officially opening the Alaska Highway.

Historian Gary Nash noted that "World War II brought the American West into the Twentieth Century," meaning that before World War II the American West was "economically isolated, underdeveloped, colonially dependent, and reliant on natural resource exploitation and contained little industrial development." However, after World War II the American West became more economically diverse and more self sufficient. There were still the traditional extractive industries but they now combined with aerospace, electronics, new service industries, and military bases. If we take Alaska to be part of the American West, how does it fare in Nash's equation?

Certainly the military presence was pronounced. In 1943, for example, there were 300,000 troops in Alaska. With three hundred military installations of one kind or another, the U.S. government spent over three hundred million federal dollars in Alaska during 1943. While some saw this influx of troops and money as a much needed boost to Alaska's development, others saw it as an end to the territory's charms. Joe Driscoll, a journalist in Alaska, thought that "the old Alaska is gone; she's wrecked. It's as bad as being invaded by the enemy." Such changes created a dichotomy in Alaska whereby Alaskans became reliant on an influx of federal money but resentful of federal interference and regulation. This pattern/attitude is familiar to anyone who has spent time in the state.

A good example of the influence of federal money in Alaska is the growth of Anchorage. In 1940 Anchorage had a population of 3,500 people and was dependent on the Alaska Railroad for its livelihood. In 1940 the government designated Anchorage as the headquarters of the militarization of Alaska. From 1940 to 1943 the permanent population grew from 3,500 to 25,000. Businesses realized the opportunity and sold everything, good or bad, at premium prices. OPA rationed prices only applied to pre-war Alaskan residents, thus new arrivals paid four times that price.

Government money updated water, lights, telephone and

sewage for the city. The military bases of Fort Richardson and Elmendorf sustained the economic growth of Anchorage after the war. By 1950 Anchorage had a population of 50,000. World War II left a permanent, large, and thriving city. In 1956 Anchorage gained the status of "All-American City." A banner proudly hung over Forth Avenue for two years. Noted Alaskan historian Stephen Haycox observed that despite Alaskan's pride in self-reliance and dislike of the federal government, "Anchorage was born of the federal government, nurtured by it, and grew to maturity from it."

Alaska Natives and World War II

World War II politicized Alaska Natives in areas beyond the Southeast. Military service and exposure to whites and the military in their communities and regions impacted the area in a variety of ways, all of them complex, ranging from encounters with racism and prejudice to an understanding of the use of citizenship. For example, Howard Rock was a Point Hope Inupiaq who served in Italy during World War II. He started the *Tundra Times*, a newspaper that dealt with Alaska Native issues on a statewide basis. It was the first such Alaska Native newspaper.

Elizabeth Peratrovich became a major civil rights leader in Alaska during the World War II era. She was born on July 4, 1911, in Petersburg, Alaska, and was the adopted daughter of Andrew and Mary Wanamaker, Presbyterian Church missionaries for Angoon, Klawock, Kake and Kluckwan. Elizabeth attended elementary school in Petersburg and graduated from Ketchikan High School. After attending Sheldon Jackson College in Sitka, she furthered her education at Western College of Education (now Western Washington University) in Bellingham, Washington, where she met and married Roy Peratrovich in 1931. The couple moved to Klawock after college. She was a mother of three children, a member of the Presbyterian Church, and Grand Camp President for the Alaska Native Sisterhood.

When Elizabeth and Roy moved to Juneau in 1941 she was shocked at the blatant discrimination against Alaska Natives. In Juneau, Roy served as the Alaska Native Brotherhood Grand President and Elizabeth as the Alaska

Native Sisterhood Grand President. They wrote a letter to territorial Governor Ernest Gruening calling his attention to the un-American signs on the Douglas Inn which read "No Natives Allowed." The letter reminded the Governor that Alaska Natives pay the required taxes to the territory, even though the system excluded Alaska Native children from the public schools.

The Peratrovichs lobbied extensively for the passage of an anti-discrimination law. In 1943 the territorial legislature finally considered such a law, but it did not pass. When the issue came before the Senate again in 1945, it was Elizabeth's powerful testimony that moved the legislature to pass the first anti-discrimination law in the country which outlawed discrimination in housing, public accommodations, and restaurants in Alaska.

Events at a movie theater in Nome also played a crucial role in the 1945 anti-discrimination bill and show some of the impacts of World War II for Alaska Natives. The civilian population of Nome at the close of the war was approximately 1,500. Roughly one-half of these were Alaska Natives. Joe Amorock was an Alaska Native with a successful business. He was the owner and operator of the only commercial laundry in Nome. One evening he took his family to the local movie house, "The Dreamland." One side of the theater was for Alaska Natives and the other side reserved for whites. Amorock entered to find the Alaska Native side full and the white side less than half-filled. So he led his family to seats together on the white side of the aisle. An usher tapped him on the shoulder and told him to "get over on the other side where you belong." Amorock rose and motioned to his family to follow him. As they left he stopped as he passed the manager's office and said, "You can remove my ad from your screen hereafter. If I can't bring my family to sit together in comfort to see a picture in your theater, then I don't want to spend my money to advertise on your screen." This would be the start of more activism at the Dreamland.

Alberta Skenk was invited to go to the movies by a white Army sergeant from the States who was stationed at the Nome base. He purchased tickets at the window and escorted her to a seat in the white section of the theater. The moment they found seats, the manager himself strode down the aisle and told her, "You can't sit here and you know it. The sergeant advised her to sit right where she was. In a few minutes the manager returned with the chief of police in tow. Together they marched down the aisle to where Skenk sat. The police seized her by the shoulders and pulled her into the aisle, pushed her down to the door, and out onto the street. The next Sunday evening Alaska Natives had lined up, bought their tickets, and literally taken over the theater, sitting wherever they wanted to. They filed charges against the theater manager and the chief of police.

Skenk also sent a message to Governor Gruening describing the situation. Within twenty-four hours the governor wired Mayor Edward Anderson of Nome, stating that his attention had been called to discrimination against Alaska Natives there. In particular he referred to the forcible ejection by city police of one Alberta Skenk from The Dreamland. The governor requested that Mayor Anderson make a full and complete investigation and report back to him. In a matter of hours, Mayor Anderson sent the following message to the governor: "A mistake has been made. It won't happen again."

The result of these and other discriminatory incidents against Alaska Natives was the anti-discrimination bill introduced at the next meeting of the territorial legislature. As a result of the war, Alaska Natives were organized and aware of all local and national affairs. Many were now for the first time exercising their right to vote and actively using American citizenship.

Overall effects of World War II in Alaska proved to be a boom greater than any gold rush. Between 1941 and 1945, the U.S. government spent over one billion dollars in Alaska, modernizing the Alaska Railroad, expanding airfields and roads, and building new docks and wharves that were then turned over to the territory after the war. The permanent population grew from a 1940 estimate of 74,000 to 112,000 in 1950.

6

The Road to Statehood and Beyond

After World War II tremendous changes took place in Alaska. Once again Alaska reflected local, national, and even international events and trends as the state transitioned from a territory to the 49th state of the Union. During the 1950s and 1960s the impacts of the Cold War, a massive earthquake, and boosts for further development set the stage for the emergence of a modern Alaska.

Alaskan Statehood

Many Alaskans had sought statehood since the 1920s but it was not until after World War II that the possibility gained serious momentum. A brief review of Alaska's political history shows that from 1867 to 1884 Alaska was under military rule as a district of the United States. With Sheldon Jackson's influence in 1884, the government passed the Organic Act, giving Alaska an appointed civilian governor, judges, clerks, marshals, and Sheldon Jackson as the education agent. However, Alaska was still officially a district; in reality there was little local control, and outside economic forces called most of the shots.

The Gold Rush Era brought more judges, marshals, and some limited town government, but those outside forces kept Alaska from gaining territorial status. The infamous "Alaska Syndicate," which formed in 1906, included such famous robber barons as J.P. Morgan and Simon Guggenheim. They came to control the Kennecott mine, steamship companies, and salmon packing. The syndicate proved to be a formidable enemy to those who promoted more home rule in Alaska, for the group could weld considerable influence in Washington, D.C. where Alaskan home rule was low on the priority list of most politicians.

As we know, James Wickersham used the Ballinger–Pinchot Affair to give the home rule advocates a much needed boost. Wickersham was correct in noting the local, national, and international impact of the affair when he wrote that it "destroyed the friendship between Theodore Roosevelt and President Taft; split the Republican Party into two great factions; defeated President Taft for re-election in 1912; elected Woodrow Wilson President of the United States; and changed the course of

Ernest Gruening
Courtesy Alaska State Library

history in our country." But the affair was positive for the Alaskan home rule cause. The 1912 Second Organic Act made Alaska a territory with a territorial legislature. Unfortunately for the home rulers, the governor of Alaska would still be appointed by the president, and federal laws regarding fish, game, and natural resources would supersede territorial legislation. Nevertheless, it was a huge step forward. Wickersham tried to follow up with a proposed bill for Alaskan statehood, but it stood little chance of success. Instead the 1920s saw the passage of federal legislation, such as the Jones Act of 1920 and the White Act of 1924, which many Alaskans saw as discriminatory and opposed to their best interests.

Interestingly, it would be a federally appointed Alaskan governor who would in the 1940s and 1950s push forward the issue of Alaskan statehood. Ernest Gruening was a progressive politician who had worked with Senator Robert LaFollette and was the editor of the liberal *Nation* magazine until 1934. That year FDR tapped him to run the Division of Territories and Islands where he became familiar with the Alaskan situation. Then in 1939 FDR appointed Gruening as governor of Alaska. Thus began a long relationship between Gruening and Alaskans.

Bob Bartlett would be Gruening's ally in the statehood cause. Bartlett served as Alaska's territorial delegate to Congress from 1944 to 1958 and thereafter became a U.S. senator representing Alaska. Alaskan historian Claus M. Naske has pointed out that both Gruening and Bartlett clearly saw that the tools of two U.S. senators and a congressional representative could be crucial to Alaska in its fight against outside control of its resources. Together they worked in steps that would eventually lead to Alaska becoming a state, but as we shall see, even after the increased population and strategic importance of Alaska in the Cold War, statehood was not easily achieved.

In 1946 a Referendum for statehood passed in Alaska by a 3 to 2 margin. It was a clear victory but not a total landslide. Some Alaskans, such as Jay Hammond, who, ironically, later became one of Alaska's most respected governors, feared the financial burden of statehood in an area with such a small tax base. Other Alaskans were not interested in further development of the land and did not want to see more people come north if the territory became a state. Nevertheless it was clear that a strong majority of Alaskans wanted the increased home rule that statehood could provide. Using the momentum of the Referendum, Bartlett introduced a bill to Congress for Alaskan statehood but it failed even to come up for a vote. Republicans in Congress killed the bill in committee due to a fear that admission of Alaska would favor the Democrats with two new senators and a congressional delegate. In response in 1949 Gruening and the territorial legislature formed the "Alaska Statehood Committee" of one hundred prominent Americans from all walks of life, including such notables as Eleanor Roosevelt, James Cagney, Pearl Buck, and historian Arthur Schlesinger, Jr. Despite the cache of celebrity endorsement, victory for the statehood advocates was still a decade away.

National politics proved to be the most difficult obstacle for Alaskan statehood, although the effort received a great boost in 1949, when another statehood bill was introduced and passed in 1950 in the House of Representatives by a vote of 186 to 146. To the displeasure of most Alaskans, the bill was then killed in the Senate. Again Senate Republicans feared that Alaska would bring in Democratic senators and congressmen. In 1954 President Eisenhower gave an address which proposed immediate admission of Hawaii as a state, with no mention of Alaska's status. Ike hoped Hawaii's delegation would be Republican.

In 1955 a Constitutional Convention for Alaska was held at the University of Alaska, Fairbanks. At the convention Governor Gruening gave a stirring speech entitled "Let Us End American Colonialism," in which he compared Alaska's struggle to the American Revolution. He drew a parallel between King George and the federal government in Alaska. Alaskans voted on and accepted the Alaska Constitution, and Bartlett and Gruening lobbied hard for another vote in Congress on Alaskan statehood.

Usually a foe of Alaskan statehood, Sam Rayburn, House Representative from Texas and Speaker of the House in 1958, changed his mind and pushed for a new bill. Interestingly, Edna Ferber's novel *Ice Palace* was crucial in changing Rayburn's mind and publicizing Alaskan issues. The book was her best-selling fictional account of Alaska's quest for home rule. A reviewer called it "practically a love letter in fiction form to Alaska." While working on *Ice Palace*, Ferber kept in close touch with Gruening. He provided Ferber an insider's perspective on Alaska's political struggles, and his influence can be seen in the novel's pro-statehood characters, Bridie Ballantyne and Thor and Christine Storm. When Alaska became the 49th state, Gruening wrote to Ferber that her work had "contributed substantially" to achieving statehood.

Another crucial maneuver toward statehood was the adoption of the "Tennessee Plan." The plan, which had been used successfully by Tennessee, Michigan, California, Oregon, Kansas, and Iowa, involved electing a Congressional delegation without waiting for an act from Congress. In the spring of 1956, Alaskans elected Ernest Gruening and William Egan as Senators-elect and Ralph J. Rivers as House Representative-elect. With support for statehood firmly established in Alaska, the stage was now set for new efforts in Congress. Egan, Gruening, and Rivers were kindly received, but were not officially seated or recognized by Congress.

Working together with Delegate Bob Bartlett, the Tennessee Plan delegation lobbied hard in the Senate and the House. When House Speaker Rayburn changed his mind, he noted Bob Bartlett's influence on his decision. Congress reconvened in January 1958 and President Eisenhower fully endorsed Alaska statehood for the first time. Senator Lyndon B. Johnson assured Bartlett that the Southern senators would not filibuster the Alaska bill. Johnson's was an important commitment, but Representative Howard W. Smith of

Virginia, Chairman of the powerful Rules Committee, obstructed the statehood bill. Additionally, Representative Thomas Pelly of Washington State demanded the right for his constituents to fish Alaskan waters on the same basis as residents.

Congress subsequently drafted an amendment seeking retention of federal jurisdiction over Alaska's fish and game resources until the secretary of the interior certified that the state met provisions for their conservation and nonresident access. The *Fairbanks Daily News-Miner* responded to Pelly by printing excerpts from Edna Ferber's *Ice Palace*. The passages featured the character of Thor Storm informing his granddaughter, Christine, about the legacy of how Seattle and San Francisco cannery operators exploited Alaska's fisheries. The clear message was that once again forces from the lower state were seeking unfair use of Alaskan resources.

After some maneuvering, the effort to bypass Representative Smith's Rules Committee succeeded when the House passed the statehood bill. The Senate, which had before it both its own version of the statehood

Famous Alaskans: Civil Servants— William A. Egan and Jay Hammond

"Born in Alaska, Raised in Alaska, and Schooled in Alaska" was how 25-year-old William A. Egan advertised himself during his first campaign for the Alaska territorial legislature in 1940. Without an opportunity to attend college, Egan received his political education in the legislature. Fifteen years later, Alaskans chose him to lead the Alaska Constitutional Convention and then serve in Washington, D.C. as an Alaska-Tennessee Plan senator. In 1959, Egan, from small-town Valdez, became Alaska's first state governor—the only governor born and educated in Alaska during the first 43 years of statehood.

Jay Hammond was governor of Alaska from 1974 to 1982. His background was varied. He had been a marine fighter pilot, had a biology degree, worked as a hunting and fishing guide, was a pilot for the Fish and Wildlife Service, was elected to the State House of Representatives, and was mayor of Bristol Bay Borough. In 1974 he narrowly defeated Egan by 287 votes. He disliked development forces but was also a fiscal conservative and feared misuse of oil monies. Some Alaskans still refer to Hammond as "St. Jay" for his part in developing the permanent fund.

bill and the House version, then passed the House version at the urging of Delegate Bartlett by a 64-20 margin.

Through the combined efforts of Ernest Gruening, Bob Bartlett, and many other Alaskans, the statehood cause was finally victorious. On January 3, 1959, President Eisenhower signed the official declaration which made Alaska the 49th state.

GREAT ALASKA EARTHQUAKE, 1964

On Friday, March 27, 1964, at 5:36 P.M., five years after Alaska became a state, one of the largest earthquakes ever recorded hit Alaska. Measuring an estimated 9.2 on the Richter scale, it was eighty times more powerful than the great San Francisco quake of 1906. This was the second largest earthquake ever recorded in the world and was the largest in North America. The earthquake caused the greatest amount of vertical uplift ever measured. While the shaking lasted four minutes in some areas, the effect on Alaska would be felt much longer. Movement of the ocean floor also caused the most disastrous waves ever to hit the west coast of the United States and Canada. The largest wave was some 220 feet high in the Valdez Inlet at Shoup Bay. One hundred twenty-three people died and 300 to 400 million dollars in property damage was reported, measured in 1964 dollars—a terrible disaster to be sure. But with federal money, some 205 million dollars, Alaska was able to rebuild. In fact, Valdez was completely remade four miles away from its original location.

Rock slides, landslides, snow avalanches and tsunami waves all hit Southern Alaska, destroying roads, railroad tracks, bridges, power facilities, radio stations, and dock structures. An area of over 50,000 square miles sustained major damage. In Anchorage alone, 120 miles northwest of the epicenter, the quake destroyed or badly damaged thirty blocks of houses and commercial buildings in the downtown area and wiped out almost all the city's schools. Luckily, the death toll was very small for an earthquake of this magnitude. Alaska's low population density and the fact that the quake occurred at night on a holiday, when schools and businesses were closed and most people at home, helped to keep the casualties low. Also, wood construction, which had been used for most of the homes, was more flexible than concrete and could bend and sway more without falling.

Two kinds of monster water waves caused damage during the Great Alaska Quake. Tsunamis are an open ocean sea wave caused by motion on the sea floor. Seiches are generated by landslides in bays or fiords. A landslide into the head of the Valdez Arm formed a seiche which killed thirty-five people who were at the docks. The water rose a terrifying 229 feet and took out the pier and waterfront. The sea continued to rise and fall within the bay throughout the night, akin to a giant bathtub, because the long narrow shape of the fiord did not allow the energy to dissipate out into the sea. When Valdez was rebuilt, planners moved the city 4.3 miles away to a location on more stable ground.

The more familiar tsunamis travel at velocities between 300 to 600 miles per hour. Interestingly, the height of the wave itself is usually less than three feet in the open ocean,

Tsunami damage at Seward following the 1964 Good Friday earthquake. Courtesy NOAA

and the wave crests can be anywhere from 60 to 435 miles apart. Many times these waves move through the open ocean without being noticed. When the wave front comes on shore, however, it piles up on itself, resulting in a huge tidal wave. At times the first warning of an approaching tsunami is the rapid withdrawal of water on the beach to exceptionally low levels. Such conditions should signal beach residents to head for the high ground if they can.

Tsunami waves generated by the Alaska quake came on shore along the Alaskan coast, the western coasts of both North and South America, and hit Hawaii and Japan. It was the second largest tsunami ever recorded. In Alaska, Chenega was completely destroyed and the port at Seward demolished. The first wave of the tsunami hit the Kenai Peninsula nineteen minutes after the quake hit and struck Kodiak Island in thirty-four minutes. It took four hours to hit the northern California coast and Crescent City.

Crescent City, California, just south of Oregon, has a sea floor that concentrated the Alaskan tsunami onto a narrow stretch of shoreline. This caused the wave height to grow and inundate more land. After the original quake, officials issued a warning to California that a tsunami was possible. The sheriff of Crescent City even received notification that it was definitely on its way and evacuated all of the coastal front areas. One hour later the waves arrived. The first wave crested 13 feet above low tide. The second wave was smaller. The third and fourth waves damaged low-lying areas around the south beach, with the third running inland 546 yards.

The waves flooded thirty city blocks, badly damaging or destroying most of the single-story wood framed houses. Sadly, after the first two waves had passed, some of the townspeople believed the threat was over and returned to their homes and businesses. One such group of seven returned to a tavern to begin cleanup. While working, they decided to have a drink. They were trapped in the building by the third wave and five of them drowned. Others returned to the shore to watch the ocean only to be surprised by a fifth wave, which crested at 20 feet. The tsunami at Crescent City caused eight million dollars worth of damage and killed eleven people.

In Achorage, three major landslides damaged water

mains, gas, sewer, telephone, and electrical systems. A layer of clay lost its strength, causing 200 acres of land to slide toward the ocean. Built on 70-foot high bluffs, Turnagain Heights housing development collapsed inland 984 feet from the bluffs' edge. The landslide destroyed over 1.7 miles of coastland, breaking the ground into blocks that collapsed and tilted at all angles and destroying seventy-five homes. The spreading caused two houses that were originally more than two hundred yards apart to collide with each other. Parts of Anchorage were never rebuilt and have been preserved in an area named Earthquake Park.

Another huge slide caused the main business district to drop ten feet. Again, fortunately, the businesses were closed for the holiday. The J.C. Penney Company building was damaged beyond repair; the Four Seasons apartment building, a new six-story structure, collapsed; and many other multistory buildings were damaged heavily. The Government Hill Grade School was almost a total loss and Anchorage High School and Denali Grade School were damaged severely.

Huge losses of life and property rocked Alaska. Many feared that the anti-state advocates were right and that with the small tax base Alaska could not pay to rebuild after the quake. Luckily, the federal government did not forget its new state; LBJ declared the Alaskan Quake a federal disaster and millions of dollars in aid, social services, and low-interest loans sped recovery efforts. But Alaskans who lived through the quake will never forget the experience and hope it is never repeated.

Boosting Alaska

Federal interest in Alaska was not limited to statehood and earthquakes. In the 1950s and 1960s, several controversial programs and projects, some proposed and some realized, affected Alaska. These plans revealed the ongoing tensions between pro-development forces and preservation forces and between state's rights advocates and the federal government.

Project Chariot

In 1957, the U.S. Atomic Energy Commission (AEC) established the "Plowshare Program" to investigate and

Tsunami damage at kodiak: fishing boats washed into town.
Courtesy NOAA Central Library

develop peaceful uses for nuclear explosives. The commission and Dr. Edward Teller, "father of the H-bomb," saw Alaska as a good spot to implement their program. In early 1958, the commission selected a site near Cape Thompson, approximately 30 miles southeast of the Inupiat village of Point Hope. It planned to use a nuclear blast to create a harbor and called the excavation "Project Chariot."

The massive explosion would carve a harbor large enough for ships to dock in order to load fossil fuels expected to be found in the area. Teller, on a tour of Alaska in 1958, spoke of "engaging in the great art of geographic engineering, to reshape the earth to your pleasure," and boasted that Project Chariot could "dig a harbor in the shape of a polar bear, if required." Officials expected the blast to be 100 times more powerful than the one at Hiroshima and scheduled it to take place in 1962.

Gaining support of the press, Teller and his associates were less successful in getting a positive endorsement by the state's financial leaders. Some were doubtful of the commercial viability of the project. Others rejected the idea that the state needed a harbor to ship out whatever minerals were found. Other dissenters included some of the science faculty at the University of Alaska at Fairbanks, environmentalists, and a few government officials. They were vocal in their criticism of the blast and its implications for the safety of the people and wildlife of the region.

Project leaders did not directly inform Inupiat leaders from Point Hope, Noatak, and Kivalina, the villages closest to the proposed blast, and thus the people remained largely unaware of the plan. It was not until the spring of 1959 that a visiting missionary from Kotzebue called Point Hope residents to an impromptu meeting, telling them the rumor about the blast was true.

Although AEC officials excluded Inupiat villagers from early discussions about Project Chariot, they did continue to promote it before Alaska's financial community and state legislature, as their support was essential to the project's implementation. After holding discussions with public officials and private industrial leaders, the commission eventually succeeded in gaining approval from the state. Realizing the skepticism of those who questioned the Project's commercial benefit, the AEC also shifted the basis of its argument for the detonation away from possible economic advantages toward the experimental aspects. Under the revised plan, presented in June of 1959, the project's Environmental Studies Program director stated that an effort would be made "... to determine the effects of a nuclear explosion on the environment—its rock substrata, soils, atmosphere, and biota, including man."

But not until the spring of 1960 did official representatives of the AEC come to the village to explain the details of the proposed blast. Among other things, the representatives told the Point Hope people that nuclear weapons tests would not make the fish radioactive and that consuming such fish posed no danger. They also claimed that the effects of nuclear weapons testing never injured anyone and that once the severely exposed Japanese people recovered from radiation sickness they suffered no side effects. The residents would not feel any seismic shock at all from Project Chariot and copies of the Environmental Program studies would be made immediately available to the Point Hope council upon the return of the AEC officials to California. There would be no need to restrict the area where the men did their hunting, and the detonation would occur at a time outside the normal caribou hunting cycle. Finally, although the AEC would compensate the residents for damage to structures, representatives claimed there was little possibility of such damage occurring.

Not surprisingly, the village council rejected assurances that Project Chariot would not be a hazard to their subsistence way of life. Immediately following the meeting, the council voted unanimously to oppose detonation of the bomb. Soon protests became more widespread. Scientists at the University of Alaska, along with those working within the AEC itself, pointed out that the tundra's "food chain" was particularly susceptible to radioactive fallout from recent atomic testing. The meat of Alaska's caribou, for example, contained approximately seven times as much strontium 90 as the meat of domestic cattle in the lower 48 states. This was because caribou fed on lichens, rootless plants deriving their nutriment from the dust in the air as it was carried down by rain and snow, directly absorbing the radioactive fallout before it became diluted in the soil.

Since the Inupiat ate the caribou, they already had a considerably greater intake of strontium 90 than other Americans. Also, above-ground testing would only add to the already existing danger. The inland Inupiat of Anaktuvuk Pass, several hundred miles northeast of Cape Thompson, also spoke out sharply against additional testing. Located high in the Brooks Range, they relied more heavily on the caribou for their subsistence than other Arctic villagers. In a plea to the outside world, Simon Paneak, head of the village council, noted that the radiation levels "keep getting higher and higher, and we just don't know what to do."

Finally, on March 3, 1961, the Point Hope village health council wrote to President John Kennedy opposing the proposed explosion, stating that such a detonation would be "too close to our hunting and fishing areas. We also know about strontium 90, how it might harm people if too much of it gets into our body. We are deeply concerned about the health of our people now and for the future."

The Inupiat of Point Hope and other North Alaskan villages all feared that the successful detonation would

Alaska Communities: McGrath

McGrath is located 221 miles northwest of Anchorage and 269 miles southwest of Fairbanks in Interior Alaska. It is adjacent to the Kuskokwim River directly south of its confluence with the Takotna River. McGrath was a seasonal Upper Kuskokwim Athabascan village used as a meeting and trading place. The Old Town McGrath site was originally located across the river. In 1904, Abraham Appel established a trading post there. In 1906 prospectors discovered gold in the area. Since McGrath is the northernmost point on the Kuskokwim River accessible by large riverboats, it became a regional supply center. By 1907 a town was established and was named for Peter McGrath, a local U.S. Marshal. In 1909 the Alaska Commercial Company opened a store. The Iditarod Trail also contributed to McGrath's role as a supply center. From 1911 to 1920, hundreds of people walked and mushed over the trail on their way to the gold districts. Mining sharply declined after 1925. After a major flood in 1933, some residents decided to move to the south bank of the river, and changes in the course of the river eventually left the old site on a slough, useless as a river stop. In 1937 the Alaska Commercial Company opened a store at its new location. In 1940 the area gained an airstrip, an FAA communications complex, and a school. McGrath became an important refueling stop during World War II as part of the Lend-Lease Program between the U.S. and Russia. In 1964 a new high school attracted boarding students from nearby villages. Slightly more than half of the population are Athabascans and Eskimos. As a regional center, McGrath offers a variety of employment opportunities, but subsistence remains an important part of the local culture. About 10 families in town have dog teams which they enter into the Iditarod, Kuskokwim 300, and Mail Trail 200 sled dog races.

cause serious health hazards, immediately making the region and their way of life untenable. Within a year, the AEC set aside Project Chariot, due in large part to the rising chorus of protest mounted against the project by Alaska Natives and many other organizations across the United States and throughout the world.

But the story did not end there. AEC scientists decided to bring fresh radioactive fallout to Alaska from an earlier nuclear explosion at the Nevada test site. Researcher Dan O'Neill found through Freedom of Information documents that in August 1962 isotopes and mixed fission products were transported to the Project Chariot location and buried. The AEC designed the experiment primarily to determine the dispersal of radioactive products from buried nuclear material. After placing radioactive fallout in measured plots, the scientists watered the ground to simulate rainfall.

This waste was left there and plowed over, leeching into the middle of prime caribou hunting ground. It was not cleaned up until 1992. In all, the AEC buried some 15,000 tons of contaminated soil in an unmarked area within traditional Inupiat hunting territory. As disturbing as Project Chariot was for many, it was certainly not the only scheme of the 1950s and 1960s that the federal government had for Alaska.

RAMPART DAM

The Army Corps of Engineers fought up through the 1960s to build a huge dam on the Yukon River. The scope of the project would have been truly mind-boggling and could have created a reservoir larger than Lake Erie, with a dam 530 feet high and 4,700 feet long at Rampart Canyon. Estimates showed it would take twenty years to fill the resulting reservoir.

Environmentalists and others pointed out that the project would effectively destroy the summer habitat for 1.5 million migratory birds. Some Alaskans agreed with the sentiment that Alaska needed the Rampart dam like it needed another earthquake. However, some editorialists and developers touted the idea, and the Alaska Legislature spent money to promote the world's largest hydroelectric project. Rampart Dam would produce twice as much power as Grand Coulee, seventeen times more than Alaska already produced, and would facilitate large-scale industrialization. But the resulting reservoir would also flood seven Athabascan villages, forcing twelve hundred Alaska Natives out of their home territory and adversely affecting many other thousands in Alaska and Canadian by the loss or reduction of salmon runs and moose hunting territory.

The Fish and Wildlife Service (FWS), however, did not back the Corps of Engineers proposal. In fact, the FWS report on the impact of the project noted that in the history of water development, Rampart Dam would be unprecedented in terms of the expected overwhelming losses of fish and wildlife. To others Rampart represented what they thought they came to Alaska to escape; it was utterly inimical to their image of Alaska as a wilderness frontier. And with tourism becoming a more important part of the economy, many decried to boosters of the project that people were not coming to Alaska to see dams and artificial lakes. The opposition of the FWS, Alaska Natives, and conservationists led to the eventual abandonment of the idea, and the Yukon remains dam-free. While public outcry may have stopped Rampart, other Cold War-era projects in Alaska would continue, unbeknownst to the general public in and outside of Alaska.

Iodine 131

As part of a larger Atomic Energy Commission program, officials gave doses of Iodine 131, a radioactive isotope, to some Alaska Natives over the course of three years (1955-1957) as part of a larger and supposedly beneficial health system project. In order to insure that the test subjects actually came in to receive their pills, the AEC awarded each subject with an apple and an orange per day. The purpose of the experiment was to explain how Alaskan Natives' thyroid glands function in cold weather, but the commission discontinued the experiment when it discovered that Alaskans had no added protection against cold weather.

The study involved 200 administrations of I-131 to 120 subjects. Animal studies suggested the thyroid gland might play a crucial role in adaptation to extreme cold. This experiment was part of a larger research mission to examine ways of improving the operational capability of Air Force personnel in arctic regions. The study required its participants to swallow a capsule containing a tracer dose of radioiodine, taking measurements of thyroid activity and samples of blood, urine, and saliva. The study's overall conclusion was that the thyroid did not play any significant role in human acclimatization to the arctic environment. Alaska Natives testifying in 1994 before a government committee could not recall any follow-up visits by physicians. Several Alaska Native subjects, including women who were pregnant or lactating, reported receiving as many as three doses. What sets the Alaska experiment

Famous Alaskans: Iditarod Champions Susan Butcher and Martin Buser

Butcher, born 1956, is the only woman to win the Iditarod Sled Dog Race for three consecutive years—placing first in 1986, 1987, and 1988. She has shown herself to be one of the top mushers in the world by breaking nine speed records in major international races. This includes the Iditarod record, which Butcher broke by 31 hours. Butcher is the first and only person to take a dog team to the summit of Denali. In 1988 a T-shirt appeared in Alaska which read, "Alaska: Where Men are Men and Women Win the Iditarod!"

Martin Buser is a four-time Iditarod champion. Since 1987 he has piled up an impressive string of 16 finishes in the top 10, including 10 in the top five. In 2003 Buser followed up his 2002 championship with a 4th place finish. In addition to his wins, he's been the runner-up twice, in 1991 and 1999. Buser set record winning times in 1994 and 1997 and again in 2002 with a time of 8 days 22 hours 46 minutes and 2 seconds, which stands as the current fastest time. Born in Zurich, Switzerland, on March 29, 1958, Buser raced dogs in his native country and came to Alaska in 1979 to expand his knowledge of training and techniques. Martin and his wife of 20 years, Kathy, own and manage Happy Trails Kennel. He often names his dogs after politicians—such as Bill, Al Gore, Hillary, and Ross Perot—or occasions. Rudolph, Prancer, and Dasher were born in December of 2002.

apart from other studies conducted on pregnant and lactating women is that this experiment was not designed to investigate a research question about any aspect of pregnancy. Their use in the experiment therefore seems highly suspect, if not outright unneccessary.

But radiation tests on Alaska Natives were not the last of federal nuclear experiments in Alaska. While the government did not explode the Project Chariot bomb, they would go ahead with detonations elsewhere in the state.

AMCHITKA ISLAND

Amchitka Island sits at the midway point on the great arc of Alaska's Aleutian Islands, less than 900 miles across the Bering Sea from the coast of Russia. Amchitka, a spongy landscape of maritime tundra, is one of the most southerly of the Aleutians. The island's relatively temperate climate has made it one of the Arctic's most valuable bird sanctuaries, a critical staging ground for more than 100 migratory species, as well as home to walruses, sea otters, and sea lions. Off the coast of Amchitka is a thriving fishery of salmon, pollock, haddock, and halibut. Visitors recognized all of these values early on. In 1913 President William Howard Taft designated Amchitka as a national wildlife refuge, yet the government used the island for three underground nuclear test detonations in 1965, 1969, and 1971, including Cannikin, the world's largest.

The dimensions of Cannikin remain staggering. The five-megaton warhead, one of the largest sub-surface nuclear blasts ever conducted by the United States, exploded on November 6, 1971, with a force equal to that produced by five million tons of TNT. For about two years, workers had drilled what was then the deepest single-lift mine shaft in the Western Hemisphere, more than a mile down. After plugging the eight-foot wide shaft, they detonated the bomb in a fifty-foot-wide cavity mined at the bottom. The blast shook forty-two-mile-long Amchitka with the power of an earthquake that at the time measured 7.0 on the Richter scale. It also widened the underground cavity at ground zero to a diameter of 200 feet. Thirty-eight hours later, an eleven-mile wide section of rock and ground above the blast site fell by as much as 50 feet.

The blast rattled the ocean nearby, bounced work-camp buildings as if they were toys, collapsed rocky outcrops into the sea, and splashed whole lakes into the air. Cannikin was the first major project in the country to fall under the requirements of the National Environmental Policy Act with the federal government furnishing the required environmental impact statement after six weeks of analysis and paperwork.

The Cannikin project cost $118 million and was the third and last test firing of a nuclear device beneath Amchitka. The Spartan warhead was intended for the U.S. Safeguard Anti-Ballistic Missile System, designed to explode at high altitude amid a cluster of incoming enemy missiles. The Nixon administration and its supporters in Congress said the test was a matter of national security. But

Cannikin had numerous opponents, including U.S. Sen. Mike Gravel, of Alaska, who urged that a delay "might be the better part of wisdom."

Despite assurances by the AEC and the Pentagon that the test sites would safely contain the radiation released by the blasts for thousands of years, some claim that highly radioactive elements and gasses, such as tritium, americium-241 and plutonium, poured out of the collapsed test shafts, leached into the groundwater, and worked their way into ponds, creeks, and the Bering Sea.

Aleuts raised objections to the tests, pointing to the risk of radiation leaks, earthquakes, and tsunamis that might overwhelm their coastal villages. Cannikin also became a rallying point for Alaska Native groups, anti-war and anti-nuclear activists, and the environmental movement. It was opposition to Cannikin by Canadian and American environmentalists who tried to disrupt the test by taking boats near the island that sparked the birth of Greenpeace.

Cannikin opponents filed a lawsuit in federal court, charging that the test violated the Limited Test Ban Treaty and the newly enacted National Environmental Policy Act. In a four to three decision, the Supreme Court refused to halt the test. What the court did not know, however, was that six federal agencies, including the departments of State and Interior, and the EPA, had lodged serious objections to the Cannikin test, ranging from environmental and health concerns to legal and diplomatic problems. Five hours after the ruling was handed down on November 6, 1971, the AEC detonated the Cannikin bomb. In an effort to calm growing public opposition, AEC chief Schlesinger dismissed environmental protesters and the Aleuts as doomsayers, taking his family with him to watch the test.

In the months following the explosion, officials took blood and urine samples from Aleuts living in the village of Adak on a nearby island. The samples showed abnormally high levels of tritium and cesium-137, both known carcinogens. But Aleuts were not the only ones exposed to Cannikin's radioactivity. More than 1,500 of the workers who helped to build the test sites, operate the bomb tests, and clean up afterward were also put at risk.

Not all the schemes and dreams of the Cold War era

Mushing in the Interior

Jack London was born in 1876 in San Francisco, California. His family struggled financially, and when he finished grammar school, he had to work to support himself. By the time he was 18, London had been a seal hunter, a fisherman, and a seaman on long ocean voyages, and he had drifted throughout a good portion of the United States, Canada, and Alaska.

He began to write and continued to read. In 1897 he traveled to Alaska's Yukon and then turned to pursue his writing seriously. His stories gained acceptance and started to be published, and he began to attract an audience who craved his adventurous tales. His travels, especially the influence of his Alaskan journeys, provided the substance for his themes of primitive instinct, violence, individualism, and the struggle for survival. He spent years searching for gold in the Klondike, and some of his best works, like *The Call of the Wild* and *White Fang*, reflect the often brutal life or death situations derived from those experiences in the wild.

The following words about mushing in Alaska open his book *White Fang*, published in 1915. Although some 90 years apart, the description is still valid for mushers in the Alaskan interior today:

> Dark spruce forest frowned on either side the frozen waterway. The trees had been stripped by a recent wind of their white covering of frost, and they seemed to lean towards each other, black and ominous, in the fading light. A vast silence reigned over the land. The land itself was a desolation, lifeless, without movement, so lone and cold that the spirit of it was not even that of sadness. There was a hint in it of laughter, but of a laughter more terrible than any sadness—a laughter that was mirthless as the smile of the sphinx, a laughter cold as the frost and partaking of the grimness of infallibility. It was the masterful and incommunicable wisdom of eternity laughing at the futility of life and the effort of life. It was the Wild, the savage, frozen-hearted Northland Wild.

> But there WAS life, abroad in the land and defiant. Down the frozen waterway toiled a string of wolfish dogs. Their bristly fur was rimed with frost. Their breath froze in the air as it left their mouths, spouting forth in spumes of vapour that settled upon the hair of their bodies and formed into crystals of frost. Leather harness was on the dogs, and leather traces attached them to a sled which dragged along behind.

were as terrifying as nuclear testing and radiation experiments. In fact, one scheme was quite successful and led to a competition that many now associate with Alaska.

THE LAST GREAT RACE

The Iditarod Trail was first used in the 1880s as towns grew up for miners with the discovery of gold nearby. One such town was Iditarod, named for the Alaska Native word *haiditarod*, meaning a far, distant place. Though full of swamps in the summer, the Iditarod Trail became a major transportation route for dog sled teams in the winter as a way to reach interior Alaska.

Train entering Nenana station

The trail became even more vital in 1925 when an epidemic of diphtheria hit the city of Nome. Though the disease could be treated with a special antitoxin, the closest antitoxin that could be found was unfortunately in Anchorage. Airplanes were still new to Alaska, so no one knew if they could fly in such cold weather. Instead officials agreed that the antitoxin liquid would be taken to Nenana (near Fairbanks) by train, and then a relay of dog sled teams would carry it to Nome.

The trip covered almost 700 miles, and about two-thirds of it followed the Iditarod Trail. Leonhard Seppala, a Norwegian who had come to Alaska looking for gold, traveled 260 of those miles. He and his lead dog, Togo, crossed the frozen Norton Bay in order to speed the journey. Gunnar Kaasen, a veteran of 21 years of dog sled running, completed the last leg of the run. His lead dog Balto led the team through blowing snow into Nome, and the antitoxins they carried stopped the diphtheria outbreak. Balto became a celebrity dog as a result, and New York City built a statue in Central Park to honor him.

As gold mining waned there was less travel on the Iditarod Trail. The use of the airplane signaled the beginning of the end for the dog team as a standard mode of transportation, and later appearance of snowmobiles in Alaska further lessened the need for dog teams in rural areas.

In 1967 a dog sled driver named Joe Redington, Sr. joined with Dorothy Page, an Alaskan interested in history, to celebrate dog sleds. The ensuing sled dog race extended to Nome in 1973, with part of it following the old Iditarod Trail. Similar to the famous Anchorage to Nome diphtheria run of 1925, the race became known as the "The Last Great Race on Earth," and Joe Redington and Dorothy Page became known as the father and mother of the Iditarod.

The race now covers over 1,150 miles of the rough and beautiful terrain complete with jagged mountain ranges, frozen rivers, dense forests, desolate tundra, and miles of windswept coast. Below-zero temperatures and winds can cause a complete loss of visibility, and the long hours of darkness and treacherous climbs add to the adventures of the contestants.

Some names associated with the race include Rick Swenson, the only five-time winner and the only musher to have entered 20 Iditarod races and never to have finished out of the top ten. Dick Mackey beat Swenson by one second in 1978 in a photo finish after two weeks on the trail. while in his 80s, Norman Vaughan finished the race four times. Four-time winner Susan Butcher was the first woman ever to place in the top ten in 1978 as a nineteen year old rookie. Libby Riddles was the first woman to win the Iditarod in 1985.

The Iditarod Race certainly shows off the natural wonders of Alaska and reveals the vastness of the land that many had sought to use and perhaps abuse during the 1960s. The end of that decade would see the next phase in the boom-and-bust cycle of Alaskan economics when a huge oil deposit was discovered in the Arctic and put out to bid for development. The oil discovery would have profound repercussions on the fortunes of the 49th state.

Modern Alaska

Oil and Alaska

In 1968 Atlantic Richfield hit oil in Prudhoe Bay, Alaska. The company estimated that the find contained some ten billion barrels of oil, making it the largest oil field ever found in the United States. This find would have a major influence on the shape of modern Alaskan history, but oil was from far from a stranger to the state.

Long before the 1968 discovery, Alaska Natives in the Artic had used oil as a fuel by soaking dried tundra blocks and burning them for heat and light, but it was not until 1886 that a Navy expedition found oil near Barrow, and in 1914, William Van Valin, a teacher at Wainwright, claimed to have seen an oil lake one mile inland from the Arctic Ocean. In 1919 Ernest Leffingwell, a geologist, found high quality oil sixty miles southeast of Prudhoe Bay. The giant corporation Standard Oil soon expressed interest, sending representatives to Barrow in 1921 to hunt for oil. The federal government then became involved in 1923 when an executive order created the Naval Petroleum Reserve Number Four in Alaska, reserving an area of 37,000 square miles on the North Slope. While it was clear that there was oil in the Arctic, getting to it and transporting it would be another matter entirely.

World War II brought many plans by the Navy to explore, map, and drill in the area. From 1946 to 1950, the U.S. Geological Survey and the Navy worked hand in hand to drill thirty-six wells. However, they only found minor deposits and deemed them not commercially significant. It was not until 1957, and not in the Arctic, that Richfield Oil Company at the Swanson River Field on the Kenai Peninsula started making money on oil in Alaska, pumping out 900 barrels a day. Gradually, from 1959 to 1965, the new state government took over oil leasing, negotiating fifteen

Alaska Communities: Soldotna

Soldotna is on the Kenai Peninsula, 150 highway miles south of Anchorage, at the junction of the Sterling and Kenai Spur Highways. It lies 10 miles inland from Cook Inlet and borders the Kenai River. The Peninsula has historically been the home to the Kenaitze, though non-Alaska Natives developed it for its rich resources, including fish, timber and oil. Named for a nearby stream, Soldotna is a Russian word meaning "soldier." Others believe the name derived from a native word meaning "stream fork." The first homesteaders were World War II veterans, given a 90-day preference over non-veterans in selecting and filing for property in 1947. That same year, the Sterling Highway right-of-way was constructed from Cooper Landing to Kenai. Soldotna was the site for the bridge crossing the Kenai River. A post office opened in 1949, with stores and a community center following shortly thereafter. Soldotna continued to develop because of its strategic location at the Sterling-Kenai Spur Highway junction. In 1957 speculators discovered oil in the Swanson River region, bringing new growth and development. The Kenai River offers top trophy king salmon fishing during June and July. One happy fisherman took a 97 lb. 4 oz. world record king salmon from these waters in 1985, and catching kings of over 60 pounds is not uncommon. The Central Peninsula Sports Center provides an ice rink, racquetball courts, weight room, and meeting facilities.

leases on 2.5 million acres and bringing in over sixty-six million dollars for Alaska. Clearly, even before developments at Prudhoe Bay, oil was becoming a major part of the state's economy in terms of jobs, transportation, and the service industry.

One of Alaska's first responses to the Prudhoe Bay find was in January 1968, when Alaska Governor Walter Hickel proposed a road from Livengood, outside Fairbanks, to the North Slope some 400 miles away. A year later in 1969, Richard Nixon named Hickel Secretary of the Interior, but his "Hickel Highway" was a mess. After being open for only a month, the highway became one long sinking trench. Officials put the plan to work again in 1969 and 1970, but made the same errors. One historian called it the biggest foul up in the history of mankind in the Arctic. Clearly another method would have to be found for oil transport through Alaska.

On September 10, 1969, the state put up 450,000 acres for bid, luring companies such as British Petroleum, Mobil, Standard, Hess, and Gulf. The high bid ended up being a whopping nine hundred million dollars.

From Prudhoe Bay to Valdez, an ice-free port in Prince William Sound, is a distance of 800 miles. Without a road system between the two places, oil companies had to construct a pipeline through Alaska that would cost another nine hundred million dollars. Richfield, British Petroleum, and Humble Oil soon created the TransAlaska Pipeline System (TAPS). But conservationists pitted themselves against the oil companies. Problems were many, including but not limited to Alaska Native land claims, environmental protection, lawsuits by the Wilderness Society and the Friends of the Earth, the impracticality of an underground pipeline, and the shipment of oil from Valdez to refineries in the lower 48. Before any construction could go forward, the companies had to clear a right-of-way. The crucial step in that process was settling the myriad of land claims issues of Alaska Natives.

Toward a Land Claims Settlement

Not long after Alaska became a state, officials in the new government began to organize, evaluate, and select appropriate lands as part of their Congressional allotment. Predictably, several of those selections brought protests from rural residents (primarily Alaska Natives) who saw the government, as jeopardizing their traditional use areas. By 1961, state officials had already selected and filed for more than 1.7 million acres near the Tanana village of Minto. In response, the Bureau of Indian Affairs that year filed protests on behalf of the villages of Northway, Tanacross, Minto, and Lake Alegnagik for a 5.8 million-acre claim that included the recent state selections. More conflicts, it appeared, were sure to follow.

The land claims process awakened Alaska Native leaders to the fact that only by organizing would they be able to have their collective voices heard. The first opportunity to organize came in November 1961, when the Association on American Indian Affairs, a New York-based charitable organization, convened a native rights conference in Barrow drawing representatives from various coastal villages, some from as far away as the lower Kuskokwim River. A report prepared at the conference stated, "We the Inupiat have come together for the first time ever in all the years of our history. We had to come together…. We always thought our Inupiat Paitot [our homeland] was safe to be passed down to our future generations as our fathers passed down to us." Later that year, conference representatives formed Inupiat Paitot, a new regional Alaska Native organization.

Other Alaska Native organizations followed in short order. In 1962 the Tanana Chiefs Conference reorganized to deal primarily with land rights and other problems. During the next few years, Alaska Natives formed several new regional organizations, such as the Bristol Bay Native Association, primarily to press for a land claims settlement. In October 1966, representatives of the newly-formed groups met in Anchorage to form an Alaska-wide Native organization, which formally organized the following spring as the Alaska Federation of Natives.

In response to a land freeze request by a thousand Alaska Natives from villages throughout western and southwestern Alaska, Interior Secretary Morris Udall in 1963 appointed a three-person Alaska Task Force on Native Affairs. The task force's report, issued later that year, urged the conveyance of 160-acre tracts to individuals for homes, fish camps, or hunting sites, the withdrawal of small acreages in and around villages, and the designation of areas for Alaska Native use (but not ownership) for traditional food-gathering activities. Alaska Natives, with the assistance of the Association on American Indian Affairs, flatly opposed the task force's recommendations and successfully fought their implementation. They lobbied the congressional delegation for a more favorable land claims settlement.

The land claims issue crystallized on December 1, 1966, when Secretary Udall, by the first of a series of executive orders, imposed a freeze on land that had been claimed by various Alaska Native groups. Udall acted in response to a request from the newly-formed Alaska Federation of Natives. The federation had protested to the secretary after the state of Alaska, having gained tentative approval to the ownership of hundreds of thousand of acres of North Slope land, announced plans to sell potentially lucrative oil and gas leases for those properties. What was "frozen" in the first executive order was potential oil-bearing acreage near Point Hope. Commercially-viable quantities of North Slope oil and gas, at this time, had not yet been discovered, but drilling rigs had been moved to other North Slope properties and geologists were hopeful of locating new deposits.

Because of Udall's action, which was soon applied to other North Slope tracts and extended to the remainder of the state's unreserved lands in August 1967, neither the state nor any private entities could secure title to any land that was subject to Alaska Native claims until Congress resolved the issue. Alaska Natives by this time had already claimed title to large tracts in western and southwestern Alaska, and within a few months of Udall's action they had filed claims for some 380,000,000 acres, approximately Alaska's entire land area. The state of Alaska, whose land selections the freeze had halted, protested the Secretary's action. The land freeze remained, however, until Congress was able to resolve the issue through appropriate legislation.

Famous Alaskans: Walter Hickel

Walter J. Hickel served as governor of Alaska, 1966–1969 and 1990–1994, and also as U.S. secretary of the interior, 1969–1970. Born 1919 in Claflin, Kansas, Hickel came to Alaska in 1940 and worked as a bartender, carpenter, and developer. During the 1950s he played a major role in the fight to get 103 million acres included in Alaska's statehood land entitlement, while developing hotels, housing, and shopping centers in Anchorage, Fairbanks, and Seward. During the 1960s, as the state's second governor, he pushed to open Prudhoe Bay to oil development and for a road to the oil known as "Hickel's Highway" that failed. As a businessman, he built the Hotel Captain Cook, which is today one of the largest individually-owned hotels in the world. He was named Alaskan of the year in 1969. Appointed secretary of the interior by President Nixon, Hickel sharply criticized (May 1970) President Nixon's hostility to student anti-war demonstrators. In the fall, relations between the two men eventually deteriorated until Hickel was forced to resign. In 1990 he was again elected governor. In his second term he settled the Exxon Valdez lawsuits, and the billion-dollar fund collected was used to buy land and support science in Prince William Sound, Kachemak Bay, and on Kodiak and Afognak Islands. He is the author of *Who Owns America?* (1971).

Sunset clouds at Camp Denali

It should be noted, however, that Udall's executive orders left one important area of the state relatively unaffected. By the mid-1920s in southeastern Alaska, the federal government had already withdrawn the overwhelming preponderance of land; either for the Tongass National Forest or the Glacier Bay National Monument. Because this state of affairs gave Alaska Natives few opportunities to acquire their own acreage, Congress had first addressed land claim issues in the Tlingit and Haida Jurisdictional Act, passed on June 15, 1935. That act authorized a central committee of Alaska Natives in that region to bring suit in the U.S. Court of Claims to compensate them for federal lands from which aboriginal title had been usurped. In response, William Paul and other lawyers representing the Alaska Native Brotherhood (ANB) filed a thirty five million dollar suit "for the value of the land, hunting and fishing rights taken without compensation." But other factors intervened, sidelining the lawsuit, and in 1941 the ANB formed a separate entity, soon to be called the Central Council of Tlingit and Haida Indians of Alaska, to take up the cause. James Curry filed the case itself in 1947. After many delays, the Court of Claims decided on October 7, 1959, that the Tlingits and Haidas had established aboriginal title to six designated areas. But it took another nine years, until January 19, 1968, for the court to award the Tlingit and Haida Indians of Alaska 7.5 million in monetary damages. Although the court awarded the plaintiffs less than one-fourth of the amount they had originally requested, an amount that Central Council president John Borbridge judged to be grossly inadequate, it also concluded that Indian title to more than 2.6 million acres of land in southeastern Alaska had not been extinguished. Eighteen months later, Congress passed a law that authorized the Tlingit and Haida Central Council to manage the proceeds of the judgment fund for the benefit of the Tlingit and Haida Indians.

The stakes involved in the land-claims controversy rose dramatically in late 1967 and early 1968 when oil, in massive quantities, was discovered on the North Slope. The State of Alaska owned or had selected most if not all of the land above the underground oil reservoirs. Further testing showed that the Prudhoe Bay field, in one geologist's opinion, was "almost certainly of Middle-Eastern proportions." Optimism about the field's potential ran to such heights that a state oil-lease sale, held in Anchorage in September 1969, brought in more than $900 million in bonus bids. The rush was on.

But the oil, valuable as it was, benefited no one unless it could reach outside markets. It was in late 1969 that the TAPS oil-company consortium applied to the Interior Department for a permit to construct a hot-oil pipeline from Prudhoe Bay to the port of Valdez on ice-free Prince William Sound.

Interior Department approval was necessary because the proposed pipeline right-of-way and the proposed North Slope haul road crossed hundreds of miles of federal lands. Secretary Hickel, well aware of the land claims controversy, favored the pipeline, and in early March 1970 he was on the verge of issuing a permit for construction of the haul road. But on March 9, five Alaska Native villages, one of which was Stevens Village, sued in district court to prevent the permit from being issued, citing claims to the pipeline and road rights-of-way. In response to that suit a temporary injunction was issued against the project until the lands issue could be resolved.

Congress had already been grappling with the land claims issue for more than three years. The issue had been the subject of at least one task force, a Federal Field Committee report, an Interior Department proposal, several congressional bills, and legislative hearings. But opposition from mining and sportsmen's groups, plus the widely divergent views of various key players, slowed progress toward a mutually acceptable solution. Oil was still a powerful incentive, however, and oil companies came to lobby for a resolution to the lands impasse; the movement toward a final bill gained new momentum.

The stage was set for Congress to act. The path toward a land claims bill would be long and tortuous, and a final bill, the Alaska Native Claims Settlement Act (ANCSA), would not emerge until December 1971.

ALASKA NATIVE CLAIMS SETTLEMENT ACT

Early in 1971, the prospects for the bill looked bleak. But in April, President Richard Nixon presented a special message to Congress that called for a forty million-acre land entitlement and a $1 billion compensation package; that same month, Chairman Henry "Scoop" Jackson of the Senate Interior Committee submitted a revised bill co-sponsored by Alaska's two newly-minted senators, Mike Gravel and Ted Stevens. Attention then shifted to a House subcommittee, which sent out its version in early August, and on October 20, the entire House passed a land claims bill.

In early November, the Senate overwhelmingly passed a bill that differed significantly from the House's version. The House-Senate conference committee sifted through these differences and reached a compromise on the legislation in early December.

Famous Alaskans: Robert Atwood

"Bob" Atwood was a long time fixture on the Alaska scene as the publisher of *The Anchorage Times* for over fifty years. He was a leader in Alaska's fight for statehood and in an attempt to move the capital from Juneau closer to Anchorage. Atwood championed the Alaska Native Land Claims Settlement, Prudhoe Bay and the Trans-Alaska Pipeline, development of Cook Inlet and the Naval Petroleum Reserve, and most recently the opening of ANWR. Atwood died Jan. 10, 1997, at the age of 89. A state office building in Anchorage is named the Robert B. Atwood Building.

That compromise, which called for a $962.5 million cash payment, a 40 million-acre land conveyance, and numerous other provisions, gained passage in both legislative bodies. President Nixon then signed the Alaska Native Claims Settlement Act (ANCSA) on December 18, 1971. ANCSA was the result of more than a decade of struggle by Alaska Natives to receive federal and state recognition of claims to land they had lived on for thousands of years. Instrumental in the land claims movement was the creation of the *Tundra Times* in 1962. This newspaper was the first publication that reached all Alaska Natives. As a method for spreading of information, it greatly increased Alaska Native participation in politics by raising awareness of issues impacting their lives.

The passing of ANCSA on December 18, 1971, granted Alaska Natives forty million acres and $962.5 million, creating twelve regional corporations to manage the funds. To be eligible for shares one had to be one-quarter Alaska Native. The act issued one hundred shares of stock per qualifying member. The final version of ANCSA extinguished Alaska Native claims to almost all of Alaska in exchange for the compensation. Of the latter, $462.5 million was to come from the federal treasury and the rest from oil revenue-sharing. Of the approximately 80,000 Alaska Natives enrolled under ANCSA, those living in villages, approximately two-thirds of the total, would receive 100 shares in both a village and a regional corporation. The remaining third would be "at large" shareholders with 100 shares in a regional corporation plus additional rights to revenue from regional mineral and timber resources. The twelve regional corporations within the state would administer the settlement. A thirteenth corporation composed of Alaska Natives who had left the state would receive monies but not land.

Along with cash compensation, these corporations could also earn income from their investments. However, the drafting of the bill did not clarify whether the corporations were expected to redistribute the proceeds from their investment income to their shareholders or could keep them for further investment instead. A shared wealth provision of the act stipulated that 70 percent of the income received by regional corporations from their resources were to be shared annually with the other corporations. To protect the land, no Alaska Native corporate shares could be sold to non-Alaska Natives for 20 years—until 1991—at which time all special restrictions would be removed. Then, non-Alaska Natives would be eligible to become shareholders, lands would be liable for taxation by the state, and the regional corporations could be open to the possibility of hostile takeovers.

Under the supervision of the regional corporations, village-level corporations would also select lands and administer local monies received under the Settlement Act. Although village corporations could choose to be non-profit entities, all selected the profit-making category.

President Nixon's signature on ANCSA completely transformed the relationship between the native peoples of Alaska and the land. No longer was ownership directly linked to Alaska Native government. Instead, by conveying land title to the twelve regional and 200 local village corporations chartered under the laws of the state of

Alaska, the act bypassed all ties to traditional governments. Alaska Natives whose earlier use and occupancy had made them owners of shared land now became shareholders in corporate-owned land. At the time of passage, most Alaska Natives were unaware of the complexities of the bill, but looked forward to having their own land and using the additional monies to improve their low standard of living.

The Alaska Federation of Natives was enthusiastic about the large settlement and felt they had achieved a considerable victory under highly adverse conditions. The limitations in the bill stemmed primarily from pressures placed on them by the government and the petroleum industry, forcing them to make compromises not of their choosing. They also saw the corporate solution both as a way to remove themselves from the bureaucratic yoke of the Bureau of Indian Affairs and as a new tool in the struggle to maintain their culture.

Not all, however, took an optimistic view. Critics feared that eventually the regional corporations could become conduits for larger multi-national corporations, enabling the latter to take land and resources held by Alaska Natives. Loss of this land would then speed up the destruction of Alaska Native culture and the rise of new class divisions mirroring those of the larger society. By these means, the government would finally achieve its long term goal of assimilating Alaska Natives into the larger mainstream. As summed up by Fred Bigjim, an Inupiat educator from Nome, "What is happening to Native people in Alaska is not a new story; it is a new chapter in an old story."

Still, whether one supported the bill or opposed it, all agreed that the implications of the land claims settlement for Alaska Natives were profound. Given the discovery of oil at Prudhoe Bay, even more pronounced changes were to occur on the North Slope. Due to this circumstance, the Inupiat and other Alaska Natives were able to create a unique development strategy—one which combined elements of both adaptation and resistance to the steadily mounting pressures impinging on them from what they had formerly referred to as the world "outside."

Since its passage in 1971, ANCSA has continued to make headlines. There have been several amend-ments to the act, and other aspects of it have spurred debate for years.

A Special Relationship

Thomas Berger is one of Canada's foremost advocates of Native American rights and a former member of the British Columbia Supreme Court. His book, *Village Journey* (1985), is a result of a commission he was given by the Inuit Circumpolar Conference and the World Council of Indigenous Peoples to review the Alaska Native Claims Settlement Act. The following reflects some of the misunderstandings he encountered from non-Alaska Natives concerning governmental and land issues.

Some person's are skeptical of the Natives' claim to a special attachment to their land. They are worried by the fact that the Native people believe in self-determination and a just settlement of their land claims, rather than letting themselves be quietly assimilated. At the other extreme, there are persons who romanticize the Natives, trying to discover in them qualities lost by urban residents, and are dismayed when Natives do not conform to an idealized image.

The government made major amendments to ANCSA in 1976, 1987, 1998, and 2000. The 1976 amendments created the 13th regional corporation for Alaska Natives living out-of-state. The amendments made in 1987 are known as the "1991 amendments" because they were made to prevent changes that were supposed to be implemented twenty years after ANCSA was signed into law. They provide protection for Alaska Native corporations in the form of tax relief, stock restrictions (the stock would not go public), and stock options and benefits (extensions to include Alaska Natives born after 1971). In 1998 the Land Bank Protection Act made clarifications concerning land provisions held by Alaska Native corporations. Finally, in the year 2000, an amendment passed allowing stock to be given as gifts to adopted-out relatives.

ANCSA is often blamed as the cause of both the native subsistence rights and the oil debates. When ANCSA was written in 1971, it extinguished aboriginal hunting and fishing rights, but did not make any special provisions for natives who continued to depend on traditional subsistence lifestyles. Instead, it stated that Alaska Native subsistence would be protected by the State of

Alaska and the U.S. Department of the Interior. As we shall see, provisions for subsistence were later added in 1980 in the Alaska National Interest Lands Conservation Act (ANILCA). ANCSA was also said to have paved the way for the Trans-Alaska Pipeline, thereby expanding the opportunity for more drilling and oil production. An amendment that the Alaska Natives have pushed to implement since the passage of the bill is a two percent revenue sharing provision from federally developed resources. Alaska Natives proposed this provision before the passage of ANCSA and it continues to be debated. Today, the debate around ANCSA is far from settled. Many wonder whether or not the act has been a just solution for Alaska Natives, and the settlement continues to be an issue that affects every Alaskan today. But in the early 1970s, ANCSA clearly was a crucial step toward making it possible for the Alaska Pipeline to move forward.

The Pipeline

For some Alaskans the Alaska Pipeline was symbolic of the beginning of the end of the last frontier wilderness of Alaska. In 1973 the Supreme Court ruled in favor of the oil companies and created a "right of way" for the pipeline. In 1974 construction of the pipeline began, launching a new boom in the state's boom-and-bust cycle. Valdez went from 1,200 to 8,000 in population. Jobs were available in Fairbanks working on the pipeline for $1,200 a week. After an oil embargo in the 1970s, the world's largest construction companies rushed north to build the 800-mile, $8 billion Trans-Alaska Pipeline. The 70,000 men and women who built the pipeline saw it as a chance to find a new life, or to escape an old one. The three-year boom was like none ever seen in Alaska, surpassing even the Gold Rush for social and economic upheaval.

Many thousands migrated north seeking fat pipeline paychecks for "seven 12s"—working seven days a week, twelve hours a day. But with the avalanche of money came trouble with drugs, prostitution, and gambling. Long lines were found everywhere, and the cost of living soared, as did the real estate and rental markets.

The pipeline's designer, builder, and operator was now Alyeska Pipeline Service Company, a consortium of British

View west from Primrose Ridge, Denali National Park

Petroleum, ARCO, Exxon, Hess, Phillips, and Unocal. Along its 800-mile length most of the pipeline is not buried due to permafrost problems. Thus the pipeline uses a system of supports (some 78,000 of them) sixty feet apart, arranged in a zigzag pattern. There are more than 800 river and stream crossings along the route. The pipeline is buried where soil conditions allowed, and insulated and jacketed where the pipe is above ground. The pipeline also includes 151 stop-flow valves along its route. The pipe itself was especially manufactured with zinc anodes to prevent corrosion. It is 48 inches in diameter and approximately one-half inch thick. Before construction, lengths of 40 to 60 feet were brought to Alaska and stored in various areas around the state until the legal issues could be resolved. In 1977 oil began to flow, running over one million barrels a day by 1978.

During the 1990s the project reached the 10-billion barrel mark for oil sent through the pipeline since its inception. The terminal of the line is in Valdez at a 1,000 acre site that has eighteen tanks, capable together of storing over nine million barrels.

ANILCA

Spanning three administrations and five sessions of Congress, what had been called the Alaska Lands Bill was enacted into law on December 2, 1980, as the Alaska National Interest Lands Conservation Act (ANILCA). Congress and various administrations spent nearly nine years, from 1971 to 1980, developing this legislation. As the agency most heavily involved with administering federal lands, the Department of the Interior had the responsibility to propose and implement most of ANILCA. However, a number of different federal agencies, as well as the state of Alaska, Alaska Native groups, and other interested organizations and individuals also had a hand in the overall process.

The origins of ANILCA date back to the late 1950s when the Alaska Statehood Act of 1958 authorized the newly established state to select, over time, 104 million acres from the total land area of 375 million acres as an economic base for the new state.

When Congress passed ANSCA in 1971, Alaska Natives were able to select approximately 44 million acres of federal

Land, Work and Oil in Alaska

Barry Lopez has been hailed as a "master nature writer" by the *New York Times Book Review*, and in *Arctic Dreams* (1986), based on 15 trips to the North Country, he reveals his ambivalence toward Alaskan development.

> … my feelings were what they had been at Prudhoe Bay—a mixture of fascination at the sophistication of the technology; sadness born out of dismalness of life for so many of the men employed here, which no amount of red velour, free arcade games, and open snack bars can erase; and misgiving at the sullen, dismissive attitude taken toward the land, the violent way in which it is addressed.

land in Alaska. The act also afforded the secre-tary of interior the opportunity to designate new natural, cultural, recreational, and wildlife areas in the nation. ANCSA authorized the secretary to withdraw 80 million acres of land to be studied for possible additions to the National Park, national Wildlife Refuge, national Wild and Scenic Rivers, and the National Forest Systems.

On December 1, 1978, the president withdrew by proclamation over 55 million acres of Alaskan land and designated them as national monuments to be administered by the National Park Service, the U.S. Fish and Wildlife Service, and the U.S. Forest Service. The secretary of interior, on February 12, 1980, withdrew 40 million acres of land for a period of 20 years. Finally, in the last days of the 96th Congress, on December 2, 1980, President Carter signed ANILCA after extensive debate and final passage by Congress.

ANILCA may be one of the most significant land conservation measures in the history of the United States. The statute protected over 100 million acres of federal lands in Alaska, doubling the size of the country's national park and refuge systems and tripling the amount of land designated as wilderness. ANILCA expanded the national park system in Alaska by over 43 million acres, creating 10 new national parks and increasing the acreage of three existing units.

From the time it was introduced in the U.S. House of Representatives in 1977 until it was enacted in 1980, the ANILCA legislation underwent a dozen versions. The final act was a compromise that reflected the struggle for balance

Alaska Communities:
Oil in Valdez and Barrow

Valdez is located on the north shore of Port Valdez, a deep water fjord in Prince William Sound, 305 road miles east of Anchorage and 364 road miles south of Fairbanks. It is the southern terminus of the trans-Alaska oil Pipeline. Don Salvador Fidalgo named the Port of Valdez in 1790 for the celebrated Spanish naval officer Antonio Valdes y Basan. Due to its excellent ice-free port, a town developed in 1898 as a debarkation point for men seeking a route to the Eagle Mining District and the Klondike gold fields. Valdez soon became the supply center of its own gold mining region. The U.S. Army established Fort Liscum in 1900 and constructed a sled and wagon road to Fort Egbert in Eagle. The Alaska Road Commission further developed the road for automobile travel to Fairbanks, completing it by the early 1920s. A slide of unstable submerged land during the 1964 earthquake destroyed the original city waterfront, killing several residents. The community rebuilt on a more stable bedrock foundation four miles to the west. During the 1970s, construction of the Trans-Alaska oil pipeline terminal and other cargo transportation facilities brought rapid growth to Valdez. In March 1989, it was also the center for the massive oil-spill cleanup after the "Exxon Valdez" disaster, and in a few short days, the population of the town tripled with scientists and workers trying to assist the work.

Barrow, the northernmost community in North America, is located on the Chukchi Sea coast, ten miles south of Point Barrow from which it takes its name. It lies 725 air miles from Anchorage. Point Barrow was named for Sir John Barrow, 2nd Secretary of the British Admiralty. Barrow's Inupiaq name is Ukpeagvik, meaning "place where owls are hunted." In 1881 the U.S. Army established a meteorological and magnetic research station near the town. The Cape Smythe Whaling and Trading Station came here in 1893, along with a Presbyterian Church in 1899 and a post office in 1901. Exploration of the Naval Petroleum Reserve Number 4 began in 1946. The Naval Arctic Research Laboratory, 3 miles north of Barrow, soon followed. The city incorporated in 1958. Formation of the North Slope Borough in 1972, the Arctic Slope Regional Corporation, and construction of the Prudhoe Bay oil fields and Trans-Alaska Pipeline have each contributed to the development of Barrow. Today, revenues from the North Slope oil fields fund borough-wide services. Sixty-four percent of the population are Alaska Native or part native with the majority of residents being Inupiat. Traditional marine mammal hunts and other subsistence practices are still an active part of the culture as Bowhead, gray, killer and beluga whales migrate near Barrow each summer.

between development and conservation of public lands in Alaska. However, battles are still being waged in Congress and the courts over the interpretation of key provisions.

In addition to controversy between development and environmental interests, ANILCA incited debates about reconciling Alaska Native and rural lifestyles with the changing demographics and technologies in the state. Questions about access were central to this debate: Where? For what purpose? By what means? In order to pass ANILCA, the opposing parties made compromises and left many tough questions to be answered later. Now increases in population, new technologies, and new motorized uses are tipping the balance in favor of development. Both Congress and the courts are considering new interpretations of access provisions designed to facilitate commercial tourism in wilderness parks. One prime example of the difficult issues related to ANILCA and subsistence can be found in the efforts of one woman who just "wanted to catch fish."

KATIE JOHN

The case of *Katie John vs. the United States of America*, informally referred to as the Katie John case, had its origin in a longstanding quarrel over fishing rights. A village located along the banks of the silty Copper River, at the confluence of a clearwater stream, was the location of a fish camp where Alaska Natives had harvested sockeye salmon each summer for hundreds of years. After World War II, the village's residents resettled in an area more accessible to the newly-developed highway system, but they still used the Copper River fish camp through the early 1960s.

In 1964, however, the Alaska Board of Fisheries and Game shut down subsistence fishing that used nets and fishwheels at the fish camps. Fisheries managers did so because the Copper River, by this time, was supporting a wide array of commercial, sport, and personal-use fisheries, and state biologists thought that if Alaska Natives caught too many fish in certain upriver streams, it would have disastrous effects, both on the various downstream users and on the viability of certain salmon stocks. After that decision, the villagers used the site less often, and before long they had effectively abandoned it. Two years later, the land was set aside for the new 8.3-million acre Wrangell-St. Elias National Park.

Famous Alaskans: Ted Stevens

A member of the Senate for 34 years, Ted Stevens is Alaska's senior senator. Stevens' tenure in the Senate makes him the fifth most senior member among his colleagues, and first among Republicans. Stevens holds the position of senate president pro tempore. He is also the chairman of the Appropriations Committee, which is responsible for annually allocating more than a half-trillion dollars in federal funds among various government programs, agencies, and departments. Ted Stevens was born in Indianapolis on November 18, 1923. During World War II he was a pilot in the China-Burma-India theater, supporting the Flying Tigers of the 14th Air Force. He received two Distinguished Flying Crosses, two Air Medals, and the Yuan Hai medal awarded by the Republic of China. Following the war he graduated from UCLA and Harvard Law School and practiced law in Washington,D.C. In the early 1950's he moved to Alaska. He practiced law in Fairbanks, and subsequently was appointed U.S. Attorney in Fairbanks in 1953, a position he held for three years. He then transferred to Washington, D.C. in 1956 to work as legislative counsel and then as an assistant to the Secretary of the Interior Fred Seaton. In 1960 President Eisenhower appointed him solicitor (chief counsel) of the Department of the Interior. While in Washington, Stevens worked successfully for Alaska's and Hawaii's admissions to the Union. Upon returning to Alaska, Stevens practiced law in Anchorage. In 1964 voters elected him to the Alaska House of Representatives. In his second term in Alaska's legislature he was the House majority Leader. Following the death of Senator E.L. Bob Bartlett in December of 1968, then-Governor Walter Hickel appointed Stevens to fill the vacancy. Under Alaska law, Stevens had to stand for election in 1970 to complete Bartlett's term, which expired in 1972. Voters subsequently elected Stevens for a full term in 1972 and re-elected him in 1978, 1984, 1990, 1996 and 2002.

During the early 1970s a newly-established regional Alaska Native corporation, Ahtna, Inc., filed a 1,600-acre claim to the lands surrounding the old village. Three local Alaska Native residents (Katie John, Doris Charles, and Gene B. Henry) also filed claims to smaller parcels in and around the village. None made an immediate attempt to resettle in the area, but by the early 1980s, Katie John and Doris Charles, both elders, began talking about going back to the former village site.

In 1984 the Alaska Board of Fisheries voted 5 to 2 against the claims and suggested instead that the claimants fish at various downstream sites. The elders persisted. Katie John

Fish wheels

noted, "We're Indian people and I don't like park rangers or game wardens coming in here telling us what to do like they own everything. That makes me mad. I don't want to be on somebody else's land. I like to do my fishing on my own land right there." Hoping to gain fishing rights for herself and for her grandchildren as well, she began talks with the Boulder, Colorado-based Native American Rights Fund (NARF), which was opening an office in Anchorage, and in 1985 filed a lawsuit, *Katie John vs. State of Alaska*, against the State of Alaska in U.S. District Court, requesting that the residents' right to fish at the old village site be recognized. In 1987 the fish board, in response to the suit, relented and allowed locals with permits to harvest a maximum of 1,000 sockeye salmon. The following year, the board further relaxed its rules and eliminated the salmon quota.

But the women pressed on, still feeling that the government was curtailing their rights, and they filed another district court suit to allow continuous fishing, without the need for permits. The plaintiffs were victorious in court, and by that fall they had won the right to a subsistence fishery that was continuously open from June 23 through October 1. Five special sessions and several governors later, the Alaska legislature had yet to comply with federal law. In August 2001 Governor Knowles dropped the state's appeal, and fisheries management of federal lands and waters, and the subsistence activities therein, are presently in the control of the federal government.

THE PERMANENT FUND

Clearly the impact of pulling oil out of the ground in the Arctic created far ranging difficulties with which Alaskans continue to cope. But one of Alaskan's favorite results was the creation of a fund from which they could individually derive benefits.

A state constitutional amendment approved by Alaska voters in 1976 established the Permanent Fund. Under this amendment, the state would invest at least twenty-five percent of certain mineral revenues, paid to the state for deposit into a public savings account, to benefit current and future generations of Alaskans. It was one of the most interesting public policy decisions Alaskans have made since statehood.

Essentially a trust fund for all residents, money in the principal must be invested and cannot be spent without the vote of the people. In 1980 the legislature established a Permanent Fund dividend payment program that provides distribution of about one-half of the fund's earnings among the citizens of Alaska. Originally, eligible residents were to receive a fifty dollar dividend for each year of residence since 1959. The U.S. Supreme Court declared the 1980 program unconstitutional on the grounds that it discriminated against short-term residents, and in 1982 a new state program was signed into law.

Under the new plan, the state paid an initial one thousand dollar dividend to residents who had lived in Alaska for at least six months prior to applying. Since then the state has paid dividends each year to established residents who apply by March 31. The amount is not fixed and has ranged from several hundred dollars to nearly two thousand dollars. The exact amount is figured by adding together the fund's net income for the last five years, multiplying that number by twenty-one percent and dividing that number in half. This half is then distributed in equal shares to those who are eligible to receive the dividend.

If Alaska's Permanent Fund were a Fortune 500 company, it would rank in the top five percent of U.S. corporations in terms of net income. It is one of the fifty largest pools of money in the country, and the only one that pays dividends to residents. Through 2002, the fund has earned approximately $25 billion.

EXXON VALDEZ DISASTER

While the fund may be the darling of Alaskans in terms of the oil industry, the spilling of oil in Prince William Sound brought home to many the potential risks of transporting oil out of the state.

The grounding of the *Exxon Valdez* oil tanker on March 24, 1989, near the southern terminal of the Trans-Alaska Pipeline System in Prince William Sound shocked many Americans and Alaskans, especially when news stations broadcast images of dead and dying animals and once-pristine waters and beaches marred by huge quantities of oil. Damage at the time included an estimated 300,000 to 645,000 dead seabirds, 4,000 to 6,000 dead marine mammals, and one hundred million dollars in other losses, including runs of salmon. Scientific disagreement persists over the legacy of the spill, but it certainly brought Alaska once again to national attention, and it serves as a watershed event that environmentalists continue to cite in their opposition to the oil industry.

On March 23, 1989, the *Exxon Valdez* arrived at berth

five of the Alyeska Marine Terminal to load a cargo of Alaska North Slope crude oil. Once the cargo was on board, the chief mate directed the third mate to go to the bridge and test the navigation equipment and the deck force to begin securing the decks for sea. With the last mooring line removed, the pilot steered the vessel away from the berth with the assistance of two tugs. What began as a normal trip would end up anything but that as events progressed.

On March 24, at 12:03 A.M., about twenty-five miles from the pipeline terminal at Valdez, the *Exxon Valdez* ran aground on Bligh Reef. Eight of the eleven cargo tanks ruptured and the North Slope crude oil gushed from the tanker into the waters of Prince William Sound. The state and federal governments estimate that 250,000 to 260,000 barrels of North Slope crude oil, or eleven million U.S. gallons, spilled from the tanker. Shortly before the collision, the captain had changed course, veering from the normal shipping lanes to avoid icebergs. At the time the tanker hit the reef, however, the third mate was piloting the vessel.

The state's response effort began with the Valdez District Office manager from the Alaska Department of Environmental Conservation, who was notified of the spill by Alyeska at 1:05 A.M. Then began a chain reaction of notification that called up responders from Anchorage, Wasilla, and Juneau. Within 24 to 30 hours more than thirty people in Valdez were setting up the aerial surveillance, general monitoring, computer mapping, and other programs that would function in one form or another for the better part of three years.

By 8:30 A.M. the magnitude of the spill was becoming clear. Governor Steve Cowper had learned of the spill about an hour earlier, from a reporter who was conducting an early-morning interview with the governor in his hometown of Fairbanks. Not pleased by the slow and inadequate response, Cowper immediately made arrangements to get to Valdez. After visiting the tanker, Cowper appeared at a community meeting and press conference at the Valdez civic center. Exxon's chief executive officer had spoken to the group earlier, noting that Exxon would be moving quickly to use dispersants on the growing slick. This made the public, especially the fishing community, uncomfortable.

What was becoming increasingly clear to the Alaska public was that no one was fully prepared to deal with a spill of this magnitude. There was not enough equipment, and technology did not provide a broad range of options. The spill overwhelmed mechanical capabilities, and the chemical possibilities had severe limitations. Burning worked for a little while, but the window of opportunity closed quickly as the oil slick gained water. The conditions were marginal for dispersants, regardless of the risks the chemicals presented.

The public was outraged. The fishing community, especially in Cordova, was suddenly and unexpectedly confronted with the fact that industry and government either did not know or did not fully explain the fragility of the safety-net underneath the Trans-Alaska Oil Pipeline System and the tankers that cruised almost daily through Prince William Sound.

The weather put a quick end to the initial response. Late on Easter Sunday, March 26, a severe, late-winter storm approached the Sound. Between Sunday and early Monday morning, the wind blew gusts up to 70 miles per hour. Flight operations were seriously curtailed. Observers noted that the oil was no longer in a single, compact slick. Breakaway patches and thick patches of oil and mousse hit shorelines. Oil stretched as far as 40 miles south-southwest of the grounding site. Skimmers and other response vessels had retreated into more sheltered areas, away from the oil, to wait out the weather.

The spill was out of control. Throughout the rest of March and most of April, various configurations of skimmers and boom and barges would attempt on-the-water cleanup, but actual recovery of oil was extremely low compared with the volume of the spill. By March 30, a week after the spill, various estimates of recovery hovered around 5,000 barrels, which was only about two percent of what was spilled.

After the Easter storm, the effectiveness of on-the-water recovery could not really be judged in a cumulative sense. Oil patches spread widely throughout the western Sound and, as the weeks went by, to the Kenai Peninsula and the Kodiak archipelago. Recovery varied from site to site, and success could most realistically be judged against a specific threat to a specific resource or shoreline. As a whole, on-the-water recovery was hampered by weathering oil, long distances, equipment limitations, storage limitations, and spotting capability. By the first week of May, no real effort remained to contain and collect free-floating oil.

The agencies and responders turned to several major tasks: planning and coordination for shoreline cleanup, defensive booming, especially at the Prince William Sound hatcheries, and stabilizing the *Exxon Valdez* and getting the remaining one million barrels of oil off the ship.

The spill eventually covered a 300-mile area noted for its salmon and herring runs. Oil from the tanker was also found later to have fouled beaches on the Alaska Peninsula, some 600 miles from the spill site. Eventually, clean-up efforts involved armies of cleaning crews who used techniques ranging from washing rocks by hand to using highly pressurized hot water. Crews also used bio-remediation, which involved applying fertilizer to oiled shorelines to accelerate oil-metabolizing bacteria. Clean-up efforts continued into 1992.

The grounding of the *Exxon Valdez* prompted both the state and federal governments to significantly alter the laws, regulations, and strategies relating to oil pollution. At the state level, between April 1989 and May 1990 the Alaska Legislature passed a dozen new laws dealing with prevention, response, and oversight. Among the most significant of these was a law boosting the state's emergency oil and hazardous substance response fund to $50 million— 50 times what the fund had contained at the time of the spill. The legislature also mandated a complete rewrite of the state's oil spill prevention, response, and contingency planning regulations, and increased both liability and penalties for polluters. The fund has since become the state's primary source for spill response planning and development, including funding for a new special division of the Department of Environmental Conservation dedicated solely to oil and hazardous substance spill issues.

Changes at the federal level came together in the Oil Pollution Act of 1990, which became law less than 18 months after the initial grounding of the Exxon tanker. This was especially significant, since the legislation had been languishing in various congressional committees for nearly 15 years. Like the state's measures, the federal act raised liability limits, mandated new prevention measures, and set up a new federal response fund.

Alaskans filed more than 29,000 claims for damages related to the oil spill. Many of them were claims from fishermen, canneries, Alaska Native groups, and business owners in the affected region. Alaska sued Exxon and the Alyeska Pipeline Service Company in 1989, and then Exxon countersued the state, claiming their officials had hampered clean-up efforts. In 1991 the two parties reached a compromise, with Exxon paying over one billion dollars to state and federal governments. In 1994 Exxon agreed to pay Alaska Natives in the spill area twenty million dollars for the loss of subsistence hunting.

Also in 1994, a jury awarded commercial fishermen $286 million in damages and ordered Exxon to pay a whopping five billion dollars in damages. Litigation continues on this aspect of the settlement to the current day, as Exxon continues to appeal the award.

THE ARCTIC NATIONAL WILDLIFE REFUGE

An executive order created the Arctic National Wildlife Refuge (ANWR) in northeastern Alaska in 1960 at the urging of environmental groups who wanted to see a section of Alaska set aside from any future development.

ANWR is an area rich in fauna, flora, and commercial oil potential. Shortages of gasoline and natural gas and resulting increased prices have renewed calls for ANWR development, debated now for over 40 years. Current law forbids energy leasing in the refuge, but President George W. Bush has included drilling in the refuge as a major feature of his proposed energy plan. Few locations stir as much industry interest as the northern portion of ANWR.

ANWR consists of 19 million acres in northeast Alaska. It is administered by the Fish and Wildlife Service (FWS) in the Department of the Interior (DOI). Its 1.5 million acre coastal plain is currently one of the most promising U.S. onshore oil and gas prospects. Together, the fields on this federal land could hold as much economically recoverable oil as the giant field at Prudhoe Bay, found in 1967 on the state-owned portion of the coastal plain west of ANWR, now estimated at 13 billion barrels. At the same time, the refuge, and especially the coastal plain, is home to a wide variety of plants and animals. The presence of caribou, polar bears, grizzly bears, wolves, migratory birds, and many other species in a nearly undisturbed state has led some to call the area "America's Serengeti." The refuge and two neighboring parks in Canada have been proposed for an international park, and international treaties protect several species found in the area, including polar bears, caribou, migratory birds, and whales.

Development proponents argue that ANWR oil would reduce U.S. energy markets' exposure to recurring crises in the Middle East. It could also boost North Slope oil production and the economic viability of the TransAlaska Pipeline System enhancing job creation. Proponents maintain that ANWR oil could be developed with minimal environmental harm using the latest techniques. But opponents argue that any intrusion on this ecosystem cannot be justified on any terms. They also maintain that the oil found would provide little energy security and could be replaced by cost-effective alternatives.

Early efforts to allow development of the coastal plain of the ANWR ended with the *Exxon Valdez* oil spill in 1989, though the 1990-91 crisis in the Persian Gulf bolstered development arguments temporarily. In May 1998, the U.S. Geological Survey released new estimates for oil in the refuge. If at least one field big enough to make development worthwhile can be found, the agency estimates that there is a 95 percent chance that eleven billion barrels or more would be present. However, not all oil present could be recovered: The agency estimates a 95 percent chance that two billion barrels or more would be economically recoverable at a market price of twenty-four dollars per barrel, and a five percent chance that 9.4 billion barrels or more would be economically recoverable at the same price. The amount actually recovered would vary with several factors, including cost and market prices for oil. The higher the price, the larger the economically recoverable amount will be. The Energy Information Administration assumes 7 to 12 years from approval to first production.

The main legislative options include authorizing development, designating the coastal area in ANWR as wilderness, which, under current law, usually ends the potential for development, or taking no action. This third choice also prevents development, since current law requires congressional action for oil development to occur. Budgetary considerations, the increased price of oil, and maintenance of the investment in the Alaskan oil infrastructure are key considerations in the renewed interest in energy development in ANWR. As of this writing the refuge is still closed to drilling despite efforts of the Bush Administration. But the battle continues as President Bush vows not to give up on the issue. Certainly oil development will continue to be a hot debate in regard to Alaska and its economic future. But as oil revenues fall, officials are seeking other avenues for the state's economic stability, one of which is the past decade's large increase in tourism.

What will be the Future of Alaska's Wilderness?

Margaret Murie was the enabling force behind the Wilderness Act and the protection of the Arctic National Wildlife Refuge. She was known as the "Grandmother of the Conservation Movement." Murie was the first woman to graduate from the University of Alaska in 1924. Bill Clinton awarded the Presidential Medal of Freedom to Murie in 1998, for her work in protecting wilderness areas. The following shows her hopes for Alaska's future:

> The shining, comforting thought now is that the parks, the forests, the refuges, the wild rivers, are there... and my feeling about it all is that when the oil and the minerals have all been found and taken away, the one hundred million acres of national parks and refuges and wild rivers and forests will be the most beneficent treasure in the whole state. I would plead with all administrators: Please allow Alaska to be different, to be herself, to nourish our souls.

> —Margaret Murie
> *Wilderness Magazine*, 1984

TOURISM IN ALASKA

When we began our exploration of Alaska, we saw John Muir paddling his way through Glacier Bay. After Muir's experiences, he urged others to come and see what he had witnessed. Perhaps it is appropriate, then, that we end with a look at the tourist trade created by the natural beauty Muir described.

After the Klondike Gold Rush brought attention to Alaska, the region's travel and tourism industry was born. Steamship companies arranged trips by rail to Washington State and then cruises through the Inside Passage of Southeast Alaska. By 1890 some 5,000 tourists had visited Alaska. But it was the development of a modern tourism industry in the early 1970s that brought in millions of visitors in a "tourist rush" of sorts. Some travelers come by car or recreational vehicle via the Alaska Highway. Most arrived by air or sea. A state-owned ferry system called the Alaska Marine Highway linked Southeast Alaska to British Columbia and the state of Washington in the early 1960s.

The industry has exploded in Alaska in the past decade, with more than 500 cruises a summer now carting 750,000 people or more north from Seattle, San Francisco, and Vancouver. According to industry reports, cruise ships generate $595 million a year in spending in Alaska. The industry contributes to local renewal projects throughout the state and is fueling a shore-side boom in everything from whitewater rafting to rock climbing.

Disembarking passengers have sparked such an economic boom in Ketchikan, which lost its timber mill in 1997, that the community of 14,000 now sports nearly 40 jewelry stores. But Juneau residents complain of being bombarded by helicopters ferrying cruise passengers on "flight-seeing" day tours. Even cruise officials once expressed fear that Juneau's downtown had so many tourists it threatened to detract from the visitors' experience.

But the industry has labored under a public relations hangover since the late 1990s, when two cruise lines paid millions of dollars in penalties after illegally dumping waste or oily residue in Alaskan waters. Although the ships were exempt from the Clean Water Act, investigators in 2000 found that even treated discharges sometimes contained 10,000 times more bacteria than the Coast Guard normally allowed. The state has since developed the nation's strictest cruise-ship pollution laws.

The ships are still transforming Southeast Alaska's sputtering economy, however, and opening untrammeled lands that otherwise might have remained virtually unknown to outsiders. Cruise ships stopped in Ketchikan, for example, 538 times in 2002. Ten years ago, the number was 421.

Alaska Communities: Attractions in North Pole, Skagway, Talkeetna, and Homer

North Pole is located 14 miles southeast of Fairbanks on the Richardson Highway. In 1944 Bon Davis homesteaded this area. Dahl and Gaske Development Company later bought the Davis homestead, subdivided it, and named it North Pole, hoping to attract a toy manufacturer who would advertise products as being made there. Con Miller and his family subsequently developed the Santa Claus House. The city incorporated in 1953, and growth from Fairbanks and the nearby Eielson Air Force Base have increased development over the years. North Pole is renowned as the "home of Santa Claus." Children all over the world mail letters to North Pole at Christmas each year, and the Santa Claus House remains a year-round attraction.

Skagway is located 90 miles northeast of Juneau at the northernmost end of Lynn Canal, at the head of Taiya Inlet. It lies 108 road miles south of Whitehorse, just west of the Canadian border at British Columbia. "Skagua" was the Tlingit name, which means "the place where the north wind blows." Capt. William Moore and Skookum Jim, a Tlingit from the Carcross-Tagish area of the Yukon Territory, discovered the White Pass route into Interior Canada in June 1887. Capt. Moore and his son Bernard staked a claim and built a cabin on the waterfront in October 1887. They called the place "Mooresville." In July 1897 prospectors discovered gold in Klondike and the first boatload of prospectors landed. By October 1897, according to a Northwest Mounted Police Report, Skagway "had grown from a concourse of tents to a fair-sized town with well-laid-out streets and numerous frame buildings, stores, saloons, gambling houses, dance houses and a population of about 20,000." Five thousand stampeders alone landed in February 1898, according to customs office records. Gold seekers used two trails to reach the headwaters of the Yukon River: the 33-mile-long Chilkoot Trail which began at nearby Dyea and the 40-mile White Pass Trail which began at Skagway and paralleled the present-day route of the White Pass & Yukon Railway. Thousands of men carried supplies up the 33-mile Chilkoot Trail or took the 40-mile White Pass trail to Lake Bennett, where they built boats to float down the Yukon River to Dawson City and the gold fields, 500 miles distant. In 1898 the area gained a 14-mile, steam-operated tramway, which eased the burdens of those able to pay. Skagway became the first incorporated city in Alaska in 1900 with a population of 3,117, the second-largest settlement in Alaska. Tales of fortune seekers, lawlessness and Soapy Smith are legendary. Once the gold rush ended in 1900, Skagway might have become a ghost town if not for the White Pass and Yukon Railroad construction in 1898. The railroad was the first in Alaska and provided freight, fuel, and transportation to Whitehorse and served the Anvil Gold Mines in the Yukon. It employed many locals until 1982, when the mine closed. Construction of the Klondike Highway in 1979 gave Skagway a link to the Alaska Highway and state ferry connection to the Southeast. Skagway is predominantly a tourist community, with historical Tlingit influences. The city has restored its downtown buildings to reflect the history of the gold rush through the Chilkoot Pass.

Located at the junction of the Talkeetna and Susitna Rivers, Talkeetna lies 115 miles north of Anchorage at mile 226.7 of the Alaska Railroad. The paved Talkeetna Spur Road runs 14 miles east off the George Parks Highway, at Milepost 98.7. The Talkeetna and Chulitna Rivers join the Susitna River at Talkeetna, a Dena'ina (Tanaina) word meaning "river of plenty." Talkeetna was settled as a mining town and Alaska Commercial Co. trading post in 1896. A gold rush to the Susitna River brought prospectors to the area, and by 1910 Talkeetna was a riverboat steamer station, supplying miners and trappers in the Cache Creek, Iron Creek, and Broad Creek districts. In 1915 the Alaska Engineering Commission, who built the Alaska Railroad, chose Talkeetna as its headquarters, and the community population peaked near 1,000. World War I and completion of the railroad in 1919 dramatically decreased the population. Talkeetna has since developed as an aviation and supply base for Denali expeditions. Several of its old log buildings are now historical landmarks, and Talkeetna earned a place on the National Register of Historic Places in April 1993. State land disposals and homestead programs helped the community grow. Talkeetna is popular for its recreational fishing, hunting, boating, flightseeing, skiing and dog mushing. Local businesses also provide services to Denali climbers.

Homer is located on the north shore of Kachemak Bay on the southwestern edge of the Kenai Peninsula. The Homer Spit, a 4.5-mile long bar of gravel, extends from the Homer shoreline. It is 227 road miles south of Anchorage, at the southern-most point of the Sterling Highway. The Homer area has been home to Kenaitze Indians for thousands of years. In 1895 the U.S. Geological Survey arrived to study coal and gold resources, and prospectors bound for Hope and Sunrise disembarked at the Homer Spit. The community was named for Homer Pennock, a gold mining company promoter, who arrived in 1896 and built living quarters for his crew of 50 on the Spit. In 1899 Cook Inlet Coal Fields Company built a town and dock on the spit, a coal mine at Homer's Bluff Point, and a seven-mile-long railroad which carried the coal to the end of Homer Spit. Various coal mining operations remained until World War I, and settlers continued to trickle into the area, some to homestead in the 1930s and 40s, others to work in the canneries built to process Cook Inlet fish. Coal provided fuel for homes, and there is still an estimated 400 million tons of coal deposits in the vicinity of Homer. The city government incorporated in March 1964. After the Good Friday earthquake in 1964, the Homer Spit sunk approximately 4 to 6 feet and several buildings had to be relocated. While commercial and sport fishing are the center of its economic activity, Homer has a large community of artists. The Homer Jackpot Halibut Derby runs from May 1 through Labor Day each year. Homer is often called the "Halibut Capital of the World."

Alaskan Snakes

One of best books written about Alaska from an outsiders perspective was by noted naturalist writer John McPhee who chronicled his journey in the state in the book *Coming Into the Country* (1977). McPhee's wry humor can be found in the following:

> In a memo to all of us written many weeks ago, Pourchot listed, under 'optional personal equipment,' "Acrtic snakebite medicine." There are no snakes in Alaska. But what if a snake should unexpectedly appear? The serum in my pack is from Lynchburg, Tennessee.

Passenger growth is even greater. In 1993, Ketchikan saw 322,000 cruise ship passengers. In the 2003 season, it expects 757,000.

Once in Ketchikan, visitors take floatplanes to Misty Fjords National Monument to watch bears feed on salmon. They rent kayaks and go hiking, see Alaska Native dance performances, or visit a

Famous Alaskans: Sports Stars—
Boozer, Gomez, and Moe

Juneau's Carlos Boozer, born in 1981, started for the Juneau-Douglas High School before going on to Duke University and currently is one the Cleveland Cavaliers. He was a McDon-ald's All-American player in High Schools and at Duke he was on the ACC All-Rookie Team and a member of the 2001 NCAA championship team. He was drafted by the Cleveland Cavaliers in the 2nd round (35th overall) in 2002 and continues to improve and is receiving increased recognition for his play now with the Utah Jazz.

Scott Gomez was born in 1979 in Anchorage and was the only Hispanic NHL 1st-round draft pick (27th selection in 1998). He led his team with 51 assists and paced all rookies with 70 points and won Calder Trophy as NHL Rookie of the Year in 1998-99. He was part of the Stanley Cup with New Jersey Devils in 2000. He is noted for an eight-game scoring streak, November 12 to December 1, in 1998. He also co-led the team with 18 goals in 2000-01.

Tommy Moe was the 1994 Olympic gold medalist (Downhill) and silver medalist (Super-G) at Lillehammer, Norway. He was the first U.S. alpine skier to win two medals in the same Olympics and has been a three-time Olympian (1992 Albertville, 1994 Lillehammer, and 1998 Nagano). He is an avid outdoorsman after growing up in Montana and Alaska where he attended Glacier Creek Ski Academy as a teenager. He also runs backcountry ski expeditions and is considered by some to be one of the top free skiers in the world. The Tommy Moe Invitational Ski Race is held annually at Mt. Alyeska, Ski Resort south of Anchorage.

collection of totem poles. And they shop: Ketchikan, an isolated island, has seen retail sales jump from $21 million a decade ago to $69 million in 2002.

The industry's allure is so tempting that even the state's largest Tlingit community, in the town of Hoonah 40 miles from Juneau, recently worked out a deal to draw cruise ships with what tribal officials describe as a journey-through-time tour that will walk them through the history of Tlingit culture and lifestyle and the history of subsistence.

Over the past 250 years, Alaska has seen a series of boom-and-bust rushes to exploit resources such as fur, gold, copper, salmon, lumber, and oil. Many gathered the rewards of the land and sea and took pleasure in them somewhere else. Alaskans often see a recurring theme of neglect by federal authorities and exploitation by "outside interests." While that feeling can be exaggerated for various purposes, the fact remains that today, decades after becoming a state, much of Alaska's economic fate remains under control of the lower 48. Certainly, conflicts within Alaska between conservationists and developers, between state's rights and federal control, and between indigenous people and later comers, have colored much of its history. Some see Alaska as the last chance for America to "get it right" in terms of the environment and Native American rights. Perhaps so, but clearly the various constituents that make up the state of Alaska will do their best to hold on to their share.

Sources

Adams, Ben. *The Last Frontier, A Short History of Alaska*. New York: Hill and Wang, 1961.

Ackerman, Robert. *Ethnohistory in Southwestern Alaska and the Southern Yukon*. Lexington, KY: University of Kentucky Press, 1970.

Alaska Geographic Society. *Alaska's Oil, Gas, and Minerals Industry*. Edmonds, WA: Alaska Geographic Society, 1982.

—-. *Alaska's Railroads, Alaska Geographic*. Edmonds, WA: Alaska Geographic Society, 1992.

Allen, Phillip. *One Came Late Over the Gold Trails of 98*. Edmonton, Canada: Self Published, 1992.

Anderson, Douglas D. "Sailing an Ancient Landbridge: A Journey into Eskimo Prehistory, from Alaska to the Russian Far East." *Archaeology 47*, no. 4 (July/August 1994): 50–54.

Andrews, C. L. "Marine Disasters of the Alaska Route." *The Washington Historical Quarterly VII* (1916): 21–37.

—-. *Sitka, The Chief Factory of the Russian American Company*. Caldwell, ID: Caxton Printers, 1945.

Andrews, Susan, and John Creed. *Authentic Alaska: Voices of Its Native Writers*. Lincoln, NE: University of Nebraska Press, 1998.

Antonson, Joan M., and William S. Hanable. *Alaska's Heritage*. Alaska Historical Commission Studies in History No. 133. Anchorage: The Alaska Historical Society for the Alaska Historical Commission, 1986.

Apostol, Jane. "Sailing with the Ruler of the Arctic Sea." *Pacific Northwest Quarterly 72* (1981): 146–156.

Atwood, Evangeline. *Frontier Politics: Alaska's James Wickersham*. Portland, OR: Binford and Mort, 1979.

Atwood, Evangeline, and Robert N. DeArmond. *Who's Who in Alaskan Politics*. Portland OR: Alaska Historical Commission, 1977.

Avery, Mary W. "The Mart A. Howard Klondike Collection." *Pacific Northwest Quarterly* 50 (1959): 53–62.

Ball, Georgiana. "The Peter Martin Case and the Provisional Settlement of the Stikine Boundary." *BC Studies* 10 (1971): 33–55.

Bancroft, Hubert Howe. *History of Alaska, 1730–1885*. Darien, Conn: Hafner Publishing Company, 1970.

Barratt, Glynn. *Russian Shadows on the British Northwest Coast of North America, 1810–1890*. Vancouver: University of British Columbia Press, 1983.

Berkh, Vasilii Nikolaevich. *A Chronological History of the*

Discovery of the Aleutian Islands: or, the Exploits of Russian Merchants: with a Supplement of Historical Data on the Fur Trade. Kingston, Ontario: Limestone Press, 1974.

Berry, Mary C. *The Alaska Pipeline: The Politics of Oil and Native Land Claims*. Bloomington: Indian University Press, 1975.

Berton, Pierre, *The Klondike Fever: The Life and Death of the Last Great Gold Rush*. New York: Knopf, 1977.

Biggar, Joan Rawlins. "Soldiers North: The Abercrombie Expedition to Alaska." *Columbia* 6.3 (1992): 40–45.

Birket-Smith, Kaj, and Frederica DeLaguna. *The Eyak Indians of the Copper River Delta, Alaska*. Kobenhavn: Levin and Munksgaard, 1938.

Birket-Smith, Kaj. *The Chugach Eskimo*. Kobenhavn: Nationalmussets publikationsfond, 1953.

Black, Lydia T. "Russia's American Adventure: For More Than a Century, Traders from Imperial Russia Pursued Their Dreams in Alaska." *Natural History* 5, no. 12 (December 1989): 46–58.

Bleakley, Geoffrey T. *Contested Ground: An Administrative History of Wrangell-St. Elias National Park and Preserve, Alaska, 1978–2001*. Anchorage, AK: National Park Service, 2002.

Bodfish, Waldo. *Kusiq: An Eskimo Life History from the Arctic Coast of Alaska*. Fairbanks, AK: University of Alaska Press, 1991.

Brodhead, Michael J. "The United States Army Signal Service and Natural History in Alaska, 1874–1883." *Pacific Northwest Quarterly* 86 (Spring 1995): 72–82.

Bowden, Henry. *American Indians and Christian Missions: Studies in Culture and Conflict*. Chicago: University of Chicago Press, 1981.

Burroughs, John, and John Muir, et al. *Alaska, the Harriman Expedition, 1899*. New York, NY: Dover Publications, 1986.

Campbell, Lawrence James, et al. *Skagway: A Legacy of Gold*. Anchorgae, AK: Alaska Geographic, 1992.

Case David S., and David A. Voluck. *Alaska Natives and American Laws*. Fairbanks, AK: University of Alaska Press, 2002.

Catton, Theodore. *Inhabited Wilderness: Indians, Eskimos, and National Parks in Alaska*. Alburquerque, NM: University of New Mexico Press 1997.

Chadwick, Douglas H. "Denali: Alaska's Wild Heart." *National Geographic* 182, no. 2 (August 1992): 62–86.

Chandonnet, Fren ed. *Alaska at War, 1941–1945: The Forgotten War Remembered*. Anchorage, AK: Alaska at War Committee, 1995.

Chevigny, Hector. *Lord of Alaska: The Story of Baranov and the Russian Adventure*.

New York, NY: Viking Press, 1942.

—-. *Russian America: The Great Alaskan Venture, 1741–1867*. New York, NY: Viking Press, 1965.

Cicchetti, Charles J. "The Route Not Taken: The Decision to Build the Trans-Alaska Pipeline and the Aftermath." *American Enterprise* 4, no. 5 (September/October 1993): 38–46.

Clifford, Howard. *The Skagway Story*. Anchorage, AK: Alaska Northwest Publishing Company, 1975.

Coates, Ken, and William R. Morrison. *The Sinking of the Princess Sophia; Taking the North Down With Her*. Fairbanks, University of Alaska Press, 1991.

Coates, Peter. "Amchitka, Alaska: Toward the Bio-Biography of an Island." *Environmental History* 1.4 (Oct. 1996): 20–45.

—-. *North to Alaska! Fifty Years on the World's Most Remarkable Highway*. Fairbanks, AK: University of Alaska Press, 1992.

—-. *The Trans-Alaska Pipeline Controversy: Technology, Conservation and the Frontier*. Fairbanks, AK: University of Alaska Press, 1993.

Cohen, Stan. *Gold Rush Gateway; Skagway and Dyea*. Missoula, MT: Pictorial Histories Publishing Company, 1986.

—-. *The White Pass and Yukon Route; A Pictorial History*. Missoula, MT: Pictorial Histories Publishing Company, 1980.

Colby, Merle. *A Guide to Alaska—Last American Frontier*. New York: MacMillian, 1939.

Cole, Terrence M. "Jim Crow in Alaska: The Passage of the Alaska Equal Rights Act of 1945." *The Western Historical Quarterly* XXIII (1992): 429–450.

—-. "Golden Years: The Decline of Gold Mining in Alaska." *Pacific Northwest Quarterly* 80 (1989): 62–71.

—-. "Raymond Robins in Alaska: The Conversion of a Progressive." *Pacific Northwest 276Quarterly* 72 (1981): 50–60.

—-. *Crooked past: The History of a Frontier Mining Camp, Fairbanks, Alaska*. Fairbanks, AK: University of Alaska Press, 1991.

Cronon, William. "Kennecott Journey: The Paths Out of Town." In William Cronon, George Miles, and Jay Gitlin, eds., *Under an Open Sky: Rethinking America's Western Past*. New York: W.W. Norton & Company, 1992.

Davidson, Art. *In the Wake of the Exxon Valdez: The Devastating Impact of the Alaska Oil Spill*. San Francisco: Sierra Club Books, 1990.

DeArmond, R.N., editor. *Early Visitors to Southeastern Alaska*. Anchorage, AK: Alaska Northwest Publishing Company, 1978.

De Laguna, Frederica. *Chugach Prehistory: The Archaeology of Prince William Sound, Alaska*. Seattle, WA: University of

Washington Press, 1956.

DeLorme, Roland L. "Liquor Smuggling in Alaska, 1867–1899." *Pacific Northwest Quarterly* 66 (1975): 145–152.

Dickrell, Jeff. *Center of the Storm: The Bombing of Dutch Harbor and the Experience of Patrol Wing Four in the Aleutians, Summer 1942*. Missoula, MT: Pictorial Histories Publishing Company, 2001.

Dmytryshyn, Basil, et al., eds. and trans. *To Siberia and Russian America: Three Centuries of Russian Eastward Expansion, 1558–1867*. 3 vols. Portland: Western Imprints, The Press of the Oregon Historical Society, 1985–1989.

Doig, Ivan. *The Sea Runners*. New York: Atheneum, 1982.

Drucker, Phillip. *The Native Brotherhoods: Modern Intertribal Organizations on the Northwest Coast*. Washington, D.C.: U.S. Printing Office, 1958.

Dunbar, Kurt, and Chris Friday. "Salmon, Seals, and Science: The Albatross and Conservation in Alaska, 1888–1914." *Journal of the West* 33 (October 1994): 6–13.

Durbin, Kathie. *Tongass: Pulp Politics and the Fight for the Alaska Rain Forest*. Corvallis, OR: University of Oregon Press, 1999.

Elias, Scott A. *The Ice Age History of Alaskan National Parks*. Washington, D.C.: Smithsonian Institution Press, 1995.

Fields, Leslie Leyland. *The Entangling Net: Alaska's Commercial Fishing Women Tell Their Lives*. Urbana, IL: University of Illinois Press, 1997.

Fisher, Raymond H. *The Voyage of Semen Dezhnev in 1648: Bering's Precursor*. London: Hakluyt Society, 1981.

Ford, Carey. *Where the Sea Breaks Its Back; The Epic Story of a Pioneer Naturalist and the Discovery of Alaska*. Boston: Little and Brown, 1966.

Fortuine, Robert. *Chills and Fever: Health and Disease in the Early History of Alaska*. Fairbanks, AK: University of Alaska Press, 1989.

Frost, O. W., ed. *Bering and Chirikov: The American Voyages and Their Impact*. Anchorage, AK: Alaska Historical Society, 1992.

Gallagher, Thomas J., and Anthony F. Gasbarro. "The Battles for Alaska: Planning in America's Last Wilderness." *Journal of the American Planning Association* 55, no. 4 (Autumn 1989): 433–445.

Garfield, Brian. *The Thousand-Mile War: World War II in Alaska and the Aleutians*. Fairbanks, AK: University of Alaska Press, 1995.

Gay, James Thomas. *American Fur Seal Diplomacy: The Alaskan Fur Seal Controversy*. Athens, GA: University of Georgia Press, 1987.

Golovin, Pavel N. *Civil and Savage Encounters: The Worldly Travel*

Letters of anImperial Russian Navy Officer 1860–1861. Trans., Basil Dmytryshyn and E. A. P. Portland, OR: Western Imprints, Oregon Historical Society, 1983.

Green, Lewis. *The Gold Hustlers*. Anchorage, AK: Alaska Northwest Publishing Company, 1977.

—-. *The Boundary Hunters: Surveying the 141st Meridian and the Alaskan Panhandle*. Vancouver: University of British Columbia Press, 1982.

Gribbin, John. "Melting Ice May Have Submerged a Migration Route Out of Alaska." *New Scientist 122* 1664 (May 13, 1989): 35.

Grinnell, George Bird. *Alaska 1899: Essays from the Harriman Expedition*. Seattle, WA: University of Washington Press, 1995.

Gruening, Ernest. *Many Battles: The Autobiography of Ernest Gruening*. New York: Liveright, 1973.

—-. *The Battle for Alaska Statehood*. Seattle, WA: University of Washington Press, 1967

Gunther, Erna. *Indian Life on the Northwest Coast of North America As Seen by the Early Explorers and Fur Traders during the Last Decades of the Eighteenth Century*. Chicago: University of Chicago Press, 1972.

Hallock, Charles. *Our New Alaska or, the Seward Purchase Vindicated*. New York: Forest and Stream Publishing Company, 1886.

Handleman, Howard. *Bridge to Victory: The Story of the Reconquest of the Aleutians*. New York: Random House, 1943.

Haycox, Stephen W. "Economic Development and Indian Land Rights in Modern Alaska: the 1947 Tongass Timber Act." *Western Historical Quarterly* 21, no. 1 (February 1990): 21–47.

—-. *Alaska: An American Colony*. Seattle, WA: University of Alaska Press, 2002.

—-. "'Races of a Questionable Ethnical Type': Origins of the Jurisdiction of the U.S. Bureau of Education in Alaska, 1867–1885." *Pacific Northwest Quarterly* 75 (1984): 156–163.

—-. *Frigid Embrace: Political Economy and Environment in Modern Alaska*. Corvallis, OR: Oregon State University, 2000.

Haycox, Steven W., and Mary Childers Mangusso, eds. *An Alaska Anthology: Interpreting the Past*. Seattle, WA, University of Washington Press, 1996.

Helms, Andrea R. C., and Mary Childers Mangusso. "The Nome Gold Conspiracy." *Pacific Northwest Quarterly* 73 (1982): 10–19.

Henry, John Frazier. *Early Maritime Artists of the Pacific Northwest Coast, 1741–1841*. Seattle, WA: University of Washington Press, 1985.

Hinckley, Ted C. "Alaska as an American Botany Bay." *Pacific*

Historical Review XLII (1973): 1–19.

—-. "Sheldon Jackson and Benjamin Harrison: Presbyterians and the Administration of Alaska." *Pacific Northwest Quarterly* 54 (1963): 66–74.

—-. "The United States Frontier at Sitka, 1867–1873." *Pacific Northwest Quarterly* 60 (1969): 57–65.

—-. "William Seward Visits His Purchase." *Oregon Historical Quarterly* LXXII (1971): 127–147.

—-. *The Americanization of Alaska, 1867–1897.* Palo Alto, CA: Pacific Books, 1972.

Holbo, Paul. *Tarnished Expansion: The Alaska Scandal, the Press, and Congress, 1867–1871.* Knoxville: University of Tennessee Press, 1983.

Holm, Bill. *Northwest Coast Indian Art: An Analysis of Form.* Seattle, WA: University of Washington Press, 1967.

Hulley, Clarence C. "A Historical Survey of the Matanuska Valley Settlement in Alaska." *Pacific Northwest Quarterly* 40 (1949): 327–340.

—-. *Alaska Past and Present.* Portland, OR: Binfords and Mort, 1958.

Johnson, James Albert. *Carmack of the Klondike.* Seattle, WA: Epicenter Press, 1990.

Jones, Dorothy. *Aleuts in Transition: A Comparison of Two Villages.* Seattle, WA: University of Washington Press, 1976.

Josephson, Karla. *Use of the Sea by Alaska Natives—A Historical Perspective.* Anchorage, AK: Arctic Environmental Information Data Center, University of Alaska, 1974.

Kaiper, Dan and Nan Kaiper. *Tlingit: Their Art, Culture, and Legends.* Saanichton, BC: Hancock House, 1978.

Kamenskii, Archimandrite Anatolii. *Tlingit Indians of Alaska: Odessa, 1906.* Fairbanks, AK: University of Alaska Press, 1985.

Keeble, John. "A Parable of Oil and Water: Revisiting Prince William Sound, Four Years After." *Amicus Journal* 15, no. 1 (Spring 1993): 35–43.

Keithahn, E. L. "Alaska Ice, Inc." *Pacific Northwest Quarterly* 36 (1945): 121–132.

Khlebnikov, K.T. *Baranov, Chief Manager of the Russian Colonies in America.* Kingston, Ontario: Limestone Press, 1973.

—-. *Colonial Russian America: Kyrill T. Khlebnikov's Reports, 1817–1832.* Trans., Basil Dmytryshyn and E. A. P. Crownhart. Portland, OR: Oregon Historical Society, 1976.

King, Robert. "Without Hope of Immediate Profit: Oil Exploration in Alaska, 1898 to 1953." *Alaska History* (Spring 1994):19–36.

Kirchhoff, M. J. *Historic McCarthy: The Town that Copper Built.* Juneau, AK: Alaska Cedar Press, 1993.

Klotter, James C., and Freda Campbell Klotter. "Mary Desha, Alaskan Schoolteacher of 1888." *Pacific Northwest Quarterly* 71 (1980): 78–86.

Kohlhoff, Dean W. *Amchitka and the Bomb: Nuclear Testing in Alaska*. Seattle, WA: University of Washington Press, 2002.

Krakauer, Jon. "Ice, Mosquitoes and Muskeg—Building the Road to Alaska." *Smithsonian* 23, no. 4 (July 1992): 102–112.

Krause, Aurel. *Journey to the Tlingits by Aurel and Arthur Krause, 1881/82*, translated by Margot Krause McCaffrey. Haines, AK: Haines Centennial Commission, 1981.

—-. *The Tlingit Indians: Results of a Trip to the Northwest Coast of America and the Bering Straits*, translated by Erna Gunther. Seattle, WA: University of Washington Press, 1956.

Kushner, Howard I. *Conflict on the Northwest Coast: American-Russian Rivalry in the Pacific Northwest, 1790–1867*. Westport, CN: Greenwood Press, 1975.

Langdon, Steve. *Contemporary Alaska Native Economies*. Lanham, MO: University Press of America, 1986.

—-. *The Native People of Alaska*. Anchorage, AK: Greatland Graphics, 2002.

Lewis, Claudia. *Indian Families of the Northwest Coast: The Impact of Change*. Chicago: University of Chicago Press, 1970.

Levi, Stephen C. "Labor History and Alaska." *Labor History* 30, no. 4 (Fall 1989): 595–608.

Lindquist, Willis. *Alaska the Forty-ninth State*. New York: Whittlesey House, 1959.

Lung, Ed, as told to Ella Martinsen. *Black Sand and Gold*. Portland, OR: Binford and Mort, 1956.

Martin, Cy. *Gold Rush Narrow Gauge: the Story of the White Pass and Yukon Route Railroad*. Corona Del Mar, CA: Trans-Anglo Books, 1974.

Matsen, Brad. "The Once and Future Spill: In the Wake of 1989's *Exxon Valdez* Oil Spill Disaster, Has Anything Really Changed?" *Audubon* 96, no. 4 (July/August 1994).

McCourt, Edward. *The Yukon and Northwest Territories*. New York: St. Martin's Press, 1969.

Meyer, Carolyn. *Eskimos Growing Up in a Changing Culture*. New York: Atheneum, 1977.

Michener, James. *Alaska*. New York: Fawcett Crest, 1988.

Miers, Earl Schenck. *Vitus Bering and James Cook Discover Alaska and Hawaii*. Newark, DE: Published by the Friends of the Curtis Papers Company, 1960.

Minter, Roy. *The White Pass: Gateway to the Klondike*. Fairbanks, AK: University of Alaska Press, 1987.

Mitchell, Donald. *Sold American: The Story of Alaska Natives and Their Land, 1867–1959*. Hanover, NH: University Press of

New England, 1997.

Mitchell, John G. "Oil on Ice." *National Geographic* 191.4 (April 1997): 104–132.

Moore, J. Bernard. *Skagway in Days Primeval*. New York: Vantage Press, 1968.

Muir, John. *Letters from Alaska*. Ed. by Robert Engberg and Bruce Merrell. Madison, WI: University of Wisconsin Press, 1993.

—. *Northwest Passages: From the Pen of John Muir in California, Oregon, Washington, and Alaska*. Edited by Scott Lankford. Palo Alto, CA: Tioga Publishing Company, 1988.

Murray, John A. ed. *A Republic of Rivers: Three Centuries of Nature Writing from Alaska and the Yukon*. New York: Oxford University Press, 1990.

Naske, Claus-M. *A History of Alaska Statehood*. Lanham, MO: University Press of America, 1985.

—. "Alaska and the Federal-Aid Highway Acts." *Pacific Northwest Quarterly* 80 (1989): 133–138.

—. "Ernest Gruening and Alaska Native Claims." *Pacific Northwest Quarterly* 82 (1991): 140–148.

—. "Some Attention, Little Action: Vacillating Federal Efforts to Provide Territorial Alaska with an Economic Base." *Western Historical Quarterly* 26 (Spring 1995): 37–68.

—. "The Case of Vuco Petrovich." *Pacific Northwest Quarterly* 78 (1987): 2–9.

—. "The Relocation of Alaska's Japanese Residents." *Pacific Northwest Quarterly* 74 (1983): 124–132.

—. *An Interpretive History of Alaskan Statehood*. Anchorage, AK: Alaska Northwest Publishing Company, 1973.

Naske, Claus-M., and Herman E. Slotnick. *Alaska: A History of the 49th State*. Norman, OK: University of Oklahoma Press, 1987.

Nelson, Richard. *Shadow of the Hunter*. Chicago: University of Chicago Press, 1980.

—. *The Athabascans: People of the Boreal Forest*. Fairbanks, AK: University of Alaska Museum, 1983.

—. *The Island Within*. New York: Vintage Books, 1991.

—. "Understanding Eskimo Science: Traditional Hunters' Insights into the Natural World Are Worth Rediscovering." *Audubon* 95, no. 5 (September/October 1993): 102–108.

Neunherz, Richard E. "'Hemmed In': Reactions in British Columbia to the Purchase of Russian America." *Pacific Northwest Quarterly* 80 (1989): 101–111.

Nichols, Robert and Robert Croskey, eds. and trans. "The Condition of the Orthodox Church in Russian America: Innokentii Veniaminov's History of the Russian Church in Alaska." *Pacific Northwest Quarterly* 63 (1972): 41 54.

Nobbe, George. "Native Culture: A New Discovery Rewrites the History of Alaska's Alutiq Eskimos." *Omni* 17, no. 6 (March 1995): 28.

Norris, Frank. "A Lone Voice in the Wilderness: The National Park Service in Alaska, 1917–1969." *Environmental History* 1.4 (Oct. 1996): 66–76.

Olson, Wallace M. *Through Spanish Eyes: The Spanish Voyages to Alaska, 1774–1792.* Auke Bay, AK: Heritage Research, 2002.

Okun, S.B. *The Russian-American Company.* New York: Octogaon Books, 1979.

O'Neill, Dan. "H-Bombs and Eskimos: The Story of Project Chariot." *Pacific Northwest Quarterly* 85 (1994): 25–34.

—-. "Project Chariot: How Alaska Escaped Nuclear Excavation." *Bulletin of the Atomic Scientists* 45, no. 10 (December 1989): 28–38.

Orth, Donald J. *Dictionary of Alaska Place Names.* U.S. Geological Survey Professional Paper 567. Washington, D.C.: U.S. Department of the Interior, 1967.

Osgood, Cornelius. *The Ethnography of the Tanaina.* New Haven, CN: Yale University Publication in Anthropology, 1966.

Patrick, Andrew. *The Most Striking of Objects: The Totem Poles of Sitka National Historical Park.* Anchorage, AK: National Park Service, 2002.

Rakestraw, Lawrence W. *A History of the United States Forest Service in Alaska.* Anchorage, AK: Alaska Historical Commission, 1981.

Ramsay, Marina, translator, and Richard A. Pierce, editor. *Documents on the History of the Russian-American Company.* Kingston, Ontario: Limestone Press, 1976.

Ray, Dorothy Jean. *The Eskimos of Bering Strait, 1650–1898.* Seattle, University of Washington Press, 1992.

Reynolds, Brad, and Don Doll. "Athapaskans Along the Yukon." *National Geographic* 177, no. 2 (February 1990): 44–70.

Ricks, Melvin B., ed. *The Earliest History of Alaska: First English Editions of Three Russian Works, Shelekhov's Voyage to Alaska, 1793; Berkh's History of the Aleutian Islands, 1823; Khlebnikov's Life of Baranof, 1835.* Anchorage, AK: Cook Inlet Historical Society, 1963.

Riggs, Thomas. "Running the Alaska Boundary." *The Beaver* September (1945): 40–43.

Ritter, Harry. *Alaska's History: The People, Land and Events of the North Country.* Anchorage, AK: Alaska Northwest Books, 1993.

Rogers, George W. *The Future of Alaska: Economic Consequences of Statehood.* Baltimore: Johns Hopkins Press, 1962.

Roppel, Pat, editor. "Sitka and Its Ocean/Island World." *Alaska*

Geographic 9 (2). Anchorage: Alaska Geographic Society, 1982.

Satterfield, Archie. *Chilkoot Pass, Then and Now*. Anchorage, AK: Alaska Northwest Books, 1973.

—. *Chilkoot Pass: the Most Famous Trail in the North*. Anchorage, AK: Alaska Northwest Books, 1978.

—. *Klondike Park: from Seattle to Dawson City*. Goldon, CO: Fulcrum, 1993.

Shalkop, Antoinette. "The Travel Journal of Vasilii Orlov." *Pacific Northwest Quarterly* 68 (1977): 131–140.

Sherwood, Morgan. *Alaska and Its History*. Seattle, WA: University of Washington Press, 1967.

—. *Exploration of Alaska, 1865–1900*. New Haven, CN: Yale University Press, 1965.

Shortridge, James R. "The Alaskan Agricultural Empire: An American Agrarian Vision, 1898–1929." *Pacific Northwest Quarterly* 69 (1978): 145–158.

—. "The Evaluation of the Agricultural Potential of Alaska, 1867–1897." *Pacific Northwest Quarterly* 68 (1977): 88–97.

Sloss, Frank H. "Who Owned The Alaska Commercial Company?" *Pacific Northwest Quarterly* 68 (1977): 120–130.

Smith, David C. "Pulp, Paper, and Alaska." *Pacific Northwest Quarterly* 66 (1975): 61–70.

Smith, E. Valerie. "The Black Corps of Engineers and the Construction of the Alaska (ALCAN) Highway." *Negro History Bulletin* 51, no. 1 (December 1993): 22–38.

Smith, J. L. *Russia's Search for America, 1716–1732*. Anchorage, AK: White Stone Press, 2002.

—. *The First Kamchatka Expedition of Vitus Bering, 1725–1730*. Anchorage: AK: White Stone Press, 2002.

Soos, Frank, and Kesler Woodward, eds. *Under Northern Lights: Writers and Artists View the Alaskan Landscape*. Seattle, WA: University of Washington Press, 2000.

Spatz, Ronald, ed. *Alaska Native Writers, Stroytellers, and Orators*. Anchorage, AK: Alaska Quarterly Review, 1999.

Spencer, Page. *White Silk and Black Tar: A Journal of the Alaska Oil Spill*. Minneapolis: Bergamot, 1990.

Steinbright, Jan. *Qayaqs and Canoes: Native Ways of Knowing*. Anchorage, AK: Alaska Native Heritage Center, 2001.

Sterling, Bryan B., and Frances N. *Forgotten Eagle: Wiley Post, America's Heroic Aviation Pioneer*. New York: Carroll and Graf, 2001.

Stoker, Sam W., et al. *Biological Conditions in Prince William Sound, Alaska: Following the Valdez Oil Spill, 1989–1992*. Anchorage, AK: Woodward Clyde Consultants, 1992.

Strohmeyer, John. *Extreme Conditions: Big Oil and the Transformation of Alaska*. New York: Simon and Schuster, 1993.

Thomas, Clive, ed. *Alaska Public Policy Issues: Background and Perspectives*. Juneau, AK: Denali Press, 1999.

Tikhmenev, P.A. *A History of the Russian American Company*. Richard A. Pierce and Alton S. Donnelly, translators and editors. Seattle, WA: University of Washington Press, 1978.

Tordoff, Dirk. *Mercy Pilot: The Joe Crosson Story*. Seattle, WA: University of Washington Press, 2002.

Twichell, Heath. *Northwest Epic: The Building of the Alaska Highway*. New York: St. Martin's Press, 1992.

VanStone, James W. "Commercial Whaling in an Arctic Ocean." *Pacific NorthwestQuarterly* 49 (1958): 1–10.

Webb, Melody. *The Last Frontier: A History of the Yukon Basin of Canada and Alaska*. Albuquerque, NM: University of New Mexico Press, 1985.

Wendell, H. Oswalt. *Alaskan Eskimos*. San Francisco: Chandler Publishing Company, 1967.

Williams, Griffith H. "Alaska's Connection: The Alcan Highway." *Pacific Northwest Quarterly* 76 (1985): 61–68.

Williams, Ted. "Alaska's Rush for the Gold." *Audubon* 95, no. 6 (November/December 1993): 50–5.

Wilson, Graham ed. *The Last Great Gold Rush: A Klondike Reader*. Whitehorse: Wolf Creek Books, 2002.

Winslow, Kathryn. *Big Pan-Out: the Story of the Klondike Gold Rush*. New York: W. W. Norton, 1951.

Wright, Allen A. A *Prelude to Bonanza: the Discovery and Exploration of the Yukon*. Sidney, B.C.: Gray's Publications, 1976.

Chronology of Major Events

1639   Cossack horsemen journey over last eastern mountain range in Siberia, and continue on to shore of Okhotsk Sea, constructing first Russian Village, facing east, across the Pacific.

1711   Russian traders learn of a "Great Land" to the east.

1725   Peter the Great of Russia commissions Danish sea captain, Vitus Bering, to explore northwest coast of Alaska. Feat is credited with "official" discovery by Russia and first reliable information on the land. Bering establishes Russia's claim to northwestern North America.

1728   Vitus Bering sails through Bering Strait.

1741   July 15 Aleksei Chirikov with Vitus Bering Expedition sights land. Chirikov, in command of the ship the *St. Paul*, sights what is believed to be Prince of Wales Island of the Alexander Archipelago. Bering's ship, the *St. Peter*, has sailed a more northerly direction and comes upon Kayak Island the next day.

1774   Spain orders Juan Perez to explore west coast; he discovers Prince of Wales Island, Dixon Sound.

1774–91 Charles III of Spain fears Russian expansion, sends expeditions north along northwest coast of North America. Spain leaves few traces except place names such as Malaspina Glacier and Valdez.

1776   Captain James Cook begins expedition to search for Northwest Passage. His maps of northern North America prove that America and Asia are separate land masses and remain the standard for over a century.

1784   First permanent Russian settlement established at Three Saints Bay on Kodiak Island in attempt to stave off British inroads. Grigory Ivanovich Shelikov brings wife Natalya to Kodiak, the first European woman in Russian America. Shelikov, a Siberian fur merchant, establishes first permanent Russian settlement on Kodiak Island as means of restricting the British fur trade. He wants to establish monopoly of fur trade in Alaska, but Empress Catherine does not allow it.

1786   Gerassin Pribilof discovers rookeries on islands now known as Pribilofs.

1789   First American expedition sets out for northwestern North American to compete with British and Russians for fur trade.

1791   George Vancouver leaves England to explore coast;

	Alejandro Malaspina explores northwest coast for Spain.
1794	Alexander Baranov builds first ocean-going vessel in northwestern America on Kenai Peninsula at Voskressenski.
1795	First Russian Orthodox Church established in Kodiak.
1799	Alexander Baranov establishes Russian post known today as Old Sitka; trade charter grants exclusive trading rights to Russian American Company.
1802	Tlingits destroy Russian fort at Old Sitka. After attack, Baranov forced to pay 10,000 rubles ransom for surviving settlers.
1804	Baranov returns to Sitka with large contingent of Russians and Aleuts and Russian warship *Neva*. Russians are successful in Battle of Sitka, and Baranov begins to build settlement of New Archangel, now known as Sitka.
1805	First cargo of Russian furs from Russian America delivered to Canton, China, by Yuri Lisiansky; Tlingits destroy the Russian settlement of Yakutat.
1812	Napoleon invades Russia, increasing isolation of Russia from its distant colonies.
1815	Otto von Kotzebue, an Estonian German, sets out on Russian round-the-world expedition, visits St. Lawrence Island and Unalaska.
1821	Russian Trading Charter renewed, extending Russian jurisdiction to 51st parallel. The Hudson's Bay Company, chartered by the British, tries to gain foothold in the Alaska fur trade. British make a deal with Russians to lease mainland south of Cape Spencer for 10 years at an annual payment of 2,000 land otter skins. The British are a presence in Alaska for next 30 years.
1824	Russians begin exploration of mainland that leads to discovery of Nushagak, Kuskokwim, Yukon, and Koyokuk Rivers; Russia and U.S. sign treaty accepting 54 degrees, 4 minutes as southern boundary of Russian America; 1848 Cathedral of St. Michael dedicated in New Archangel (Sitka).
1832	First gold in Alaska discovered in the Kuskokwim River Valley.
1833	Fort St. Michael constructed close to mouth of Yukon River.
1834	Father Veniaminov moves to Sitka and consecrated Bishop Innokenty in 1840.
1836	Baranov Castle built in Sitka, in memory of Alexander Baranov.
1840	Russian Orthodox Diocese forms; Bishop Veniaminov

given permission to use Alaska Native languages in
liturgy.

1841   Edward de Stoeckl assigned to secretariat of Russian
legation in U.S.

1847   Fort Yukon established.

1848   Cathedral of St. Michael dedicated at New Archangel
(Sitka).

1851   Alaska Natives, upset with Russian treatment, attack
Fort Nulato on Yukon.

1853   Russian explorer-trappers and employees of the
Russian–America Company Oil find oil seeps in Cook
Inlet.

1855   Port Graham opens Alaska's first coal mine.

1859   De Stoeckl returns to U.S. from St. Petersburg with
authority to negotiate sale of Alaska. Economics of time
and Crimean war have disastrous effects on Russian
domestic affairs which brings about Russians attempts
for sale.

1861   Gold discovered inland of the present city of Wrangell,
on Stikine River near Telegraph Creek.

1865   Western Union Telegraph Company prepares to put a
telegraph line across Alaska and Siberia.

1867   U.S. purchases Alaska from Russia and places Pribilof
Islands under jurisdiction of Secretary of Treasury. Fur
seal population, stabilized under Russian rule, declines
rapidly. Secretary of State William H. Seward
negotiates purchase of Russian America: 375 million
acres for $7.2 million—less than 2 cents per acre. Many
call this "Seward's Folly" because little is known about
Alaska. Major General Jefferson, U.S. Army, assumes
command of the Department of Alaska. A decade of
military rule begins.

1868   Alaska's first salmon cannery built in Klawock, on
Prince of Wales Island; First newspaper office
established, producing the *Sitka Times* with first issue on
September 19.

1872   Gold discovered near Sitka and in British Columbia.

1874   George Halt said to be first white man to cross Chilkoot
Pass in search for gold.

1876   Gold discovered south of Juneau at Windham Bay.

1877   U.S. troops withdrawn from Alaska.

1878   School opens at Sitka, to become Sheldon Jackson
College; First canneries in Alaska established at
Klawock and Sitka; Sitka also becomes home to
Alaska's first steam operated sawmill.

1880   Richard Harris and Joseph Juneau, with help of local clan leader Kowee, discover gold on Gastineau Channel. Juneau founded. In 1880, George Pilz, a German-born mining school graduate living in Sitka, grubstaked his employee Joe Juneau and another man, Richard Harris. A mining district is established and called Harrisburg, and soon a town first named Harrisburg, then Rockwell, and finally Juneau begins to flourish at a shallow bay called Miners Cove.

1881   Promotor John Treadwell obtains claim on Douglas Island from prospector "French Pete" for sum of $5 to $400. A Geologist said the site contained only low-grade ore, making it worthless to French Pete, who did not possess capital to develop it. Treadwell recognizes potential and develops profitable enterprise. The year-round employment at mine gives town economic base. Eventually, four mines open—the Treadwell, the 700, the Mexican, and the Ready Bullion—and five stamp mills.

1882   First commercial herring fishing begins at Killisnoo; first two central Alaska salmon canneries built. U.S. Navy bombs, then burns Tlingit village of Angoon.

1884   Steamers begin bringing first tourists to Alaska; President Chester Arthur signs Harrison Act, creating "District of Alaska," which provides for governor and judge; Congress passes Organic Act. $15,000 funding approved to educate native children.

1885   Dr. C. H. Townsend suggests introduction of reindeer into Alaska; Sheldon Jackson appointed General Agent for Education.

1887   Reverend William Duncan brings 1,000 Tsimshian followers from Metlakatla in British Columbia to Annette Island. On land obtained through a congressional grant, he builds new Metlakatla, designed to make the Tsimshian self-sufficient. They learn trades such as carpentry, seamanship, and boat-building, build their own sawmills and a cannery, and engage in other enterprises.

1888   Dr. W. H. Dall of U.S. and Dr. George Dawson of Canada start boundary survey.

1890   Large corporate salmon canneries begin construction. Sheldon Jackson explores Arctic Coast, introduces reindeer husbandry.

1891   First oil claims staked in Cook Inlet area.

1892   Afognak Reserve established, beginning Alaskan Forest Service System.

1894   Gold discovered at Cook Inlet. Baranov Castle destroyed by fire. Gold discovered on Mastadon Creek, founding of Circle City.

1896   Dawson City founded at mouth of Klondike River; gold discovered on Bonanza Creek.

1897   First shipment of fresh halibut sent south from Juneau.

1898   Skagway largest city in Alaska; Congress appropriates money for telegraph from Seattle to Sitka and passes laws making way for construction of railroads in Alaska. Work starts on White Pass and Yukon Railroad; Nome gold rush begins. The Klondike produced $200 million in gold.

1900   Alaska moves capital to Juneau. State divided into three judicial districts, with judges at Sitka, Eagle, and St. Michael; White Pass and Yukon Railroad completed; First exploratory well drilled in Cook Inlet. 20,000 gold miners on Nome beach.

1902   First oil production in Alaska; Felix Pedro discovers gold near Fairbanks. Pedro and merchant Barnette play leading role in establishment of Fairbanks; President Theodore Roosevelt establishes Tongass National Forest.

1903   Alaska-Canada border settled.

1904   Last great Tlingit potlatch held in Sitka. Submarine cables laid from Seattle to Sitka and from Sitka to Valdez, linking Alaska to "outside."

1905   Tanana railroad built; telegraph links Fairbanks and Valdez; Alaska Road Commission established under Army jurisdiction.

1906   Native Allotment Act passes; first opportunity for Alaska Natives to obtain land under restricted title.

1906   Alaska authorized to send voteless delegate to Congress; Governor's Office moved from Sitka to Juneau.

1907   Gold discovered at Ruby; Richardson trail established; Tongass National Forest, largest U.S. forest, created by presidential proclamation.

1908   Cache Creek Mining Company formed; Ketchikan becomes home for first cold storage plant.

1909   Gold discovered at Iditarod River.

1911   International agreement between U.S., Great Britain, Canada, Russia, and Japan controls fur seal fisheries; sea otters become protected species; Copper River and Northwestern Railroad begins service to Kennecott Copper Mine.

1912   Territorial status for Alaska provides for legislature; Alaska Native Brotherhood organizes in Southeast; Mount Katmai explodes, forming Valley of Ten

Thousand Smokes.

1913   First Alaska territorial legislature convenes; first law
        grants women voting rights.

1914   Surveying begins for Alaska Railroad; City of
        Anchorage born as construction campsite.

1915   Alaska Native Sisterhood holds first convention in
        Sitka.

1916   Delegate James Wickersham introduces first Alaska
        statehood bill in Congress; Congress creates the
        National Park Service through passage on Organic Act;
        1917 Pribilof fur seal exports exceed $274,000. Total
        Alaska fur exports: $1,338,599; Treadwell Mine caves in
        at Douglas.

1918   Congress creates Alaska Agricultural College and
        School of Mines as land grant college.

1918   Alaska salmon pack exceeds six million cases, valued at
        over $51 million.

1918   Father William Duncan of Metlakatla dies.

1920   Anchorage city government organized; Alaska Air
        Expedition from New York to Nome, sponsored by
        U.S. Army, successful. "Black Wolf" squadron of
        wheeled biplanes land at Wrangell, Fairbanks, Ruby,
        and finally at Nome's Fort Davis. For Alaska, flight is
        significant because demonstrates that airplanes capable
        of carrying heavy loads can fly to and across Alaska.

1922   Alaska Native voting rights established through court
        case. Alaska Agricultural College & School of Mines,
        later University of Alaska in 1935, opens at College near
        Fairbanks. When opened in 1922, the Alaska
        Agricultural College and School of Mines had six
        students, one building, and annual budget of $30,000.

1923   President Warren G. Harding drives golden spike near
        Nenana completing Alaska Railroad; Naval Petroleum
        Reserve No. 4 created.

1924   Congress extends citizenship to all Native Americans in
        U.S.; Tlingit William Paul, Sr. first Alaska Native
        elected to Alaska Legislature; Start of airmail delivery
        to Alaska.

1926   Alaska Native Townsite Act allows natives to obtain
        restricted deeds to village lots; design for Alaska flag
        selected in contest for Alaska students in grades seven
        through 12 in 1926. Winning design, submitted by 13-
        year-old Benny Benson, consists of eight gold stars on
        field of blue, representing Big Dipper and North Star.

1927   Alaska Legislature adopted Benny Benson's design as
        official flag for the Territory of Alaska on May 2, 1927.

It later became official state flag.

1928   Court case resolves right of Alaska Native children to attend public school.

1929   U.S. Navy begins 5-year survey to map parts of Alaska; Alaska Native Brotherhood convention at Haines resolves to pursue land claims settlement in Southeast Alaska.

1932   Radio telephone communications established in Juneau, Ketchikan, and Nome.

1935   Matanuska Valley Project established; Nine hundred Alaska–Juneau Gold Mine workers go on strike that lasts 40 days and ends in violence. Jurisdictional Act allows Tlingit and Haida to pursue land claims in U.S. Court of Claims; Salmon pack peaks at 8,437,603 cases.

1936   Indian Reorganization Act of 1935 amended to include Alaska. Nell Scott of Seldovia becomes first woman elected to territorial legislature.

1938   Kennicott Mine closes at McCarthy.

1940   Fort Richardson established; construction begins on Elmendorf Air Force Base.
Pan-American Airlines begins regular scheduled flights to Alaska from Seattle.

1942   Japan bombs Dutch Harbor, invades Aleutians; Pioneer Service Road (Alaska–Canada Military Highway) built between February 14 and September 24 from Dawson Creek, B.C., to Delta Junction, Alaska.

1943   Upgrading and bridge building continues on Alaska Highway providing first start for some of today's largest construction contractors; American forces retake Aleutian Islands of Attu and Kiska from Japanese; Secretary of the interior creates Venetie Reservation.

1944   Alaska–Juneau Gold Mine shuts down. Oil and Gas Exploration begins. Alaska-Juneau Gold Mine shuts down.

1945   Governor Gruening signs Anti-Discrimination Act, first such legislation passed in U.S. and its possessions since post-Civil War.

1946   Boarding school for Alaska Native high school students opens at Mt. Edgecombe, Sitka.

1947   Alaska Command established; first unified command of the U.S. staffed by Army, Air Force, and Navy officers; First Alaska Native land claims suit, filed by Tlingit and Haida people, introduced in U.S. Court of Claims.

1948   Alaska Highway opens to civilian traffic; Alaskans vote to abolish fish traps by 10 to 1 margin.

1949   Alaska Statehood Committee launches campaign for

Alaska Statehood.

1953   Oil well drilled near Eureka on Glenn Highway marks beginning of Alaska's modern oil history; First plywood operations begin at Juneau; First big Alaskan pulp mill opens at Ketchikan; First Alaskan television broadcast by KENI, Anchorage.

1955–56 Constitutional convention held at University of Alaska. Territorial voters adopt Alaska Constitution, send two senators and one representative to Washington under Tennessee Plan.

1957   Atlantic Richfield discovers oil at Swanson River on Kenai Peninsula, beginning Alaska's modern oil era. Swanson River field on the Kenai Peninsula is first commercial production site for oil and gas in Alaska's modern oil era. During next ten years, additional oil fields discovered offshore in nearby Cook Inlet and production platforms installed to bring production on-line for Middle Ground shoal field, Granite Point field, MacArthur River field and Trading Bay field. By 1968, Cook Inlet producing nearly 200,000 barrels per day, and income generated by oil production constributes more than 20% of state government's total revenues.

1958   Congress passes Alaska Statehood Act conveying ownership of 104 million acres.; President Eisenhower signs statehood bill.

1959   Alaska admitted to Union as 49th state, and William A. Egan becomes Alaska's first governor; Sitka pulp mill opens. State revenues: $25.4 million. British Petroleum begins to explore for oil on Alaska's North Slope; U.S. Court of Claims issues judgment favoring Tlingit and Haida claims to Southeast Alaska lands.

1960   Amoco finds offshore oil in Cook Inlet.

1963   Stevens Village and other Yukon villages protest proposed Rampart Dam.

1964   Alaska's population reaches 250,000; Good Friday earthquake at 5:36 pm. Fortunately, loss of life caused by earthquake relatively low, but property damage estimated at almost $500 million. Earthquake more than 10 million times force of atomic bomb. Town of Valdez completely destroyed.

1965   State revenues total $82,964,000.

1966   Alaska Federation of Natives organized; Interior Secretary Udall imposes "land freeze" to protect Alaska Native use and occupancy of Alaska lands.

1967   August 15: Chena River floods Fairbanks. First bill introduced in Congress to settle Alaska Native land claims.

1968   Oil pumped from well at Prudhoe Bay on North Slope. Governor Hickel establishes Alaska Lands Claims Task Force that recommends 40 million acre land settlement for Alaska Natives.

1969   North Slope Oil lease sale brings $900 million. First live satellite telecast in Alaska.

1970   State revenues: $1,067,264,000; First bill introduced in legislature to establish Permanent Fund; Alaska's population totals 295,000; Environmental studies measuring impact of pipeline construction on Alaska wildlife begin.

1971   Congress passes Alaska Native Claims Settlement Act, transfers ownership of 44 million acres to newly established Alaska Native corporations.

1972   Alaska Constitution amended to prohibit sexual discrimination.

1973   Congress passes the Trans-Alaska Pipeline Authorization Act; Salmon fisheries limited entry program becomes law; War in the Middle East in October causes oil prices to rise from $3 to $16 per barrel.

1974   Alaska voters approve capital move initiative; construction begins on the pipeline. Thousands of workers flock to Alaska in search of jobs. Construction lasts 39 months, costs $8 billion, including Marine Terminal in Valdez.

1975   Alaska Legislature appropriates funds to initiate purchase and installation of 100 satellite earth stations for establishment of statewide satellite communications network; First Permanent Fund bill passes legislature. Governor Hammond vetoes it and urges establishment of Permanent Fund by amendment to State Constitution.

1976   Natural gas pipeline proposals filed; Alaska voters pick Willow as new capital site; voters approve constitutional amendment establishing Alaska Permanent Fund to receive "at least 25 percent" of all state oil revenues and related income.

1977   Trans-Alaska Pipeline completed from Prudhoe Bay to Valdez. February 28: Permanent Fund receives first deposit of dedicated oil revenues: $734,000.

1980   Alaska Legislature increases Permanent Fund share of oil revenues from 25 to 50 percent, repeals Alaska personal income tax, establishes Alaska Dividend Fund to distribute Permanent Fund earnings to Alaska residents. Congress passes Alaska National Interests Lands Conservation Act (ANILCA).

1981   Alaska Legislature approves second special appropriation to Permanent Fund, this time for $1.8 billion.

1982   Alaska voters repeal law relocating capital to Willow and establish state spending limit; First Permanent Fund dividends distributed.

1983   Time zone shift: All Alaska except westernmost Aleutians Islands move to Alaska Standard Time, one hour west of Pacific Standard time; Crab stocks so low that most commercial seasons cancelled; Drinking age raised from 18 to 21 by legislature.

1985   State purchases Alaska Railroad from federal government; declining oil prices cause budget problems.

1986   Price of oil drops below $10 per barrel, causing Alaska oil revenues to plummet; legislature passes a new bill governing subsistence hunting and fishing.

1987   Economic doldrums from oil prices continue to affect state, causing many to lose jobs and leave, banks to foreclose on property, and businesses to go bankrupt; a new military build-up in Alaska begins when first troops of new Sixth Infantry Division arrive in Fairbanks; Congress passes amendments to the Alaska Native Land Claims Settlement Act, which protects lands and stocks; Trans-Alaska Pipeline celebrates its 10th anniversary.

1988   International efforts to rescue two whales caught by ice off Barrow captures world-wide attention; The state's economic woes continue and Anchorage loses 30,000 in population; Soviets allow one-day visit of group of Alaskans to Siberian port city of Provideniya; Anchorage loses bid to host 1994 Olympic Games to Lillehammer, Norway.

1989   *Exxon Valdez* grounds on Bligh Reef spilling 11 million gallons into Prince William Sound; Permanent Fund passes $10 billion mark; Alaska Supreme Court throws out Alaska's rural preference law.

1990   Alaska Legislature meets in special session and struggles unsuccessfully to resolve subsistence issue. Federal authorities take over subsistence management on federal lands; oil prices temporarily double after Iraq's invasion of Kuwait; Walter Hickel makes a political comeback with lieutenant governor candidate Jack Coghill on Alaskan Independence Party ticket and wins gubernatorial race; Congress sets aside more Southeast Alaska as wilderness by passing Tongass Reform Act.

1991   State of Alaska, U.S. Justice Department, and Exxon reach $1 billion settlement resulting from *Exxon Valdez* oil spill which is rejected by U.S. District Court.

Amended settlement earmarking more money for restoration work in Prince William Sound wins judicial approval. Congress effectively closes the Arctic National Wildlife Refuge to oil development; Bristol Bay fisherman strike over low salmon prices; Hickel administration and legislature unable to resolve subsistence issue.

1992   Final repercussions of Alaska's recession are felt as oil industry retrenches with major job losses; *Anchorage Times*, once Alaska's largest newspaper folds; reapportionment challenges delay primaries by two weeks; Spurr Volcano erupts three times, one blast dumping ash on Anchorage; Juneau's Hillary Lindh wins Olympic Silver Medal in downhill skiing; Alaska Highway celebrates 50th anniversary; Denali National Park 50 years old; Anchorage now largest city in Alaska with more than 250,000 residents.

1993   Alaska Legislature passes largest capital works appropriation in ten years; Court-mandated new reapportionment scheme re-draws boundaries of some election districts; Greens Creek Mine near Juneau closes due to low silver, zinc, and lead prices; Sitka Pulp Mill announces indefinites suspension of mill operations, affecting 400 workers; Alaskan Independence Party Chairman Joe Vogler mysteriously disappears.

1994   Federal trial results in $5 billion dollar verdict in *Exxon Valdez* case; Alaska's Tommy Moe brings home Olympic gold in downhill ski competitions; Joe Vogler's body discovered buried off Chena Hot Springs Road near Fairbanks; Voters defeat latest proposal to move Alaska capital from Juneau; mental health lands case decided after years in court; Suit initiated by Vern Weiss of Nenana and several other plaintiffs revolved around 1977 legislature's dissolution of trust established in territorial days.

1995   Canadian fisherman attack Alaska ferry with paint and ball bearings projected from sling shots in frustration over inconclusive U.S.–Canada Pacific Salmon Treaty talks, which hinder Southeast Alaska's troll king salmon fishery; MarkAir faces bankruptcy while ticket holders stranded and employees all over the state laid off; $267 million dollar Healy Clean Coal Project launched with substantial backing by U.S. Department of Energy; Villagers from Alatna return to newly rebuilt village after being one of several Koyukuk River communities washed out by fall floods in 1994.

1996   Federal judge rules against State of Alaska in case brought by Governor Hickel and continued by Governor Knowles over state's interpretation of how Alaska Statehood Act affects federal government's management of federal lands in state; U.S. Congress lifts ban on exportation of Alaska crude oil; One of most devastating fires in state history destroys homes and property in South Central area near Big Lake.

1997   High winds and seas cause Japanese refrigerator ship to go aground near Unalaska, spilling approximately 39,000 gallons of fuel; Fairbanks Municipal Utilities System sold to three private companies, ending 50 years of public utility ownership; MAPCO, owner of Alaska's largest oil refinery, bought by Williams Co. Inc; Canadian fishermen in Prince Rupert blockade Alaskan ferry for three days in protest of Alaskan salmon-fishing practices; ferry service to Prince Rupert disrupted for 19 weeks; issue of 20-year-old Trans-Alaska Pipeline safety in the news, but both Alyeska and Joint Pipeline Office maintain pipeline well-monitored and safe.

1998   Statewide, 6,700 jobs added and unemployment rate sets record low at 5.8%; Moose adopted as Alaska's official state land mammal; in May, estimated 4,000 people march in Anchorage to show solidarity and bring attention to Alaska Native Rights' issues; New Seward SeaLife Center is western hemisphere's first cold-water marine research facility and includes two floors of public displays; U.S. Supreme Court of in case No. 96-1577 rules that approximately 1.8 million acres owned by native village of Venetie Tribal Government is not "Indian country."

1999   Two legendary dogmushers die—Joe Redington, Sr., founder of Iditarod Trail Sled Dog Race, and Edgar Nollner, Sr., last surviving musher of diphtheria serum run to Nome; State's top two oil producers, BP and ARCO, announce intent to merge; University of Alaska Museum in Fairbanks receives $1,000,000 from Bill Gates Foundation to help with expansion project; In Anchorage, Alaska Native Heritage Center, 26 acre cultural park, opens doors. Center expected to attract 130,000 visitors a year; In September, proposal to spend Alaska Permanent Fund earnings on state government soundly rejected by voters, 83% to 17%; state's largest financial institution, National Bank of Alaska, announces buyout by Wells, Fargo & Co; Derailment of two Alaska Railroad trains in Susitna River Valley in

November and December result in jet fuel spills totaling approximately 100,000 gallons. Cleanup hampered by extreme weather and remote terrain.

2000   Alaskans welcome year 2000 with fanfare and firecrackers; tragedy strikes on January 31 when Alaska Airlines jet crashes near Los Angeles, killing 88, including Morris Thompson, Interior Alaska Native leader and former BIA director; snow slides strand dozens of people in Girdwood for week. Avalanche conditions in area among worst in decades; in April, after more than year of anti-trust investigations by FTC, agreement signed for BP to take over ARCO, with exception of ARCO Alaska which is purchased by Phillips Petroleum; after more than 40 years, bodies of 133 people, mostly Native Alaskans, returned to villages for burial. Patients at Mt. Edgecumbe TB hospital when died, they had been buried in nearby WWII bunker; Elmer Rasmuson, Anchorage banker and Alaskan philanthropist, dies in December. Once again Alaska offers unique challenges to intrepid federal census takers. Census 2000 results show state population of 626,932, increase of 14% from 1990, and Alaska moves to 47th in state population rankings.

2001   Governor Knowles declined to appeal the Katie John subsistence case and held a summit on subsistence.

2002   On November 3rd, Interior Alaska experienced a 7.9 earthquake centered 90 miles south of Fairbanks; On November 5, Alaska voters rejected moving the State Legislature by 67% to 33%. Senator Frank Murkowski (R) elected Governor.

2003   Alaskans hike the minimum wage from $5.65 to $7.15. This gave Alaska the highest minimum wage on the West Coast. Wolf control became an issue in April, after the Board of Fish and Game voted to allow it, and environmental groups threatened tourism boycotts.

2004   In the election for U.S. Senate Lisa Murkowski (R), daughter of Governor Murkowski, defeated former Governor Tony Knowles (D) in a close race; Don E. Young (R) was again overwhelming re-elected in the U.S. House.

Cultural Highlights

Noted Alaskan Writers and Books

Anderson, Jean. *In Extremis and Other Alaskan Stories*. New York: Talman, 1989.

Armstrong, Michael. *Agviq: The Whale*. United States: Popular Library, 1990.

Bruchac, Joseph and James Ruppert, eds. *Raven Tells Stories: An Anthology of Alaskan Native Writing*. Greenfield Center, NY: Greenfield Review Press, 1991.

Carlstrom, Nancy White. *Northern Lullaby*. New York: Philomel Books, 1992.

Chadwick, Jerah. *Absence Wild: Aleutian Poems*. Seattle, WA: Jugum Press, 1984.

Chandonnet, Ann Fox. *Canoeing in the Rain: Poems for My Aleut-Athabascan Son*. Forest Grove, OR: Published for Mr. Cogito Press by Meredith L. Bliss, 1990.

Dauenhauer, Nora Marks. *The Droning Shaman: Poems*. Haines, AK: Black Current Press, 1988.

Dauenhauer, Richard. *Frames of Reference: Poems 1987*. Haines, AK: Black Current Press, 1987.

Gutheridge, George and Janet Berliner. *Child of the Light*. Clarkston, GA: White Wolf, 1995.

Guttenberg, Elyse. *Summer Light*. New York: HarperPrism, 1995.

Hildebrand, John. *Reading the River: A Voyage Down the Yukon*. Boston: Houghton Mifflin, 1988.

Jans, Nick. *The Last Light Breaking: Living Among Alaska's Inupiat Eskimos*. Anchorage: Alaska Northwest Books, 1993.

Kremers, Carolyn. *Place of the Pretend People*. Anchorage: Alaska Northwest Books, 1996.

Kusz, Natalie. *Road Song: A Memoir*. New York: Farrar Straus Giroux, 1990.

Lord, Nancy. *Survival: Stories*. Minneapolis, MN: Consortium Book Sales and Distribution, 1991.

Mergler, Wayne, ed. *The Last New Land: Stories of Alaska Past and Present*. Anchorage: Alaska Northwest Books, 1996.

Morgan, John. *Walking Past Midnight*. Tuscaloosa AL: University of Alabama Press, 1989.

Murray, John, ed. *A Republic of Rivers: Three Centuries of Nature Writing from Alaska and the Yukon*. New York: Oxford University Press, 1990.

Nickerson, Sheila. *On Why the Quiltmaker Became a Dragon*. Fairbanks: Vanessapress, 1985.

Parry, Richard. *Ice Warrior*. New York: Pocket Books, 1991.

Scarborough, Elizabeth. *The Goldcamp Vampire*. New York:

Bantam Books, 1987.

Sexton, Tom. *The Bend Toward Asia*. Anchorage: Salmon Run Press, 1993.

Shumaker, Peggy. *Wings Moist from the Other World*. Pittsburgh, PA: University of Pittsburgh Press, 1994.

Simpson, Sherry. *Alaska's Ocean Highways*. Fairbanks: Epicenter Press, 1995.

Stabenow, Dana. *Play With Fire*. New York: Berkley Prime Crime, 1995.

Wallis, Velma. *Two Old Women: An Alaska Legend of Betrayal, Courage, and Survival*. Fairbanks: Epicenter Press, 1993.

Non-Alaskan Writers & Books about Alaska

Hawkes, John. *Adventures in the Alaskan Skin Trade*. New York: Penguin Books, 1985.

Kesey, Ken. *Sailor Song*. New York: Viking, 1992.

Lopez, Barry. *Arctic Dreams*. New York: Vintage Books, 1986.

McGinniss, Joe. *Going to Extremes*. New York: New American Library, 1980.

McPhee, John. *Coming into the Country*. New York: Bantam Books, 1977.

Quick, Barbara. *Northern Edge*. San Francisco: HarperCollins West, 1990.

Smith, Martin Cruz. *Polar Star*. New York: Random House, 1988.

Noted Alaskan Artists

Amason, Alvin—Painter
Barker, James—Photographer
Behlke, Jim—Painter
Brody, Bill—Painter
Cutler, Enid—Painter
Dahluger, Jules—Painter
DeRoux, Ken—Painter
Evans, Dan—Photographer
Fejes, Claire—Painter
Hayes, Deborah—Painter
Heurlin, Rusty—Painter
Hill, Thomas—Painter
Keith, William—Painter
Kent, Rockwell—Painter
Lambert, Ted—Painter
Laurence, Sydney—Painter
Machetanz, Fred—Painter
Mangus, Marvin—Painter
Mason, Charles—Photographer
Michaels, Mary Beth—Painter

Mollett, David—Painter
Niebrugge, Gail—Painter
Rabener, Nancy—Photographer
Reed, Fran—Fiber Artist
Schneider, Shelly—Photographer
Senungetuk, Ron—Carver
Sherman, Todd—Painter
Simpson, Glen—Metalsmith
Steinbright, Jan—Painter
Stock, Marionette—Painter
Stonington, Nancy—Painter
Van Zant, Charlottee—Tapestries
Ver Hoef, Mary—Painter
Vienneau, Larry—Painter
Wright, Myron—Photographer
Ziegler, Eustace —Painter

Alaska Movies/Television Shows
The Hunt for Red October (1990)
Mystery, Alaska (1999)
Nanook of the North (1922), documentary
North to Alaska (1960)
Northern Exposure, televison series
Runaway Train (1985)

Facts and Figures

Territorial Governors of Alaska
John Kinkead, July 4, 1884–May 7, 1885
Alfred Swineford, May 7, 1885–April 20, 1889
Lyman Knapp, April 20, 1889–June 18, 1893
James Sheakley, June 18, 1893–June 23, 1897
John Brady, June 23, 1897–March 2, 1906
Wilford Hoggatt, March 2, 1906–May 20, 1909
Walter Clark, May 20, 1909–April 18, 1913
John Strong, April 18, 1913–April 12, 1918
Thomas Riggs Jr., April 12, 1918–June 16, 1921
Scott Bone, June 16, 1921–Aug. 16, 1925
George Parks, April 16, 1925–April 19, 1933
John Troy, April 19, 1933–Dec. 6, 1939
Ernest Gruening, Dec. 6, 1939–April 10, 1953
Frank Heintzleman, April 10, 1953–Jan. 3, 1957
Mike Stepovich, April 8, 1957–Aug. 9, 1958

Governors Since Statehood
William A. Egan, Jan. 3, 1959–Dec.5, 1966
Walter J. Hickel, Dec. 5, 1966–Jan. 29, 1969 (Appointed Secretary
    of Interior in 1969)
Keith H. Miller, Jan. 29, 1969–Dec. 5, 1970
William A. Egan, Dec. 5, 1970–Dec. 2, 1974
Jay S. Hammond, Dec. 2, 1974–Dec. 6, 1982
Bill Sheffield, Dec. 6, 1982–Dec. 1, 1986
Steve Cowper, Dec. 2, 1986–Dec. 2, 1990
Walter J. Hickel, Dec. 3, 1990–Dec. 5 1994
Tony Knowles, Dec. 5, 1994–Dec. 2, 2002
Frank Murkowski, Dec. 2, 2002–Present

Alaska's U.S. Senators
E.L. Bartlett, 1958 to 1968
Ernest Gruening, 1958 to 1968
Mike Gravel, 1968 to 1980
Ted Stevens, 1968 to present
Frank Murkowski, 1980 to 2002
Lisa Murkowski, 2002 to present

Alaska's U.S. Representatives
Ralph Rivers, 1958 to 1966
Howard Pollock, 1966 to 1970
Nicholas Begich, 1970 to 1972
Don Young, 1972 to Present

Alaska's State Symbols

Bird: the Willow Ptarmigan, chosen in 1955 by Alaskan school children.

Capital: Juneau located in the Southeast. Juneau became the state capital in 1906.

Fish: the King Salmon, adopted in 1962.

Flower: the Forget-me-not, adopted in 1949.

Fossil: the Woolley Mammoth, adopted in 1986.

Gem: Jade, adopted in 1968.

Insect: the Four-spot Skimmer Dragonfly (no not the Mosquito), adopted in 1995.

Mammal: the Moose.

Marine Mammal: the Bowhead Whale, adopted in 1983.

Mineral: Gold, adopted in 1968.

Motto: "North to the Future" adopted in 1967.

Nicknames: "Land of the Midnight Sun" and "The Last Frontier."

Sport: Dog mushing, adopted in 1972.

Tree: the Sitka Spruce, adopted in 1962.

State Song

Eight stars of gold on a field of blue—
Alaska's flag. May it mean to you
The blue of the sea, the evening sky,
The mountain lakes, and the flow'rs nearby;
The gold of the early sourdough's dreams,
The precious gold of the hills and streams;
The brilliant stars in the northern sky,
The "Bear"—the "Dipper"—and, shining high,
The great North Star with its steady light,
Over land and sea a beacon bright.
Alaska's flag—to Alaskans dear,
The simple flag of a last frontier.

GLOSSARY OF COMMON ALASKAN TERMS

Bear bells: A bear will normally try to avoid contact with humans if given warning. Talking, singing, playing a portable radio, or making some other noise is good insurance in bear country. Bear bells are small bells like cow bells or sleigh bells that are worn on boots or some other place on your body that will let them make a noise as you walk.

Breakup: The point in time in the spring when the ice breaks up in the local rivers and disappears.

Bush: Any area outside a city or town with limited access to the rest of the state.

Cheechako: The Alaska native term for newcomers to the area.

Denali: The Alaska native term for Mount McKinley. It has been translated as "The High One." Many Alaskans prefer to use it as the name of the mountain, rather than McKinley.

LightBox: A device containing a strong, concentrated source of light. Used for thirty minutes to an hour each morning in dark months to simulate daylight. Helps prevent or cure Seasonal Affective Disorder (SAD), a form of depression.

Lower 48: What Alaskans call the original 48 contiguous states.

North Slope: The sloping tundra region from the foothills of the Brooks Range north to the Beaufort Sea and Arctic Ocean. It contains the Prudhoe Bay oil field and is often called simply "The Slope."

Overflow: Water or ice that appears on top of earlier ice in a body of water when it is unable to run underneath.

Pepper spray: A pressurized can of hot pepper in a propellant, which can be aimed and discharged like a fire extinguisher. The spray will reach a distance of about twelve feet and will almost certainly disable a human or animal attacker for up to thirty minutes if eyes or mucus membranes are hit. Pepper spray is fast becoming the protection of choice for Alaskans who prefer not to carry a gun.

Permanent Fund Dividend: In 1976, a constitutional amendment to the Alaska Constitution established the Alaska Permanent Fund as a depository for a percentage of rental, royalties, and other sources of income from state mineral deposits, principally oil. In 1980, the dividend payment program was set up to give to eligible state residents a portion of the proceeds from the fund each year.

Sourdough: The miners of the Gold Rush era carried sourdough starter to mix with their flour to make bread, biscuits, pan cakes, etc. They called themselves "Sourdoughs." The definition is one who has spent at least a year in Alaska.

Southeast: The southeastern panhandle portion of the state, which includes the cities of Skagway, Juneau, Sitka, and Ketchikan.

Termination dust: During the gold mining days, when the first autumn snow fell, it was the signal to the miners that they should terminate operations for the year and retreat to town for the winter.

The Valley: The valley between the Chugach and Talkeetna Mountains at the confluence of the Matanuska, Susitna, and Knik Rivers. It is officially called the Matanuska-Susitna Valley or, locally, the Mat-Su Valley.

SPECIAL EVENTS

January

Statehood Day—Jan. 3—Statewide.

Orthodox Christmas—Jan. 7—Statewide.

Alcan 200 International Snowmachine Race—Jan. 16–18—Haines.

Polar Bear Jump-off Festival—Jan. 16–18—Seward.

Martin Luther King Day—Jan. 19—Statewide.

Anchorage Folk Festival—late January—Anchorage.

February

Ski for Women—Feb. 1—Anchorage. Largest women-only ski event in North America.

Tent City Festival—Feb. 4–8—Wrangell. Celebrates gold and timber history of this Inside Passage city.

Ice Worm Festival—Feb. 6–8—Cordova.

State Winter Carnival—Feb. 6–8—Willow.

Winter Ice Festival—Feb. 13–15—Seward.

Winter Carnival—Feb. 13–15—Homer.

Yukon Quest—Feb. 14—Fairbanks. Hard sled-dog race to Whitehorse, Yukon Territory, starts in downtown Fairbanks. (In 2005 it starts in Whitehorse and ends in Fairbanks.)

Susitna 100—Feb. 14—Big Lake. A 100-mile and 50K winter race along the National Historic Iditarod Trail within the Susitna Valley, with ski, bike, snowshoe, and triathlon divisions.

Iron Dog Snowmachine Race—Feb. 16—Fairbanks. 2,000-mile snowmobile race starts in Fairbanks and passes through Nome and Big Lake on its way to Wasilla.

Fur Rendezvous Festival—Feb. 20 to March 7—Anchorage.

Iditarod Days Festival—Feb. 27 to March 7—Wasilla.

Winterfest—Feb. 27–29—Denali National Park.

Alaska Ultra Sport, Iditarod Trail Invitational—Feb. 28—Wasilla to Nome. A human-powered ultramarathon race from Wasilla to McGrath and on to Nome by bike, foot, ski, snowshoe, or snowmachine.

Ski Train South Grandview—Feb. 28—Anchorage. Take a 3-hour Alaska Railroad journey to the Kenai Peninsula's locale of Grandview for backcountry touring, telemark skiing, snowshoeing, and snowboarding.

March

McNeil River bear permits deadline—March 1—Anchorage. Deadline to enter lottery to see bears catch salmon in June, July and August at McNeil River State Game Sanctuary on western shore of Cook Inlet.

World Ice Carving Championship—March 3–31—Fairbanks.

Iditarod Trail Sled Dog Race—March 6 to mid-March— Anchorage, Wasilla to Nome. Race has ceremonial start in downtown Anchorage and goes to Eagle River on March 6. The next day, the official start occurs in Wasilla. Parties and contests in Nome until the winner arrives.

Ice Classic Tripod Weekend—March 6–7—Nenana. River town near Fairbanks puts tripod on Tanana River in contest to see when ice will go out.

Tour of Anchorage—March 7—Anchorage. Cross-country ski marathon.

Limited North American Championship Sled Dog Race—March 12–14—Fairbanks.

Chatanika Days—March 13–14—Chatanika. Gold-mining hamlet celebrates winter.

Ski Train North to Curry—March 14—Anchorage. Alaska Railroad carries Nordic ski enthusiasts north of Talkeetna to explore the Curry area.

Spring Equinox—March 19—Statewide. 12 hours of daylight. Equinox is 9:49 P.M.

Winter King Salmon Tournament—March 20—Homer.

Pillar Mountain Golf Classic—March 26–28—Kodiak. Tournament to drive golf ball up Pillar Mountain in fewest strokes.

April

Arctic Man Ski and Sno-Go Classic—April 9–11—Paxson. Skiers and machines combine in breakneck runs down a mountain.

Whalefest—April 9–18—Kodiak. Watch migrating whales.

Garnet Festival—April 10–17—Wrangell. Bald eagles gather at Stikine River mouth.

Alaska Folk Festival—April 12–18—Juneau.

Alyeska Resort Spring Carnival and Slush Cup—April 17–18— Girdwood. Resort town south of Anchorage begins farewell to ski season.

Native Youth Olympics—April 22–24—Anchorage. Youths from around state compete in traditional games at University of Alaska.

Old Harbor Whaling Festival—April and May—Kodiak.

May

Jackpot Halibut Derby—May 1 to October 1—Homer.

Kachemak Bay Shorebird Festival—May 6–9—Homer.

Copper River Delta Shorebird Festival—May 7–9—Cordova.

Alaska State Railroad—May 15—Railbelt towns. Daily service

begins between Anchorage and Seward, and between
Anchorage, Talkeetna, Denali National Park, and Fairbanks.

Syttende Mai—May 17—Petersburg. Scandinavian town
celebrates Norwegian indepedence day.

Koniag's Kodiak Crab Festival—May 27–31—Kodiak.

Great Alaska Craftbeer and Homebrew Festival—May 28–29—
Haines.

Kachemak Bay Kayak Fest—May 28 to June 6—Homer. Ten days
of kayaking and related events, seminars, demonstrations
and workshops for all ages and skill levels.

Park opening—May 29—Denali National Park.

June

Summer Music Festival—All June—Sitka. Renowned artists
perform classical music.

Ship Creek King Salmon Derby—June 4–13—Anchorage.

Anchorage Festival of Music—June 11–19—Anchorage. White
nights and lots of music. *Mayor's Midnight Sun Marathon*—
June 19—Anchorage.

Kluane-Chilkat Bike Race—June 19—Haines.

Spirit Days—June 19–20—Anchorage. Alaska Natives celebrate
heritages.

Seldovia Summer Solstice Music Festival—June 19–20—Seldovia.

Summer Solstice—June 20—Statewide. Any town worth its salt
has a festival, concert or race this weekend as days reach their
longest. Solstice is 4:57 P.M.

Midnight Sun Baseball Game—June 21—Fairbanks. Annual
Midnight Sun game features the Fairbanks Gold Panners.
Play begins at 10:30 P.M.

Yukon 800 Boat Race—June 21–22—Fairbanks. Down Chena
and Tanana rivers to the Yukon and back. Race starts at
Pike's Landing.

Gold Rush Days—June 26–27—Juneau.

July

Midnight Sun Intertribal Powwow—July 2–4—Fairbanks.

Girdwood Forest Fair—July 2–4—Girdwood.

Independence Day—July 4—Statewide.

Mount Marathon race—July 4—Seward. Racers go up and down
3,022-foot mountain.

Bear Paw Festival—July 7–11—Eagle River.

Moose Dropping Festival—July 10–11—Talkeetna. Raucous
party includes the Mountain Mother contest, a parade, the
moose nugget (moose poop) toss game, and a moose nugget
dropping contest.

Crow Pass Crossing—July 17—Girdwood to Eagle River.

Runners cover a marathon-length mountain route.

Midnight Sun Ultra Challenge Race—July 18–23—Fairbanks
to Anchorage. Longest wheelchair and handcycle race in
world: six days, 267 miles.

Summer Arts Festival—July 18 to Aug. 1—Fairbanks.

Bear Country Music Festival—July 16–17—Kodiak.

Golden Days—July 21–25—Fairbanks.

World Eskimo-Indian Olympics—July 21–25—Fairbanks.
Competitors from arctic lands compete in traditional games.

Fort Seward Days—July 24–25—Haines.

Anderson Bluegrass Festival—late July—Anderson.

August

Gold Rush Days—Aug. 4–8—Juneau.

Talkeetna Bluegrass Festival—Aug. 5–8—Talkeetna.

Tanana Valley State Fair—Aug. 6–14—Fairbanks.

Silver Salmon Derby—Aug. 7–21—Seward.

Founder's Day—Aug. 7—Metlakatla.

Ship Creek Silver Salmon Derby—Aug. 13–22—Anchorage.

SE Alaska State Fair and Bald Eagle Music Festival—Aug. 11–15—
Haines.

Humpy's Marathon—Aug. 15—Anchorage.

Kenai Peninsula State Fair—Aug. 21–22—Ninilchik.

Golden North Salmon Derby—Aug. 22–24—Juneau.

Alaska State Fair—Aug. 26 to Sept. 6—Palmer.

September

Alyeska Blueberry & Mountain Arts Festival—Sept. 4–5—Girdwood.

Kodiak State Fair and Rodeo—Sept. 4–5—Kodiak.

Park closing—Sept. 8—Denali National Park. Park officially
closes for season, although it open for people who win
passes in park road lottery.

Alaska State Railroad—Sept. 13—Railbelt towns. Daily service ends.

Autumn Equinox—Sept. 22—Statewide. Days and nights are
each 12 hours long. Equinox is 8:30 A.M.

Silver Salmon Derby—Sept. 24 to Oct. 15—Kodiak.

October

Hockey Classic—Oct. 15–16—Anchorage. Four college teams
meet in a tournament.

Alaska Day—Oct. 18—Statewide. Anniversary of date when
U.S. flag was first raised over Alaska after territory was
bought from Russia (1867 in Sitka).

Alaska Federation of Natives Convention—mid-October—
Anchorage. Alaskans come from all corners for week of
meetings and shopping.

November

Alaska Bald Eagle Festival—Nov. 17–21—Haines. Four
thousand eagles gather to eat as much as they can of the late
run of chum. Eagles are present en masse from October
through January.

Top of the World Classic—Nov. 18–21—Fairbanks. National
college men's basketball tournament.

Great Alaska Shootout—Nov. 23–27—Anchorage. National
college men's and women's basketball tournament.

December

Talkeetna Winterfest—Weekends—Talkeetna. Bachelor Society
Ball, Wilderness Woman Contest, a parade and a tree-
lighting ceremony.

Anchorage Film Festival—early, mid-Dec.—Anchorage.

Winter Solstice—Dec. 21—Statewide. Shortest daylight of year.
Solstice is 3:42 A.M.

Julebukking—Dec. 24—Petersburg. Merchants offer food and
drink in customer appreciation.

Contact Information

Alaska Airlines: www.alaska-air.com/

Alaska.com: Includes local news, weather, travel information, fishing reports, and more. www.alaska.com/

Alaska Legislature: www.legis.state.ak.us/

Anchorage Daily News: www.adn.com/

Cruises: Offers information on various cruise options. www.alaskacruise.com/

Department of Fish and Game: www.adfg.state.ak.us/

Internet Travel Guide: Loads of information about culture, people, products, and businesses. www.alaskaone.com/

Railroads: Offers travel packages and freight service. www.akrr.com

State of Alaska: Official site. Includes departments, job listings, visitor guide, and more. www.state.ak.us/

Travel Industry Association: state-sponsored Alaska travel guide and vacation planner. www.travelalaska.com/

University of Alaska: www.alaska.edu/

Visitor Information: Information about the state for travelers and travel agents. www.dced.state.ak.us/tourism

Further Reading

Travel Guides

DuFresne, Jim. *Lonely Planet Alaska*. Victoria, Australia: Lonely Planet Publications, 2003.

Fodor's 2004 Alaska. New York, NY: Foder's Publications, 2004.

Frommer's Alaska Cruises and Ports of Call, 2004. Hoboken, NJ: Wiley and Sons, 2004.

Halliday, Jan. *Native Peoples of Alaska: A Traveler's Guide to Land, Art and Culture*. Seattle, WA: Sasquatch Books, 1998.

Nienhaueser, Helen. *55 Ways to the Wilderness of Southcentral Alaska*. Seattle, WA: Mountaineers Books, 2002.

Quick, Daniel. *Kenai Canoe Trails*. Soldotna, AK: Northlite Books, 1995.

Romano-Lax, Andromeda. *Alaska's Kenai Peninsula: A Traveler's Guide*. Lansing, MI: AAA Publishing, 2001.

Romano-Lax, Andromeda. *How to Rent a Public Cabin in Southcentral Alaska: Access and Adventures for Hikers, Kayakers, Anglers, and More*. Berkeley, CA: Wilderness Press, 1999.

The Milepost 2001: Trip Planning for Alaska, Yukon Territory, British Columbia, Alberta & Northwest Territory. Augusta, GA: Morris Communications, 2001.

Arts and Culture

Berry, William D. *William D. Berry: 1954–1956 Alaskan Field Sketches*. Fairbanks, AK: University of Alaska Press, 1989.

Campbell, John Martin. *North Alaska Chronicle: Notes From the End of Time: —The Simon Paneak Drawings*. Santa Fe, NM: Museum of New Mexico Press, 1998.

Chandonnet, Ann. *Alaska's Arts, Crafts and Collectables*. Anchorage, AK: Todd Communications, 1998.

Decker, Julie. *Icebreakers: Alaska's Most Innovative Artists*. Anchorage, AK: Decker Art Services, 1999.

Fienup-Riordan, Ann. *Freeze Frame: Alaska Eskimos in the Movies*. Seattle, WA: University of Washington Press, 1995.

Jonaitis, Aldona, ed. *Looking North: Art from the University of Alaska Museum*. Seattle, WA: University of Washington Press, 1998.

Kent, Rockwell. *Wilderness: A Journal of Quiet Adventure*. Hanover, NH: University Press of New England, 1996.

Niebrugge, Gail. *Gail Niebrugge's Alaska Wildflowers: An Artist's Journey In Painting and Prose*. Seattle, WA: Epicenter Press, 2000.

Ray, Dorothy. *Legacy of Arctic Art*. Seattle, WA: University of Washington Press, 1996.

Naturalist Field Guides

Armstrong, Robert. *Guide to the Birds of Alaska*. Anchorage, AK: Alaska Northwest Books, 1995.

Conner, Cathy. *Roadside Geology of Alaska*. Missoula, MT: Mountain Press, 1988.

Davis, Neil. *Alaska Science Nuggets*. Faribanks, AK: Geophysical Institute, 1982.

Ewing, Susan. *Great Alaska Nature Factbook: A Guide to the State's Remarkable Animals, Plants and Natural Features*. Anchorage, AK: Alaska Northwest Books, 1996.

Lethcoe, Jim. *Geology of Prince William Sound*. Valdez, AK: Prince William Sound Books, 1994.

Matkin, Craig. *Killer Whales of Southern Alaska*. Valdez, AK: Prince William Sound Books, 1994.

O'Clair, Rita. *Nature of Southeast Alaska*. Anchorage, AK: Alaska Northwest Books, 1996.

Pielou, E.C. *After the Ice Age: The Return of Life to Glaciated North America*. Chicago, IL: University of Chicago Press, 1991.

Schofield, Janics. *Discovering Wild Plants*. Anchorage, AK: Alaska Northwest Books, 1993.

Wynne, Kate. *Guide to Marine Mammals of Alaska*. Narragansett, RI: University of Rhode Island, 1996.

Zimmerman, Jenny. *Naturalist Guide to Chugach State Park*. Anchorage, AK: A.T. Publishing and Printing, 1993.

Children's Books

Cobb, Vicki. *This Place is Cold*. New York: Walker, 1989.

Ewing, Susan. *Lucky Hares and Itchy Bears*. Anchorage, AK: Alaska Northwest Books, 1993.

Joosse, Barbara. *Mama, Do You Love Me?* San Francisco, CA: Chronicle Books, 1991.

Kreeger, Charlene. *Alaska ABC Book*. Wasilla, AK: Alaska ABC Books, 1986.

Raffi. *Baby Beluga*. New York, NY: Crown Publishing, 1997.

Hunting in Alaska

Adams, Mary. *Out of Season: The Johnny Luster Story*. Wasilla, AK: Northern Publishing Company, 2003.

Atamian, Sarkis. *The Bears of Manley*. Anchorage, AK: Publications Consultants, 1995.

Bartlett, Larry. *A Complete Guide to Float Hunting Alaska*. Fairbanks, AK: Pristine Press, 2003.

Batin, Christopher. *Hunting in Alaska: A Comprehensive Guide*. Fairbanks, AK: Alaska Hunter, 1995.

Castle, Lynn and Jimmie Rosenbruch. *Hunting and Fishing Alaska*. [United States]: Amwell Press, 1991.

Conkle, Lenora. *Hunting : The Way It Was to Our Changing Alaska*. Anchorage, AK: Publication Consultants, 1997.

Gilchrist, Duncan. *Quest for Dall Rams*. Butte, MT: International Hunting Consultants, 1981.

Kaniut, Larry. *More Alaska Bear Tales*. Anchorage, AK: Alaska Northwest Books, 1990.

Massey, Jay. *A Thousand Campfires*. Girdwood, AK: Bear Paw Publications, 1985.

—-. *Bowhunting Alaska's Wild Rivers*. Girdwood, AK: Bear Paw Publications, 1983.

Russ, Tony. *Quest for Dall Sheep*. Wasilla, AK: Northern Publishing, 1994.

Schetzle, Harold. *Alaska Wilderness Hunter*. Anchorage, AK: Great Northwest Publishing, 1987.

Sherwood, Morgan B. *Big Game in Alaska: A History of Wildlife and People*. New Haven, CT: Yale University Press, 1981.

Suits, Chauncey. *Big Game, Big Country*. Anchorage, AK: Great Northwest Publishing, 1987.

Walker, Tom. *Shadows on the Tundra: Alaskan Tales of Predator, Prey and Man*. Harrisburg, PA: Stackpole Books, 1990.

Fishing Alaska

The Alaska Atlas & Gazetteer: Topographic Maps. Freeport, ME: DeLorme Mapping, 1999.

Armstrong, Robert H. *Alaska's Fish: A Guide to Selected Species*. Anchorage, AK: Alaska Northwest Books, 1996.

Batin, Adela and Chris. *Fishing Alaska on Dollars a Day*. Fairbanks, AK: Alaska Angler Publications, 1992.

Batin, Chris and Rudnick Terry. *How to Catch Trophy Halibut*. Fairbanks, AK: Alaska Angler Publications, 1988.

Batin, Chris. *Chris Batin's 20 Great Alaska Fishing Adventures*. Fairbanks, AK: Alaska Angler Publications, 1991.

Jettmar, Karen. *The Alaska River Guide: Canoeing, Kayaking, and Rafting*. Anchorage, AK: Alaska Northwest Books, 1998.

Marsh, Ken. *Breakfast At Trout's Place: Seasons of An Alaska Flyfisher*. Boulder, CO: Johnson Books, 1999.

Rosenberg, Bernard R. *Alaska Fishing on a Budget*. Portland, OR: Frank Amato Publications, 2003.

Route, Anthony. *Flyfishing Alaska*. Boulder, CO: Spring Creek Press, 1995.

Russ, Tony. *Alaska Wear*. Wasilla, AK: Northern Publishing, 2001.

Thomas, Donnall E. *Dream Fish and Road Trips: Alaska, Montana, and Beyond*. New York, NY: Lyons & Burford, 1996.

Index of Places